FUNDAMENTALS OF

CLINICAL REHABILITATION

COUNSELING

FUNDAMENTALS OF

CLINICAL REHABILITATION
COUNSELING

Mary-Anne M. Joseph and Mona Robinson, Editors

Alabama State University and Ohio University

Bassim Hamadeh, CEO and Publisher
Amy Smith, Senior Project Editor
Alia Bales, Production Editor
Stephanie Kohl, Licensing Coordinator
Natalie Piccotti, Director of Marketing
Kassie Graves, Vice President of Editorial
Jamie Giganti, Director of Academic Publishing

Printed in the United States of America.

3970 Sorrento Valley Blvd., Ste. 500, San Diego, CA 92121

Brief Contents

Detailed Contents

4. Models of Disability   45

Bilal Urkmez, PhD, CRC
Chanda Pinkney, MA

5. People With Disabilities   61

Ajasha M. Long, MS
Louvisia Conley, MEd, EdS
Juwanna Kindred, MS
Sharon Brown, PhD, CRC
Chrisann Schiro-Geist, PhD, CRC, D/ABVE

6. The Duplicity of Disability and Abuse   79

Dr. Brian L. Bethel, PhD, LPCC-S, LCDC III, RPT-S

Preface

Clinical Rehabilitation Counseling provides students and professionals with a vast range of knowledge and skills to aid them in working effectively with people with disabilities. This is a growing profession that views the individual in a holistic manner while assessing their psychiatric, developmental, cognitive, emotional, sensory, and physical disabilities in relation to their individual goals, aspirations, worldview, and perspective on quality of life. The text provides an overview of the historical context of clinical rehabilitation counseling, relevant rehabilitation legislation, the global perspective of disability, the impact of abuse and neglect on persons with disabilities, and the applicability of ethical concepts in clinical rehabilitation counseling. Furthermore, this text will introduce the concepts of vocational rehabilitation, work and disability, as well as the role of assessment, case management, independent living, assistive technology, and forensic rehabilitation in clinical rehabilitation counseling. In addition, insight, guidelines, and resources for the implementation of basic skills in the area of clinical rehabilitation counseling are provided.

The text is organized to escort the reader through the chief concepts of clinical rehabilitation counseling and prepare them to move into expanded explorations of these topics as they move further in their training. By beginning with historical and legislative perspectives combined with definitions, global perspectives, and models of disability, the text enables the reader to develop foundational knowledge about the field of clinical rehabilitation counseling prior to moving into applicable concepts. In the heart of the text, readers are presented with applicable concepts that speak to the challenges clinical rehabilitation counselors are called to champion when aiding people with disabilities to improve their quality of life on a global scale. Framed around the understanding of disability, ethical responsibilities, and abuse and neglect, this portion of the text sets the tone of responsibility for clinical rehabilitation counselors. The information in the associated chapters can be used as a resource to increase the readers' understanding of clinical rehabilitation counseling and prepare them for the expansion of their knowledge throughout the clinical rehabilitation counseling curriculum. The remaining components of the text highlight, explore, and expand upon the core specialty areas associated with clinical rehabilitation counseling to assist readers in grasping the diverse complexities of the field.

This text is the first in the field to present a view of clinical rehabilitation counseling in an introductory text. It takes the readers on a collaborative journey, providing students and educators a text that aligns with the innovative, expansive, and developmental arena that is clinical rehabilitation counseling. The purpose of this text is to help readers understand the needs of people with disabilities in today's society. It also aims to provide readers with practical resources and examples for application in the field of clinical rehabilitation counseling. This text is well suited to serve as a core textbook for clinical rehabilitation counseling and clinical mental health counseling.

Acknowledgments

The development of this valuable resource would not have been possible without the multifaceted group of professionals who contributed their time and effort to this project. We would like to thank you all for your hard work and dedication that made this textbook a possibility. Additionally, we would like to extend our sincerest gratitude to everyone on the Cognella publishing team for your guidance and support throughout the production of this book. We would like to extend special thanks to Kassie Graves and Amy Smith for their patience, guidance, and support in the completion of this text. Last, but certainly not least, we would be remiss if we did not thank our friends and family for their unwavering encouragement and uplifting support as we championed this project.

CHAPTER 1

Historical Background of Modern Rehabilitation Practice

John Tooson, PhD, CRC
Malik Raheem, EdD

Learning Objectives

As a result of reading this chapter, the student will be able to:

- Outline views toward people with disabilities throughout history.
- Describe the history of treatment of persons with disabilities.
- Explain the significance of various individuals who were instrumental in changing our understanding of disabilities.
- Describe how rehabilitation services treatment has changed over time.
- Define the practice of clinical rehabilitation counseling.
- Identify the unique elements of clinical rehabilitation counseling.
- Outline the history of evolution of rehabilitation counseling to clinical rehabilitation counseling.
- List the range of services provided by rehabilitation counselors and clinical rehabilitation counselors.

INTRODUCTION

Clinical mental health and rehabilitation counseling is a growing profession that views the individual in a holistic manner while assessing their psychiatric, developmental, cognitive, emotional, and physical disabilities in relation to their individual goals, aspirations, worldview, and quality of life. Rehabilitation is a set of interventions needed when a person is experiencing or is likely to experience limitations in everyday functioning due to aging or a health condition, including chronic diseases or disorders, injuries, or traumas (Merriam-Webster.com, n.d.). Becoming a professional clinical rehabilitation counselor will be contingent on your individual training and development, your values and beliefs, and how you are able to apply these in the counseling process.

Counselors who are in training programs need to become familiar with and have an understanding of the history of rehabilitation and how the treatment of people with disabilities has evolved over the last few centuries. Having a passion for people and a desire to assist them in their life endeavors is significant and necessary in this profession.

Ancient Greece and Rome

The Greeks and Romans considered themselves to be superior to all other races and viewed any disability as a mark of inferiority. The Greeks referred to people with intellectual deficiencies as idiots. Until this time, people who had seizures, or "fits," as they were called, were often said to be touched by the finger of God and were considered sacred. Hippocrates (460–357 BCE), the Father of Medicine, challenged this notion by speculating that seizures were the result of physical causes and not divine intervention. Aristotle recommended that there should be a law "to prevent rearing of deformed children" and that deformed children should be killed. In the city of Sparta, the abandonment of "deformed and sickly" infants was a legal requirement (Minnesota Governor's Council on Developmental Disabilities, n.d.).

In Rome, children with disabilities were treated as objects of scorn. Children who were blind, deaf, or mentally retarded were publicly persecuted and reported to have been thrown in the Tiber River by their parents. Some children born with disabilities were mutilated to increase their value as beggars. Other children with disabilities were left in the woods to die, their feet bound together to discourage anyone passing by from adopting them. It was not unusual for the wealthy to keep a person with a physical or mental disability, referred to as a fool, for their amusement. The royal courts commonly kept fools or court jesters as playthings (Minnesota Governor's Council on Developmental Disabilities, n.d.).

Middle Ages

After the fall of the Roman Empire in the 5th century CE, Western Europe fell apart. The value that had been placed on education, science, and art during the Roman Empire was gone. For people with disabilities, the period was marked by indifference, neglect, and fear, and as in Roman times people with physical disabilities, mental illness, or intellectual deficiency were kept as fools and court jesters to entertain the nobility (Minnesota Governor's Council on Developmental Disabilities, n.d.). Those who were lucky enough to provide entertainment for the monarchy often were well looked after; however, those not lucky enough to live in the royal palace would have their property taken away from them if they were deemed to be incapable of looking after themselves (Squire, 2016).

During the Middle Ages, the Roman Catholic Church provided refuge to those in need, establishing orphanages, hospitals, and homes for the blind and the aged. In 787 CE the archbishop of Milan founded the first asylum for abandoned infants (Minnesota Governor's Council on Developmental Disabilities, n.d.).

The great majority of people with disabilities had no occupation, no source of income, limited social interaction, and little religious comfort. Their lives were severely limited by widely held beliefs and superstitions that justified the pervasive prejudice and callous treatment. During this period, people with disabilities were killed, exorcised, ignored, exiled, or exploited, although some were set apart because they were considered divine (Rushton, 2013).

The history of disabilities prior to the 17th and 18th centuries has been referred to as a time of confusion due to the lack of understanding of and services for persons with disabilities (Minnesota Governor's Council on Developmental Disabilities, n.d.). Later in the Middle Ages, however, scientists such as Sir Isaac Newton and Galileo contributed to an understanding of the physical world, and philosophers tried to understand human nature.

17th- and 18th-Century America

The energies of the American colonists were devoted to survival. The overburdened settlers preferred to avoid assuming responsibility for those incapable of self-support in this highly challenging environment (Rubin & Roessler, 2008). Perceptions of mental illness were largely guided by folk beliefs and traditions, and the belief that the moon caused lunacy (the Latin word for *moon* is "luna") persisted well into the 19th century.

In the 18th century, having a disability was a death sentence in some instances. Although not all beggars were people with disabilities, most individuals with disabilities in the 1700s survived through begging. Because life in poverty required exhausting physical labor to simply earn enough to survive, those who were not able to work were often left destitute and without any other option aside from begging (Brainard, 2020).

During the 1800s, institutions were founded that catered to people with disabilities. However, most of these facilities focused on restraining and controlling patients, not on treatment or therapy. They housed people with cognitive, developmental, physical, and emotional disabilities, often for the entirety of a person's life (Action for Access, n.d.).

Rehabilitation in the 19th Century

During the 19th century, idiots were hardly an unfamiliar sight to most Americans, and yet idiocy was somewhat ill-defined medically and would remain so well into the 20th century. Idiocy was defined by English and early American legal theorists and social commentators as a permanent, "natural" lack of understanding (or mental deficiency) that typically dated from birth, which prevented self-support and moral judgment (Rose, 2017). Some viewed idiocy as being the result of sin. Puritans, as well as 19th-century charities officials, considered idiots to be evidence of parental sins such as intemperance and unchaste behavior. Others viewed idiocy as an appropriate object of study for those seeking to understand the natural world and as an innate characteristic of certain races (Rose, 2017).

The first major change regarding the concept of intellectual deficiency came in the 19th century from the famous French psychiatrist Jean-Etienne Dominique Esquirol. He divided intellectual deficiency into two levels: (1) idiocy, a person with little or no intellectual functioning (i.e., incapable of attention, cannot control their senses) and (2) imbecility, a person who has intellectual and affective faculties, but to a lesser degree than others, that can be developed only to a certain extent (Minnesota Governor's Council on Developmental Disabilities, n.d.). It is essential to note that rehabilitation professionals no longer utilize such language to describe individuals with psychiatric and intellectual disabilities.

Rehabilitation of People With Hearing Disabilities

The ancient Hebrews may have been the first to distinguish between those who are born deaf and those who lose their hearing later in life (Nomeland & Nomeland, 1940). Some of the earliest accounts of deaf education come from Iberia in Spain during the late 16th and early 17th centuries, with Fray Melchor de Yebra, a hearing Benedictine monk, being the first to publish an illustration of a manual method of communicating (essentially a fingerspelling chart; Zimmerman & Horejes, 2017).

Many early American settlers who were deaf came from Europe and arrived in ports in Massachusetts. Although the first formalization of American signing took place in 1817, when the first school for the deaf opened, the roots of signing in America date back to the 1600s (Nomeland & Nomeland, 1940). Research suggests that deaf individuals had been signing since the early 1700s in Martha's Vineyard.

The debate over communication methods long predated the establishment of the first school for the deaf in America. Ancient philosophers such as Plato and Aristotle pondered whether people who were deaf could learn speech or process knowledge (Burch, 2001). In Europe, by the mid-18th and early 19th centuries, some pupils who were deaf received instruction through sign language. In America, most schools founded between 1817 and the 1860s adopted the French method of sign-based teaching (Burch, 2001). No formal classes for teaching sign language were available, but schools used signing as a source of communication, and because of this it became a central part of the developing Deaf Culture.

In mid-18th-century France, sign-based education became well established and began to spread to other European countries. Private tutoring in England and Germany in the late 18th and early 19th centuries evolved into schools that implemented oral and lip-reading techniques (Burch, 2001). In the early 1800s, the American educator Thomas Gallaudet was able to collect enough funding to travel to Europe to study methods of teaching the deaf. Upon Gallaudet's arrival in Edinburg, Scotland, he found that he was not able to meet with the Braidwood family to share their knowledge to train prospective teachers of the deaf. However, the director of the Institution Nationale des Sourds-Muets à Paris was in London at the time giving lectures and demonstrations on the teaching of the deaf using manual communication, and Gallaudet was given an invitation to their French school. Gallaudet was able to persuade one of the school's faculty, Laurent Clerc, to accompany him on his return trip to America. During the return voyage, Gallaudet learned the language of signs from Clerc and in return taught the Clerc English (American School for the Deaf, n.d.). In 1864, deaf people gained the opportunity for advanced education with the establishment of Gallaudet College, which is the only liberal arts university in the world exclusively for the deaf (Burch, 2001). The oldest existing school for the deaf in America opened in Bennett's City Hotel on April 15, 1817. The school became the first recipient of state aid to education in America when the Connecticut General Assembly awarded its first annual grant to the school in 1819. By the mid-19th century, Deaf Culture and self-awareness were established and expanding (American School for the Deaf, n.d.).

The latter half of the 19th century saw the rise of oral theories of deaf education, and although there are a variety of these theories, they all emphasize the importance of oral skills (speechreading and speech) in the education of deaf children. The difference in philosophy between the proponents of traditional sign language and supporters of the oral method was a crucial division throughout the second half of the 19th century and well into the 20th century. During the latter 20th century, sign language regained legitimacy as the preferred communication method (American School for the Deaf, n.d.).

Rehabilitation of Persons Who Are Blind

In France, Valentin Hauy (1745–1822) was sufficiently impressed by the work of his countryman Abbe de l'Eppe with the deaf that Hauy opened the National Institute for Blind Youth in Paris in 1784. Hauy's school was the first charity school for the blind, funded by the Philanthropic Society. In 1786, Hauy published his "Essay on the Education of the Blind," in which he discussed his methods of teaching, writing, arithmetic, geography, music, and handicrafts for occupational purposes, endeavoring to make the education of children who were blind similar to that of children who were sighted (Nordstrom, 1986). The most famous pupil of Hauy's school was undoubtedly Louis Braille (1809–1852). Hauy had experimented with the use of embossed print for people who were blind to read, but Roman letters are not sufficiently distinct to the touch. In 1829, Braille, who was blind himself, introduced a system of raised dots that represented the letters of the alphabet; these dots had the advantages of being easier to feel; of taking little space; and, with the aid of a stylus, of being easy and quick to write (Nordstrom, 1986).

In 1829, Dr. John Dix Fisher chartered the first school for the blind in the United States after being inspired by what he saw while visiting the National Institute for Blind Youth in Paris while studying medicine there. The first school for the blind in America, the New England School for the Blind, opened in Boston with Samuel Gridley Howe, who also visited the school for the blind in Paris, as its first director. This school is now called the Perkins Home for the Blind. In 1839, the school moved to its third location, a former hotel in South Boston. The move was made possible by Thomas Handasyd Perkins who facilitated the sale of the mansion he had donated in 1833, and for this generosity, the school was renamed the Perkins Institution and Massachusetts School for the Blind (Perkins School for the Blind, n.d.).

Rehabilitation of Persons With Mental Illness

The earliest explanation for mental illness was that it was caused by evil spirits. Researchers think that early human societies used trephination, the drilling of a hole in the skull, to allow such spirits to escape. Skulls and cave art from as early as 6500 BCE show surgical drilling of holes in the skulls, most likely to treat injuries and epilepsy as well as to allow evil spirits trapped within the skull to be released (Farreras, 2020). Around 2700 BCE, Chinese medicine's concept of complementary positive and negative bodily forces (yin and yang) attributed mental (and physical) illness to an imbalance between these forces (Tseng, 1973).

Mesopotamian and Egyptian papyri from 1900 BCE describe women suffering from mental illness resulting from a wandering uterus (later called *hysteria* by the Greeks). In their view, the uterus could become dislodged and attached to parts of the body such as the liver or chest cavity, preventing their proper functioning and producing various and sometimes painful symptoms (Ferreras, 2020). As a result, the Egyptians, and later the Greeks, employed a somatogenic treatment of using strong smelling substances to guide the uterus back to its proper location (pleasant odors to lure; unpleasant odors to dispel).

Greek physicians rejected supernatural explanations of mental disorders, but it was not until 400 BCE that Hippocrates (460–370 BCE) attempted to separate superstition and religion from medicine by systematizing the belief that a deficiency in, or especially an excess of, the four essential bodily fluids (i.e., humors)—blood, yellow bile, black bile, and phlegm—was responsible for physical and mental illness.

Beginning in the 13th century, people with mental illness, especially women, began to be persecuted as witches who were possessed. In the mid- to late 16th century, attempts were made to convince the public that accused witches were actually women with mental illnesses and that mental illness was not due to demonic possession but rather to faulty metabolism and disease. However, witch-hunting did not decline until the 17th and 18th centuries, after more than 100,000 presumed witches were burned at the stake (Schoenberg, 1977; Zilboorg & Henry, 1941).

Typically, the family was responsible for custody and care of their mentally ill family member. Outside interventions and facilities for residential treatment were rare; it wasn't until 792 CE in Baghdad that the first mental hospital was founded. In Europe, having a family member with a mental illness was long seen as a source of shame and humiliation. Many families resorted to hiding their loved ones in cellars, sometimes caging them, delegating them to servants' care, or simply abandoning them, leaving them on the streets as beggars (Sunrise House, 2019).

Other options for care included placing the mentally ill in workhouses, public institutions where the poorest people in a church parish were given basic room and board in return for work. Others were sometimes checked into general hospitals, where they were often abandoned and ignored.

Two reformers greatly influenced the spread of what is known as the humanitarian movement: Phillipe Pinel and William Tuke. Pinel was a prominent French physician who believed that patients who were mentally ill would improve if they were treated with kindness and consideration. Tuke, an English philanthropist, founded the York Retreat, where mentally ill patients were treated with respect and compassion (Hardy, 2015).

In the 1840s, American activist Dorothea Dix lobbied for better living conditions for people with mental illness after witnessing the dangerous and unhealthy conditions in which many patients lived. Over a 40-year period, Dix successfully persuaded the U.S. federal government to fund the building of 32 state psychiatric hospitals through land grants (Minnesota Governor's Council on Developmental Disabilities, n.d.). In 1943, Dix was instrumental in getting legislators to the pass the Barden-LaFollette Act. The Barden-Lafollette Act broadened the definition of disability, allowing persons with mental illness or psychiatric disabilities to be eligible for rehabilitation services (Fox & Marini, 2018).

Along with the creation of state psychiatric hospitals, various organizations, such as Mental Health America (MHA) and legislative acts, such as Community Mental Health Centers Act of 1963, sought to improve the lives of the mentally ill in the United States (Minnesota Governor's Council on Developmental Disabilities, n.d.).

Rehabilitation of Persons With Physical Disabilities

In colonial America, caring for people with disabilities was often the responsibility of the town. Towns provided poor farms and almshouses to house and support those in need, and individuals with disabilities, criminals, and paupers were often lumped under one roof. These facilities were overcrowded, dirty, and unregulated, with men and women in the same space with little oversight. By the 1800s, inmate numbers swelled, and doctors blamed the overcrowding on the rapid development of cities, machinery, and industry. Many physicians of that time believed that industrialization created pressure and stress on individuals, and in response, state governments took responsibility for these populations and often removed them to the countryside. Groups were divided and placed in institutions that were thought to be specific to their needs; however, individuals with disabilities—whether physical or cognitive—were commonly sent to "lunatic" and "insane" asylums (National Park Service, 2017).

The 1800s also brought other changes. People with disabilities were considered meager, tragic, and pitiful individuals, unfit and unable to contribute to society, except to serve as ridiculed objects of entertainment in circuses and exhibitions (Anti-Biased Education, n.d.). They were assumed to be abnormal and feeble-minded, and numerous persons were forced to undergo sterilizations. People with disabilities were forced to enter institutions and asylums where they would spend most of their lives. The purification and segregation of persons with physical disabilities were considered merciful actions but ultimately served to keep people with disabilities invisible and hidden from a fearful and biased society (Anti-Biased Education, n.d.).

The impact of the return of veterans with disabilities after World War II and the fights for rights of women and racial and ethnic minorities contributed to changing perspectives on disability in the United States. A growing number of people with disabilities and their advocates saw that it was not the disability but rather an inaccessible environment and the negative attitudes of others that were the greatest contributors to the restrictions they encountered. Their view that access to programs and services was a civil right led to legislation such as the Architectural Barriers Act of 1968, the Rehabilitation Act of 1973, the Education of All Handicapped Children Act of 1975 (later updated and renamed the Individuals with Disabilities Education Act, IDEA), and the Americans with Disabilities Act of 1990 (ADA). These and other laws allowed people with physical and mental disabilities to have full access to the services, communities, and opportunities they did not have before (Disabilities, Opportunities, Internetworking, and Technology, 2020).

Near the end of the 19th century, greater support was given to the education and training of children with physical disabilities (Rubin & Roessler, 2008). Several states took the initiative in developing special schools for children with disabilities and providing additional support for their education through specialized training or vocational training that was designed to assist in their employment. The Individuals with Disabilities Education Act (IDEA) was passed in 1975, and amendments to the law were passed in 1990, and the name was changed to IDEA. The law states that all children with an identified disability have a right to receive special education and related services to address their individual needs (Disabilities, Opportunities, Internetworking, and Technology, 2020).

Historical Lineage of Clinical Rehabilitation Counseling

Any discussion of the historical lineage of clinical rehabilitation counseling must include the history of counseling and the roots of vocational guidance. During the growth of vocational guidance, specialization of vocational rehabilitation counseling also increased (Chan, 2003). Traditionally, the primary role of vocational rehabilitation counselors was to provide services such as vocational and career counseling, consultation, counseling interventions, community-based rehabilitation services, research, assessments, professional advocacy, and case management (Leahy et al., 2003; Maki & Tarvydas, 2012). The field of counseling expanded from vocational guidance to a holistic approach of providing professional counseling services to individuals with mental, emotional, and developmental disabilities (American Counseling Association, 2014).

The roots of clinical rehabilitation counseling can be traced to the 1960s with the specialization of psychiatric rehabilitation counseling that came from the intersection of rehabilitation counseling and mental health counseling (Jenkins et al., 1988). Psychiatric rehabilitation and community counseling specializations arose in the 1960s in response to the deinstitutionalization movement, whereby individuals with severe psychiatric disabilities were discharged from long-term psychiatric hospitals into the community (Jenkins et al., 1988; Maki & Tarvydas, 2012).

Over the next couple of decades, conversations occurred regarding the merger of vocational rehabilitation counseling and mental health counseling as society began to recognize the importance of integrated care for both physical and mental disorders. In 2015, a merger between the two counseling accrediting bodies that provide curriculum for counseling degree programs, the Council for Accreditation of Counseling and Related Educational Programs (CACREP) and the Council on Rehabilitation Education (CORE), took place. Prior to the merger, rehabilitation counseling programs accredited by CORE were required to offer a minimum of 48 credit hours focusing on preparing vocational rehabilitation counselors to work with people with disabilities (Chan et al., 2003). During the merger, the specialization of clinical rehabilitation and mental health counseling was created, and the educational requirements increased from 48 credit hours to 60 credit hours to account for the additional clinical coursework and experiential training. In addition to taking additional clinical courses, clinical rehabilitation counselors were required to do an internship in a setting that treats and diagnosis mental and emotional disorders. Specifically, students pursuing clinical rehabilitation counseling were required to take coursework that included diagnosis and treatment of mental and emotional disorders and personality assessment so that they would be eligible to sit for the National Counselor Examination (NCE), the exam used for licensure as a professional counselor in most states' mental health licensure boards, while some states provide reciprocity with the Commission on Rehabilitation Counselor Certification. The field of clinical rehabilitation and mental health counseling is a profession that addresses the holistic needs of consumers. Many of the consumers served by clinical rehabilitation counselors have psychiatric, developmental, cognitive, emotional, and/or physical disabilities. In order to achieve their maximum level of independence and wellness to be able to fully integrate and participate in the community and the world of work in accordance with their career aspirations, they need counselors who are equipped to address all of these needs (Leahy et al., 2003; Maki & Tarvydas, 2012).

Clinical rehabilitation counselors are highly trained professionals who use a consumer-centered approach to assist individuals with disabilities, physical, emotional, and psychological, to have optimal functioning with personal goals, abilities, and quality of life (Chan et al., 2003). Rehabilitation counselors' primary professional focus is on job development and placement of individuals with disabilities, career counseling, employer consultation, and vocational planning and assessment. Their professional interventions were organized into three primary areas, including providing individual, group, and family counseling; building consumer–counselor relationships; and assisting consumers to adjust and handle psychosocial aspects related to disabilities (Leahy et al., 2003; Maki & Tarvydas, 2012).

Historical Lineage of Clinical Rehabilitation Counseling Accreditation

Counseling is a dynamic field of practice that affords counselors the potential to influence and impact consumers. Clinical rehabilitation counseling developed from a range of historical influences into its current role and continues to develop. Credentialing has helped tremendously in aiding in the establishment of the professional identity of counselors by providing professional standards that all counselors must adhere to. The training that both clinical mental health counselors and clinical rehabilitation counselors receive before entering the field is pursuant to professional standards of educational accrediting bodies, licensure laws, and best practice research.

In 1972, CORE was incorporated with the mission of promoting "the effective delivery of rehabilitation services to individuals with disabilities by promoting and fostering continuing review and improvement of master's degree level rehabilitation counseling educational programs (CORE, 2001, p. 2). Nine years after CORE, CACREP was established and incorporated in 1981. For years, these two accrediting organizations worked separately to accredit educational programs responsible for preparing counselors. However, in 2015, the two accrediting bodies merged and established guidelines as well as criteria for the training of clinical rehabilitation counselors. With the merger of CORE and CACREP, many traditional rehabilitation programs began the process of seeking accreditation under the Clinical Rehabilitation and Clinical Mental Health program, a specialty established by CACREP with the input of CORE pursuant to the CACREP and CORE affiliation in 2009 (Newsome & Gladding, 2014). The clinical rehabilitation counseling program utilizing CACREP standards has operated as a sophisticated professional model in the preparation of new clinicians (Newsome & Gladding, 2014). When accredited by CORE, rehabilitation programs were only required to provide a minimum of 48 credit hours. While the educational curriculum fully prepared rehabilitation counselors for assisting vocational rehabilitation consumers, it did not meet the new standards for licensure by state organizations that required a minimum of 60 credit hours. Students who graduated from a program accredited by CORE were prepared to sit for the Certified Rehabilitation Counselor examination. The primary purpose of certification is to provide assurance that rehabilitation counselors have the requisite knowledge to provide quality services to their consumers with disabilities (Leahy et al., 2003).

Clinical Rehabilitation Counseling as a Specialized Practice

Counselors seek to understand and connect with their consumers by establishing a therapeutic working relationship or therapeutic alliance (Smart, 2016). Clinical rehabilitation counselors' professional focus is with individuals with physical, cognitive, emotional, and psychiatric disabilities (Smart, 2016). According to Koch (2016), one of the leading disabilities in the world is mental illness. According to Koch (2016), 1 in 5 U.S. adults has a mental illness. The Substance Abuse and Mental Health Administration (SAMHA, 2014) estimates that approximately 10 million Americans meet the criteria for a serious mental illness. According to SAMHA (2014), a psychiatric disability exists when an individual with a mental illness is unable to perform major life activities such as work, community activities, and independent living. Despite the fact that disability is a natural part of human existence and a condition that anyone can experience at any time, clinical rehabilitation counseling is the primary specialization that is prepared to work with this unique population (Smart, 2016).

SUMMARY

This chapter focused on the history of rehabilitation counseling, including the treatment of people with disabilities over the years. Understanding varying perspectives of how people with disabilities were viewed enables one to understand how individuals with disabilities were treated in the past as compared to the current treatment modalities. Viewing rehabilitation from different lenses (clinical rehabilitation vs. vocational rehabilitation) facilitates a deeper understanding of what is involved in practice and how practitioners are better equipped to provide different levels of treatment as a clinical versus vocational counselor. Although there are many distinct differences between vocational rehabilitation counseling and clinical rehabilitation counseling, consumers will benefit from a clinical rehabilitation counselor who is equipped to provide integrated care that addresses vocational and mental health needs.

Discussion Questions

1. How were children with disabilities treated in ancient Greece and Rome?
2. What services were available for individuals with mental illness during the early 1900s?
3. How did services for individuals with hearing disabilities emerge in the United States?
4. What is the significance of schools that were created for the blind?
5. Trace the treatment of individuals with physical disabilities from the distant past to the present.
6. When did rehabilitation emerge as a treatment?
7. How has the specialization of clinical rehabilitation counseling changed the role of vocational counselors?

Case Study: Tracey and George

Tracey and George have been married for 9 years. Tracey is a 45-year-old Trinidadian woman, and George is a 55-year-old African American man. He is a Gulf War veteran and served 20 years in the U.S. Army. During the conflict in Iraq, he was wounded and lost his left arm. He was granted an honorable discharge and awarded a Purple Heart. Tracey has been married to George for 3 years. Two years ago George was diagnosed with anxiety and posttraumatic stress disorder. Tracey has been feeling overwhelmed for the past 3 months. Tracey and George have one child together, a daughter, Alicia, who is 13 years old and is in high school. Currently, her grades are good, and her teachers enjoy her work. Tracey has started joining George in therapy with his clinical rehabilitation counselor because she has been feeling overwhelmed and they fear it is affecting Alicia and their marriage. Also, George is requesting vocational/career counseling.

Tracey is an assistant dean for the College of Education and starts her day at 8:30 a.m. with university meetings. Tracey usually has breakfast on the road, and she frequents the drive-thru on her way to work for convenience. She is the only person of color in the College of Education and feels anxious and stressed. She feels no one understands her. At night, George prepares a balanced meal for himself, Alicia, and Tracey. Tracey has gotten to the point to where she isolates herself, preferring to go to her home office and snack all night in front of the computer writing instead of spending time with family or friends.

1. Discuss a possible diagnosis for Tracey.
2. Discuss specific efforts made to ensure multicultural competences are demonstrated.
3. Discuss possible cultural biases a clinical rehabilitation counselor might have when conducting an assessment on Tracey.

REFERENCES

Action for Access. (n.d.). *Changing perceptions of disability in America life: Early movement.* https://www. actionfor access.mohistory.org

American Addiction Services. (2020). *Treatment options for those with physical disabilities.* https://www. greenhousetreatment.com/therapy/physical-disabilities/

American Counseling Association. (2014). *State of the profession.* http://www.counseling.org

American School for the Deaf. (n.d.). *History of deaf education in America.* https://www.asd-1817.org/about/ history--cogswell-heritage-house

Anti-Biased Education. (n.d.). *A brief history of disability rights movement.* https://www.adl.org/education/ resources/backgrounders/disability-rights-movement

Brainard, R. (2019). Living with a disability in the 18th century. https://www.history.com/index

Burch, S. (2001). *Reading between the signs: Defending deaf culture in early twentieth-century America.* New York University Press.

Chan, F. (2003). Training needs of rehabilitation counselors for contemporary practices. *Rehabilitation Counseling Bulletin, 46,* 86–91.

Commission on Rehabilitation Counseling Certification. (2016). *Rehabilitation counseling.* http://www. crccertification.com/pages/rehabilitation_counseling/30.php

Council on Rehabilitation Education. (2002). *CORE standards revised draft.* Retrieved October 18, 2002, from http://www. core-rehab.org/CoreStandardsReview.pdf

Disabilities, Opportunities, Internetworking, and Technology. (2020). *History and current trends regarding people with disabilities.* https://www.washington.edu/doit/history-and-current-trends-regarding-people-disabilities

Emener, W. G., & Cottone, R. R. (1989). Professionalization, deprofessionalization, reprofessionalization of rehabilitation counseling. *Journal of Counseling and Development, 67,* 576–581.

Ferreras, I. G. (2020). *History of mental illness.* In R. Biswas-Deiner & E. Diener (Eds.), *NOBA textbook series: Psychology.* DEF publishers.

Fox, D., & Marini, I. (2018). History of treatment towards persons with disabilities in America. In C. Stebnicki & I. Marini (Eds.), *The psychological and social impact of illness and disability* (7th ed.). Springer Publishing.

Hardy, J. (2015). *A beautiful mind: The history and treatment of mental illness.* https://www.historycooperative.org

Jenkins, W. M., Patterson, J. B., & Szymanski, E. M. (1998). Philosophical, historical, and legislative aspects of the rehabilitation counseling profession. In R. M. Parker & E. M. Szymanski (Eds.), *Rehabilitation counseling: Basics and beyond* (3rd ed., pp. 19–40). PRO-ED.

Koch, L. C., Donnell, C. C., & Lusk, S. L. (2016). Introduction to the special issues of psychiatric rehabilitation counseling. *Rehabilitation Research Policy, and Education, 30*(3), 198–203.

Leahy, M., Chen, F., & Saunders, J. (2003). A work behavior analysis of contemporary rehabilitation counselors. *Rehabilitation Counseling Bulletin, 46,* 66–81.

Maki, D. R., & Tarvyadas, V. (Eds.). (2012). *The professional practice of rehabilitation counseling* (2nd ed.). Springer Publishing.

Minnesota Governor's Council on Developmental Disabilities. (n.d.). *Parallels in time: A history of developmental disabilities.* https://wn.gov/mndd/parallels/two/1.html

National Park Service. (2017). *Disability history: Early and shifting attitudes of treatment.* https://www.nps.gov

Newsome, D. B., & Gladding, S. T. (2014). *Clinical mental counseling in community and agencies settings* (4th ed.). Pearson.

Nomeland, M. M., & Nomeland, R., E. (1940). *The deaf community in America: History in the making.* McFarland & Company, Inc.

Nordstrom, B. H. (1986). *The history of the education of the blind and deaf.* Retrieved from ERIC.files.ed.gov.

Perkins School for the Blind. (n.d.). *The 1800s.* https://www.perkins.org/history/timeline/1800s

Merriam-Webster. (n.d.). Rehabilitation. In *Merriam-Webster.com dictionary.* https://www.merriam-webster.com/dictionary/rehabilitation

Rose, S. E. (2017). *No right to be idle: The invention of disability, 1840s–1930s.* University of North Carolina Press.

Rubin, S. E., & Roessler, R. T. (2008). *Foundation of the vocational rehabilitation process* (5th ed.). Pro-Ed.

Rushton, C. J. (2013). *Disability and medieval law: History, literature, society.* Cambridge Scholars Publishing.

Schoenberg, T. J. (1977). The role of mental illness in European witch hunts of the sixteenth and seventeenth centuries: An assessment. *Journal of the History of Behavioral Sciences, 13*(4), 337–351.

Smart, J. (2016). Counseling individuals with disabilities. In I. Marini & M. A. Stebnicki (Eds.), *The Professional Counselor Desk Reference* (2nd ed.; pp. 417–421). Springer Publishing.

Squire, A. (2013). *Disability in the medieval period.* https://www.quadlife.com

Sunrise House. (2019). *The history and evolution of mental health and treatment.* https://sunrisehouse.com

Tseng, W. (1973). The development of psychiatric concepts in traditional Chinese medicine. *General Archives of Psychiatry, 29,* 569–575.

Unite for Sight. (n.d.). *Early history of mental illness: Mental health hospitals and deinstitutionalization.* https://www.uniteforsight.org

Young, J. S., & Cashwell, C. S. (2017). *Clinical mental health counseling: Elements of effective practice.* SAGE.

Zilboorg, G., & Henry, G. W. (1941). *A history of medical psychology.* W. W. Norton.

Zimmerman, H. G., & Horejes, T. (2017). The origins of deaf education: From alphabets to America an introduction to educating children who are deaf/hard of hearing. In *Teach to learn* (Chapter 6). [E-book]. https://www.infanthearing.org/ebook-educating-children-dhh/

CHAPTER 2

Disability Law

Camilla Drake, PhD, LPC
Angela Hall, PhD
Sekeria Bossie, PhD, LPC-S, NCC, CAMS, ACAS
Dothel Edwards, RhD, CRC, CLCP

> Lawmaking is a basic power approach designed to give freedom and equity to groups of people. Transcendence of power approaches ... is an individual's step toward liberation of a different kind. It becomes more attainable, it seems, after individuals have experienced the sense of being powerful in ways meaningful to them. (Wright, 1983)

Learning Objectives

As a result of reading this chapter, the student will be able to:

- Describe the basic facts, arguments, and decisions of six landmark disability court cases.
- Outline the evolution of legislative acts related to the employment and civil rights of individuals with disabilities.
- Describe the development and amendments of the Rehabilitation Act of 1973.
- Describe the Education for All Handicapped Children Act of 1978.
- Explain the disability policy that was mandated between 1988 and 2014.

INTRODUCTION

Individuals with disabilities have endured inadequate services, rejection, devaluation, and externally imposed limitations based on their identified disabilities. Several significant court cases have led to the development and passage of groundbreaking legislation that has positively impacted the lives of individuals with disabilities. Laws have been passed that ensure that individuals with disabilities have the right to attend school, the right to employment, the right to serve on a jury, the right to serve in the military, the right to be admitted into a professional organization, the right to take a professional licensure exam, and the right to be admitted into a residency program Additionally, legislative amendments have expanded definitions, services, monetary support, and accountability for a number of federal and private entities that provide services to individuals with disabilities.

Significant Court Cases

Mills v. Board of Education, 1972

Facts

Seven children between the ages of 7 and 16 years of age who exhibited behavior problems were attending school in the District of Columbia. Some of the children were labeled as mentally retarded, emotionally disturbed, and/or hyperactive. All of the students had been excluded from school and were not allowed to participate in educational services. It was believed that some of these educational services that the youth could not participate in would have been able to address some of the needs that arose from their identified disabilities. The Board of Education for the District of Columbia claimed that these children were not able to be educated by the schools due to their special needs. The Board of Education did not make any alternative provisions or efforts to attempt to meet the children's academic needs. In fact, the Board of Education claimed that to address the behaviors of the children they would have to provide extra services and that such services would be too expensive. The Board of Education also chose not to enroll and/or expel and/or suspend/transfer students due to their disabilities. The parents of the seven children banded together and filed suit against the Board of Education for the District Columbia for failing to provide their children with a free public school education.

Arguments

The parents and guardians of the students argued that the failure of the school board in the District of Columbia to provide a public school education constituted a denial of their children's right to an education. The Board of Education argued that they had insufficient funds to serve the children based on their needs.

Decision

The decision by the United States District Court for the District of Columbia in *Mills v. Board of Education* produced the following findings:

- The actions taken by the District of Columbia School Board were in violation of the children's right to a public school education.
- School-age children must receive a free and public education regardless of their mental, physical, or emotional ability.
- A free public education or a suitable alternative education, paid for by the Board of Education, must be provided to all students regardless of their needs and regardless of the cost.
- A free and public education cannot be denied to a child with a disability unless they are granted due process proceedings.

- The school board's failure to provide an education for the children could not be due to insufficient funds available for services and that funds should be apportioned as best as possible to ensure that no child is denied the opportunity for a public school education.

In light of these findings, the court ordered a remediation plan.

Galloway v. Superior Court of District of Columbia, 1993

Facts

Donald Galloway was a blind citizen of the District of Columbia and had been blind since his youth. He had lived his life blind and had become adjusted to his blindness. He was an active member of society. Galloway received a summons to present himself for jury duty, a task he proudly viewed as a civic duty. After arriving to make himself available for jury duty, Galloway was informed by personnel of the Superior Court of the District of Columbia that the court's policy was to exclude all blind persons from jury service. He was prevented from serving as a juror, which Galloway viewed as a violation of his rights. Specifically, he believed that the Superior District Court of the District of Columbia was in violation of the Rehabilitation Act of 1973, the Civil Rights Act of 1871, and Title II of the Americans with Disability Act. Galloway's affidavit articulated how he endured substantial emotional pain and mental anguish from his barring of being able to be a juror.

Arguments

Galloway asserted that his rights were violated by the court's failure to adhere to the Rehabilitation Act of 1973, the Civil Rights Act of 1964, and the Americans with Disability Act. He expressed that not being able to engage in being a juror had had a negative emotional impact. His lawyers argued that the United States has substantial responsibility for enforcing Section 504 of the Rehabilitation Act of 1973 and that Title II of the Americans with Disability Act, which was patterned after Section 504 of the Rehabilitation Act of 1973, provided broad prohibitions against discrimination on the basis of disability. They also argued that the Civil Rights Act of 1964 provided for compensatory damages. They also noted that there were several active judges who were blind and that individuals who were deaf had been able to serve as jurors. Galloway's lawyers held that he should be compensated for the indignity, humiliation, stigmatization, and emotional distress of being prohibited, because of his disability, from exercising one of the most important privileges and duties this country asks of its citizens.

Decision

The United States District Court for the District of Columbia stated three important findings in the case. First, the court acknowledged that the policy of the Superior Court of the District of Columbia of categorically excluding blind individuals from jury service was a violation of the Rehabilitation Act of 1973, the Americans with Disabilities Act, and the Civil Rights Act of 1964. Second, it was ordered that the Superior Court of the District of Columbia, and all acting on its behalf, were prevented from categorically excluding blind persons from jury service in the Superior Court of the District of Columbia. It was also concluded that Mr. Galloway was entitled to seek compensatory damages under both Title II of the American Disabilities Act and Section 504 of the Rehabilitation Act.

Lane v. Pena, Secretary of Transportation, 1996

Facts

James Griffin Lane enrolled at the United States Merchant Marine Academy and entered as a first-year student in July 1991. Part of the process for him being able to enroll was Lane's ability to meet the Academy's health requirements. Lane completed and passed a physical examination conducted by the Department of Defense. During his first year, however, Lane was seen by his private physician and was diagnosed with diabetes mellitus. He communicated the new diagnosis appropriately. He reported the diagnosis to the Academy's chief medical officer. He later became aware that his diagnosis of diabetes mellitus might be problematic for his continuance in the Academy. According to the case summary, in September 1992, the Academy's Physical Examination Review Board conducted a hearing to determine his medical suitability to continue at the Academy. As a result, the Review Board reported to the superintendent of the academy that Lane suffered from insulin-dependent diabetes. As a result of his diagnosis, in December 1992, Lane was separated from the Academy on the ground that his diabetes mellitus was a disqualifying condition rendering him ineligible to be commissioned for service in the Navy/Merchant Marine Reserve Program or as a Naval Reserve Officer. He worked to challenge the findings and the decision to dismiss him from the Academy. He was unsuccessful in having the dismissal modified. After his unsuccessful efforts at challenging his separation, he brought suit in the Federal District Court against the secretary of the Department of Transportation and other defendants, alleging that his separation from the Academy violated Section 504 of the Rehabilitation Act. He sought reinstatement to the Academy as well as compensatory damages, attorney fees, and cost.

Arguments

Lane asserted that his rights had been violated according to Section 504 of the Rehabilitation Act. Section 504 provides that "no otherwise qualified individual with a disability in the United States … shall, solely by reason of her or his disability, be excluded from the participation in, be denied the benefits of, or be subjected to discrimination under any program or activity receiving Federal financial assistance." Lane had demonstrated that he met the qualifications for the Academy previously, and it was believed that, notwithstanding his diagnosis of diabetes mellitus, he would still meet the qualifications for the Academy.

Decision

The District Court concluded that his separation from the Academy solely on the basis of his diagnosis of diabetes mellitus violated Section 504 of the Rehabilitation Act. The court ordered Lane to be reinstated but denied any awards for compensatory damages.

Petition of Rubenstein, 1994

Facts

Kara B. Rubenstein received a bachelor's degree from the University of Pennsylvania and a juris doctorate from Temple University Law School. From 1989 to 1990 she served as a law clerk, and in the fall of 1990, she was certified under Supreme Court Rule 55 that provides limited permissions to practice law in Delaware's courts. Subsequently, in 1990 she became employed by the Department of Justice of the State of Delaware as an assistant deputy attorney general and worked as an attorney in that capacity for 2 years until December 1992.

Although she was engaging in the work of being an attorney and exhibiting a high level of skill, she had not passed the Delaware bar examination. However, it was not due to her failing to make an attempt to pass the examination. Rubenstein applied for admission to the Delaware bar in 1990, as well as 1991, 1992, and 1993. The test had two parts: (1) the Professional Conduct Examination and (2) the Delaware Bar Examination, which included both an essay portion and the Multistate Bar Examination. According to the petition, in 1990 Ms. Rubenstein failed both portions of the test; in 1991, she passed the Professional Conduct Examination but not the Delaware Bar Examination; in 1992, she passed the Multistate Bar Examination but failed the essay portion. This caused her to consider why she was able to perform at a high level as an attorney but was struggling with the examination. After three unsuccessful attempts to pass the Delaware Bar Examination, Ms. Rubenstein sought out an expert to gain clarity and an explanation for the anomalous dichotomy between her inability to pass the Delaware Bar Examination and her undisputed ability to function effectively as a prosecuting attorney in Delaware courts. After careful testing, Rubenstein was advised that she suffered from a learning disability that had been previously undiagnosed. This allowed her to gain information about assistance she might need to be able to pass the examination. The disability had no bearing on her level of intelligence or acumen but related exclusively to the means by which she processed information. With this new information in hand, in April 1993 Rubenstein filed a petition with the board requesting an exercise of its discretion to permit her a fourth opportunity to take the Delaware Bar Examination. Her petition alleged that she suffered from a learning disability that had been previously undiagnosed. In June 1993, the board granted her petition to take the Delaware Bar Examination a fourth time. They made this decision based on the new information that was provided to them related to her current and previously undiagnosed condition. The board made accommodations by allowing her to take the essay section in a separate room and to have one additional hour for each 3-hour essay. The board did not permit additional time or any other accommodations on the Multistate Bar Examination. She passed the Delaware Bar Examination, but did not pass the Multistate Bar Examination. She followed up this disappointment by petitioning the board to be qualified for admission to the Delaware Bar, and it was denied. She made that additional petition due to believing that she should have been provided accommodations with both sections.

Arguments

Ms. Rubenstein argued that the decision to grant her additional time on the essays but not on the Multistate Bar Examination was both arbitrary and manifestly unfair. Her limitations were applicable to both portions of the examination. She further argued that the board's accommodations to her were an unreasonable response to her undisputed learning disability. This led her to believe that the Americans with Disability Act was a standard that was applicable to her circumstances. The Americans with Disabilities Act provides that persons or entities make reasonable accommodations or modifications for the disability.

Decision

The Delaware supreme court determined that the board's decision to deny Rubenstein any additional time to take the Multistate Bar Examination portion of the Bar Examination in 1993 was manifestly unfair and that the court had to identify an appropriate and equitable remedy. They ruled that efforts to address accommodations be manifestly fair. Under the facts of this case, the board was directed to deliver to Rubenstein the certificate required by the Supreme Court. It was concluded that due to the special circumstances both sections of the Delaware Bar Examination did not have to be passed in one setting.

Bartlett v. New York State Board of Law Examiners, 1997

Facts

Dr. Marilyn Bartlett was a 49-year-old woman with a reported cognitive disorder that impaired her ability to read. While this impairment might have negatively impacted others academically, Dr. Bartlett earned a PhD in educational administration from New York University and a law degree from Vermont Law School. After graduating from law school, she decided to pursue her licensure. Dr. Bartlett experienced significant difficulties in being able to pass the licensure exam. From 1991 to 1993, Dr. Bartlett took the bar examination five times, requesting accommodations on at least three of those occasions due to having what she labeled a reading disability. On three agreed-upon occasions and one contested occasion, when applying to take the licensure exam, Dr. Bartlett sought reasonable accommodations. She had been seeking an extension related to time allotted to her to take the licensure exam. She was denied each time. The New York State Board of Law Examiners expressed that the content of her application did not support a diagnosis of a reading disability or dyslexia. She was also administered a test (Woodcock Johnson Test of Cognitive Abilities) that initially yielded similar findings. On July 20, 1993, the Board denied her application for accommodations, and she took legal actions, alleging that her rights had been violated.

Arguments

Dr. Bartlett notified the Board of her disability and put forth the efforts to request accommodations. She sought unlimited or extended time to take the test and permission to tape record her essays and to circle her multiple choice answers in the test booklet rather than completing the answer sheet. These accommodations were perceived as reasonable, and their supportive nature related to the area of her disability could have been beneficial. The Board denied her request each time. They expressed that her application does not support a diagnosis of a reading disability or dyslexia. According to the court documents, these findings were grounded on a Dr. Vellutino and his assessment of her capacity. Dr. Vellutino reportedly based his interpretations of the results of the Woodcock Johnson Test of Cognitive Abilities. It was noted that the Woodcock Johnson Test of Cognitive Abilities was specifically designed to assess children, and this resulted in discrepancies in the findings.

Due to this final denial, Dr. Bartlett argued that Title II of the Americans with Disabilities Act and Section 504 of the Rehabilitation Act had been violated due to the Board's denial of reasonable accommodations that she was entitled to due to her learning disability.

Decision

The United States Court of Appeals, Second Circuit, concluded that Dr. Bartlett had a disability and that the Board's failure to accommodate her constituted violations of the Americans with Disability Act and Section 504 of the Rehabilitation Act. The court found that Bartlett was not substantially limited with respect to major life activities such as reading or learning but that she was substantially limited with respect to the major life activity of working. After coming to that conclusion, the court held that the New York State Board of Law Examiners was required to provide Bartlett with reasonable accommodations on the New York State Bar Examination.

Should she decide to retake the bar exam in the future, the court awarded Dr. Bartlett the following reasonable accommodations:

- Double the normally allotted time (more than 4 days).
- Use of a computer.
- Permission to circle multiple choice answers in the exam booklet.
- Large print on both the state and multistate exams.

In addition to the award of reasonable accommodations, the court also awarded compensatory damages of $12,500.00 to compensate for fees that she incurred when taking the test multiple times without accommodations.

Pushkin v. Regents of the University of Colorado, 1981

Facts

Joshua Pushkin was a medical doctor. He was attempting to be admitted into a psychiatry residency program at the University of Colorado. He had a diagnosis of multiple sclerosis and was ambulatory with the use of a wheelchair. In addition to not being able to walk, he was not able to write. He worked with Dr. Carter and others to complete all procedural requirements pertaining to the application process. Dr. Pushkin completed the interview process (four separate interviews), and each of his interviewers noted his disability as a concern in their documentation as a factor in determining if he should be accepted into the program. Dr. Pushkin had recommendations from others that indicated he was able to work effectively with others and that his medical treatments could be arranged to minimally impact his availability. While his interviews were conducted by several other professors, Dr. Carter was responsible for exercising final power to make the decision as to appointments or rejections of applicants for positions as a psychiatric resident at the University of Colorado. Ultimately, Dr. Carter rejected Dr. Pushkin's application but did not identify a direct reason as to why he was not accepted. Dr. Pushkin expressed that he felt he was not admitted into the psychiatric residency program based on his disability. He believed his rights had been violated.

Argument

In rejecting Dr. Pushkin's application, Dr. Pushkin's lawyers argued that Dr. Carter and the University of Colorado were excluding him and denying Dr. Pushkin the ability to participate in the residency program based on the disability concerns identified by the four interviewers. It was noted that Dr. Pushkin would not have needed substantial modifications of the residency program to be able to participate. Additionally, his difficulty with writing was not considered a problem because he could dictate his documentation. The process of dictating one's documentation is a common practice in the medical field. The specific statutory provision alleged to have been violated is Section 504 of the Rehabilitation Act which provides: "No otherwise qualified handicapped individual in the United States, as defined in section 706 of this title, shall, solely by reason of his handicap, be excluded from the participation in, be denied the benefits of, or be subjected to discrimination under any program or activity receiving federal financial assistance." Dr. Pushkin's lawyers stated that Dr. Pushkin was an "otherwise qualified handicapped individual."

Decision

The United States Court of Appeals for the 10th Circuit found that the residency program of the University of Colorado had discriminated against Dr. Pushkin and was in violation of Section 504 of the Rehabilitation Act.

Impact of Cases on Individuals With Disabilities

These court cases were integral in transforming the lives of individuals with disabilities. Not only were these individuals and their families involved in the court cases afforded the opportunities and experiences that they were seeking, but they also created opportunities for others as well. Overall, these court cases have increased the assurance of equal treatment, equal access to services, and equal opportunities to individuals with disabilities. Additionally, these court cases have led to the development of key legislation that generalized the impact of these court cases for others.

Legislation

Years 1917–1938

The course of legislation improving the lives of those with disabilities has been a relatively short one for this country, considering that most of the legislation has occurred during the past 50 years or so. The following legislative acts, while not all-encompassing, give some indication as to how the premise of "providing vocational opportunities" has progressed into the concept of "equal rights and access." For individuals with disabilities, these legislative acts are more than just words; they represent major sociological events for the disability rights movement.

Beginning in 1917, the Smith-Hughes Act established a federal–state program in vocational education and created a Federal Board of Vocational Education with the authority and responsibility for vocational rehabilitation of disabled veterans. This was the first time in U.S. history that a law was created to address the needs of individuals with disabilities, specifically those returning from war. In 1918, The Smith-Sears Veterans Rehabilitation Act expanded the role of the Federal Board of Vocational Education to provide services for vocational rehabilitation of veterans disabled during World War I. This act is also referred to as the Soldier's Rehabilitation Act.

In 1920, The Smith-Fess Act, also known as the Civilian Rehabilitation Act, expanded on the Smith-Hughes Act and the Smith-Sears Veterans Rehabilitation Act with the beginnings of rehabilitation programs for all Americans with disabilities. It established a federal–state program in rehabilitation and provided funds to states at a 50/50 match primarily for vocational services, including vocational guidance, training, occupational adjustment, prosthetics, and placement services. However, this act was specific only for persons with physical disabilities and did not include physical restoration or social orientation rehabilitation.

Fifteen years later, in 1935, the Social Security Act was passed to establish an income maintenance system that targeted those unable to work and included provisions furnishing medical and therapeutic services for children with disabilities and made permanent the Vocational Rehabilitation program, as well as provided for continuous authorizations, increased grant awards, and increased support from the federal government. The next year, in 1936, the Randolph-Sheppard Act recognized that persons who were blind had vocational potential. This legislation gave states the authority to license qualified persons with blindness to operate vending stands in federal buildings. In 1938, the Wagner-O'Day Act, also aimed at helping persons with blindness in the vocational arena, required the federal government to purchase designated products from workshops for persons who were blind.

Years 1943–1971

In 1943, the Vocational Rehabilitation Amendments, also known as the Barden-LaFollette Act, made significant and important changes in the federal–state rehabilitation program. The act broadened the program's financial provisions, offered a comprehensive definition of vocational rehabilitation, and expanded services to include physical restoration. In addition, each state had to submit a written plan for approval by the federal agency as to how federal and state dollars would be used. It also included an expansion of services on a limited basis for those with mental disabilities and mental illness and fostered separate agencies for general rehabilitation and rehabilitation of persons who were blind. Five years later, in 1948, in order to aid returning World War II Veterans, Congress passed legislation prohibiting discrimination based on physical disability for employment in the U.S. Civil Service.

In 1954, the Vocational Rehabilitation Amendments reshaped the roles of the federal and state governments in the federal–state rehabilitation program, as well as established the basis for a working relationship between public and private rehabilitation providers. These amendments also expanded the role of the state agency and established funding sources for college and university training of rehabilitation professionals, the improvement and remodeling of rehabilitation facilities, research and demonstration grants, which increased federal funding to states, a federal dollar match for every two dollars from the states, and increased services to persons with mental disabilities and mental illness.

With the civil rights movement in full swing, the 1960s brought about many legislative changes, including several amendments to the Vocational Rehabilitation Act. In 1961, the American National Standards Institute (ANSI) issued the first minimum requirements for individuals with disabilities relating to architectural access to common structures. In 1965, the Vocational Rehabilitation Act Amendments expanded services to include individuals with social rehabilitation issues, such as alcoholism, educational deficits, and prison records, and expanded evaluations to determine individual eligibility for services where feasibility was not easily determined. The 1965 amendments also allowed rehabilitation counselors to take more risks in serving individuals with disabilities that affected employability, thereby serving more individuals with severe disabilities, as well as established a National Commission on Architectural Barriers and removed economic need as a general requirement for services. Finally, these 1965 amendments increased the federal dollar match to 75%.

In 1967, the Vocational Rehabilitation Act Amendments began to provide rehabilitation services to migratory workers, eliminated the state residency requirement, and supported the construction and operation of the National Center for Deaf/Blind Youth and Adults. Near the end of the decade, in 1968, the Vocational Rehabilitation Act Amendments added follow-up services for maintaining an individual with a disability in employment and provided services to family members. Additionally, the 1968 amendments gave authority to provide vocational evaluation and work adjustment services to persons at a disadvantage due to age, level of vocational attainment, and ethnicity, and the federal match was increased to 80%. This same year, the Architectural Barriers Act (1968) required buildings constructed with federal funds or leased by the federal government to be accessible to individuals with disabilities.

In 1970, the Urban Mass Transportation Act required local transportation authorities to plan and design mass transit systems to be accessible to individuals with disabilities, and in 1971, the Javits-Wagner-O'Day Act retained priority for blindness in the provision of products for the federal government and added people with severe disabilities as eligible for participation. Two court cases—*Pennsylvania Association for Retarded Children vs. Pennsylvania* and *Mills vs. Board of Education*—established that denying education to disabled children or treating them differently within the educational system was a denial of equal protection and due process under the U.S. Constitution.

Years 1973–1986

The Rehabilitation Act of 1973 was enacted by the 93rd United States Congress and signed into law on September 26, 1973, by Richard Nixon. It protects qualified individuals with disabilities from employment discrimination. Specifically, it "prohibits discrimination on the basis of disability in programs conducted by federal agencies, in programs receiving federal financial assistance, in federal employment, and in the employment practices of federal contractors" (U.S. Department of Justice, 2020). The legislation also attempted to address societal barriers faced by individuals with disabilities, including isolation by placement in institutions, limited access to buildings, and discrimination in education and employment (Wilcher, 2018). Employment discrimination under the Rehabilitation Act are the same as those used in Title I of the Americans with Disabilities Act.

Section 501: Employment of Individuals With Disabilities

Section 501 of the Rehabilitation Act prohibits discrimination against individuals with disabilities in the federal sector to also include the United States Postal Service, Postal Regulatory Commission, and the Smithsonian Institution. Federal agencies must adopt employment goals and subgoals for individuals with disabilities, provide personal assistant services, and execute affirmative action to recruit, retain, and advance individuals with disabilities in the federal workforce (Rehabilitation Act of 1973, Pub. L. 93–112, title V, § 501, Sept. 26, 1973, 87 Stat).

Section 502: The Access Board

Section 502 of the Rehabilitation Act addresses the development and composition of the Architectural and Transportation Barriers Compliance Board. This board is composed of 25 members; 13 individuals are appointed and represent the general public, with the majority of those appointees being individuals with disabilities. The remaining members are current heads of departments from a number of different federal agencies. The access board is responsible for ensuring compliance with the Architectural Barriers Acts (ABA) of 1968 by developing and maintaining guidelines upon which the standards are based and promoting access throughout all segments of society. Additionally, the board is also responsible for

- Determining how and to what extent transportation barriers impede the mobility of individuals with disabilities and aged individuals with disabilities and consider ways in which travel expenses in connection with transportation to and from work for individuals with disabilities can be met or subsidized when such individuals are unable to use mass transit systems or need special equipment in private transportation;
- Considering the housing needs of individuals with disabilities and determining what measures are being taken, especially by public and other nonprofit agencies and groups having an interest in and a capacity to deal with such problems;
- Eliminating barriers from public transportation systems (including vehicles used in such systems) and preventing their incorporation into new or expanded transportation systems;
- Making housing available and accessible to individuals with disabilities or meeting sheltered housing needs; and

- Preparing plans and proposals for such further actions as may be necessary to the goals of adequate transportation and housing for individuals with disabilities, including proposals for bringing together in a cooperative effort, agencies, organizations, and groups already working toward such goals or whose cooperation is essential to effective and comprehensive action (United States Access Board, 2015).

Section 503: Compliance of Federal Contractors and Subcontractors

Section 503 speaks specifically to federal contracts and subcontracts in excess of $10,000. It prohibits employment discrimination and requires that these entities take affirmative action to recruit, hire, promote, and retain individuals with disabilities (Rehabilitation Act § 503, 87 Stat at 393).

Section 504: Civil Rights for Individuals With Disabilities

Section 504 prohibits any program or activity receiving federal financial assistance or any program or activity conducted by a federal executive agency or U.S. Postal Service from discriminating against individuals with disabilities (Rehabilitation Act § 504, 87 Stat at 394, 29 USC § 794). This section protects qualified individuals with disabilities as well as job applicants and the employees of the organizations that provide them. It was not until 1977, during Jimmy Carter's administration, that this section of the Rehabilitation Act was enforced as written.

Section 508: Electronic and Information Technology

Section 508 is a 1998 amendment requiring federal agencies' information and communication technology to be accessible to individuals with disabilities. Federal agencies must give individuals with disabilities that are employed as well as individuals with disabilities that are members of the public access to information comparable to the access available to others (Rehabilitation Act Pub. L. 93–112, title V, § 508).

Rehabilitation Act Amendments of 1974

These amendments included a broader definition of handicapped individuals; transferred the Rehabilitation Services Administration to the Department of Health, Education and Welfare; strengthened the Randolf-Sheppard Act; and provided for convening a White House Conference on handicapped individuals (Rehabilitation Act Amendments of 1974).

The Education for All Handicapped Children Act of 1975

The Education for All Handicapped Children Act was enacted by the 94th United States Congress and signed by Gerald Ford on November 29, 1975. The law guaranteed a free, appropriate public education to each child with a disability in every state and locality across the country (U.S. Department of Education, 2007). Four purposes were outlined in the law to ensure that changes made to improve the education for children with disabilities included efforts to improve methods of locating and identification of children with disabilities, to provide due process protections for these children and their families, and to authorize the use of financial incentives to allow states and localities the ability to comply with this public law. Specifically, the law outlined four purposes:

1. "To assure that all children with disabilities have available to them … a free appropriate public education which emphasizes special education and related services designed to meet their unique needs"
2. "To assure that the rights of children with disabilities and their parents … are protected"

3. "To assist states and localities to provide for the education of all children with disabilities"
4. "To assess and assure the effectiveness of efforts to educate all children with disabilities"

The Rehabilitation Act Amendments of 1978

The 1978 amendments to the Rehabilitation Act of 1973 provided comprehensive services for independent living through Title VII to include provisions for comprehensive services, centers for independent living, independent living services for older blind individuals, and protection and advocacy of individual rights. It also mandated that applicants for funds under Title VII provide assurance that individuals with disabilities would be employed, substantially involved in policy, and consulted on the direction and management of independent living centers; this major focus recognized that achievement of substantially gainful activity (employment) was not the only significant outcome that could be gained from the rehabilitation system and expanded the view of the person with needs that cut across the bureaucracy; it also provided vocational rehabilitation service grants to Native American tribes (Comprehensive Rehabilitation Services Amendments of 1978).

The Rehabilitation Act Amendments of 1984

The 1984 amendments to the Rehabilitation Act established consumer assistance programs in each state and inserted "qualified" before the word "personnel" for training programs in the act. Specifically, the amendments "revise and extend the Rehabilitation Act of 1973, to provide for the operation of the Helen Keller National Center for Deaf-Blind Youths and Adults, to extend the Developmental Disabilities Assistance and Bill of Rights Act, and for other purposes."

The Rehabilitation Act Amendments of 1986

The 1986 amendments enacted by the 99th United States Congress stipulated that rehabilitation services are to be provided by qualified personnel; defined and established supported employment as an acceptable goal; provided grants for special projects and demonstrations in supported employment; and established a program to assist state agencies to develop and implement supported employment services as well as added rehabilitation engineering as a vocational rehabilitation service. https://disabilitycenter.colostate.edu/awareness/disability-history/

Years 1988–2014

The Technology-Related Assistance for Individuals With Disabilities Act of 1988

The focus of the Technology-Related Assistance for Individuals with Disabilities Act (Tech Act) of 1988 was to improve on the role that assistive technology (AT) can have in meeting the functional needs of individuals with disabilities. The fundamental premise of the legislation was to develop and to apply technology projects that will better the quality of life for individuals with disabilities (Wallace et al., 1995).

The Assistive Technology Acts of 1998 and 2004

The Assistive Technology Act of 1998 (P.L. 105–394) extended operative terms and programs that were mentioned in the Tech Act of 1988 and its 1994 amendments. For example, the Assistive Technology Act of 1998 states the following: *assistive technology device* means "any item, piece of equipment, or product system, whether acquired commercially, modified, or customized, that is used to increase, maintain, or improve functional capabilities of individuals with disabilities; and *assistive technology service* means "any service that directly assists an individual with a disability in the selection, purchase, or use of an assistive technology device." This includes: (1) the needs of an individual with a disability, including an evaluation of the functional use of assistive technology and services to the individual in the life of the individual; (2) services consisting of purchasing, leasing, or otherwise providing for the purchase of assistive technology devices; (3) services consisting of selecting, designing, fitting, customizing, adapting, implementing, maintaining, repairing, or replacing of assistive technology devices; (4) planning and use of required therapies, interventions, or services with assistive technology devices; (5) training or technical assistance for an individual with disabilities or, if applicable, the family members, guardians, advocates, or authorized representatives of the individual; and (6) training or technical assistance for professionals providing education and rehabilitation services, employers, or other individuals that are significantly involved in the major life activities of individuals with disabilities (Alpers & Raharinirina, 2006).

The Assistive Technology Act of 1998 also includes the following aspects between the relationship of assistive technology and how it is utilized by individuals with disabilities to perform activities such as education, work, and social/cultural life: it is strongly believed that disability is a natural part of the life experience and should not prevent individuals the right to (1) live independently; (2) secure self-determination and have the right to make their own life choices; (3) profit from a quality education; (4) pursue meaningful employment; and (5) enjoy full inclusion and integration in all aspects of society.

The Assistive Technology Act of 2004 (P.L. 108-364) amends the Assistive Technology Act of 1998 (29 U.S.C. 3001 et seq.) by including an addition to the term *assistive technology service* by stating that it also "includes a service consisting of expanding the availability of access to technology, including electronic and information technology" (Alpers & Raharinirina, 2006).

The Americans With Disabilities Act of 1990 and Subsequent Amendments

The Americans with Disabilities Act (ADA) of 1990 was modeled after civil rights legislation through the avoidance of discrimination among individuals with disabilities within private and public businesses, programs, and services. The law defines an individual with a disability as an individual with "a physical or mental impairment that substantially limits one or more of the major life activities of such individual; a record of such an impairment; or being regarded as having such an impairment" (ADA, 1990).

Title I: Employment

This title is established to assist individuals with disabilities access equal employment advancements and benefits. Employers must provide reasonable accommodations to qualified persons with disabilities. The Title disability and establishes, establish reasonable accommodation guidelines. However, medical examinations and inquiries can demonstrate "direct threat" when there is significant risk of substantial harm to the health or safety of the individual employee with a disability or others, which is an acceptable reason for disqualification. (ADA National Network, n.d.).

Title II: State and Local Government

Title II of the ADA precludes discrimination against qualified individuals with disabilities within programs, activities, and services of public entities. The title applies to state and local governments. It includes the requirements of section 504 of the Rehabilitation Act of 1973, as amended, for public transportation systems that receive federal financial assistance. The title extends coverage to public entities that provide public transportation, whether or not they receive federal financial assistance (ADA National Network, n.d.).

Title III: Public Accommodations

This title precludes individuals with disabilities from discrimination in private places of public accommodation such as privately owned, leased, or operated facilities such as hotels, restaurants, retail merchants, doctors' offices, golf courses, private schools, day care centers, health clubs, sports stadiums, movie theaters, etc. The title establishes the minimum standards for accessibility for alterations and new construction of facilities. It also requires public accommodations to remove barriers in existing buildings without creating an undue hardship (ADA National Network, n.d.).

Title IV: Telecommunications

This title requires telephone and internet companies to provide individuals with hearing and speech disabilities a national system of interstate and intrastate telecommunications relay services. Further, the title requires closed captioning of federally funded public service announcements. The title is overseen by the Federal Communication Commission (ADA National Network, n.d.).

Title V: Miscellaneous Provisions

This title contains a plethora of ADA requirements to include the law's connection to other laws, state immunity, its impact on insurance providers and benefits, exclusion of retaliation and coercion, illegal use of drugs, and attorney fees. In addition, the title offer conditions that are not recognized as disabilities (ADA National Network, n.d.).

Key Definitions of the ADA

The following are key definitions of the ADA:

- *Essential job function:* Fundamental job duties of the employment position the individual with a disability holds or desires. The term does not include the reduced functions of the position (ADA National Network, n.d.).
- *Qualified individual with a disability:* An individual with a disability who meets vital skill, experience, education, and other associated job requirements of the employment position who can perform the essential functions of the job (ADA National Network, n.d.).
- *Reasonable accommodation:* A workplace modification or adjustment, the work environment, or the work processes that enables a qualified individual with a disability to enjoy an equal employment opportunity.

ADA Amendments Act of 2008

The U.S. Congress sought to improve upon the original focus of the ADA through the passage of the ADA Amendments Act (ADAAA) of 2008, which went into effect on January 1, 2009. With the passage of the ADAAA, the premise leans toward interpreting and implementing titles under the ADA, as amended. Part II provides an overview of the three-prong definition of *disability*. These three prongs maintain the definition of disability as explained in the ADA. Parts III and IV discuss the definition of disability under the first and second prong. Part V observes the guidelines of the first and second prong. Lastly, Part VI evaluates the definition of disability under the third prong. To provide clarity, Congress redefined the terms in each prong of the definition of disability and also added a rule of construction requiring that the definition of disability provide for broad coverage of individuals. The primary reason in amending the ADA with the ADAAA was to respond to the Supreme Court's interpretation of the definition of disability, which had the effect of severely reducing coverage for individuals with disabilities who were intended to receive coverage. In the ADAAA, Congress mentions that the Supreme Court and the Equal Employment Opportunity Commission have imposed too great of a degree of limitation in their interpretations of disability, specifically the terms "substantially limits" and "major" in life activities. Congress achieved the outcome of establishing a lower standard by rejecting these past Supreme Court decisions and requiring that the definition of disability be interpreted broadly (Benfer, 2009). The amendment complements the ADA by focusing on whether an individual who has been discriminated against has proven that the discrimination was based on a disability (Benfer, 2009).

Rehabilitation Act Amendments of 1992

The Rehabilitation Act Amendments of 1997 (Public Law 102-569) provided significant modifications in the guidelines, purpose, process, and goals of the rehabilitation program to support individuals across a diverse range of disability to attain and maintain employment outcomes that match their interests and abilities.

The amendments are directed by the individual's capabilities. With the needed services and support, an individual with a disability can achieve meaningful employment. Therefore, the primary responsibilities of the vocational rehabilitation system are to:

- Assist the individual with a disability to have full autonomy as it relates to potential employment outcomes.
- Develop an individualized rehabilitation program that is mutually agreed by the individual with a disability.
- Establish needs and interests reflected in the individualized programs with the right services and supports, including rehabilitation technology, supported employment, and others.
- Establish mutually agreed upon relationships with other agencies and programs.
- Emphasize the quality of services and the accountability that service personnel need to advocate for individuals with disabilities as their employment interests develop as they are being served.

Workforce Investment Act of 1998

The Workforce Investment Act of 1998 provided "workforce investment activities, through statewide and local workforce investment systems, that increase the employment, retention, and earnings of participants, and increase occupational skill attainment by participants, and, as a result, improve the quality of the workforce, reduce welfare dependency, and enhance the productivity and competitiveness of the Nation." The law was enacted to supplant the Job Training Partnership Act and certain other federal laws. The goal of the legislation was to encourage businesses to participate in workforce development through Workforce Investment Boards (WIBs), which were chaired by private-sector members of the local community.

Workforce Innovation and Opportunity Act of 2014

The Workforce Innovation and Opportunity Act (WIOA) of 2014 replaced the Workforce Investment Act of 1998. The goal of the act is to establish increased coordination among federal workforce development and related programs.

WIOA includes five titles:

- *Title I: Workforce Development Activities.* Authorizes job training and related services to unemployed or underemployed individuals and establishes the governance and performance accountability system for the WIOA.
- *Title II: Adult Education and Literacy.* Authorizes education services to assist adults in improving their basic skills, completing secondary education, and transitioning to postsecondary education.
- *Title III: Amendments to the Wagner-Peyser Act.* Amends the Wagner-Peyser Act of 1933 to incorporate the U.S. Employment Service (ES) into the one-stop system sanctioned by WIOA.
- *Title IV: Amendments to the Rehabilitation Act of 1973.* Authorizes employment-related vocational rehabilitation services to individuals with disabilities, integrating vocational rehabilitation into the one-stop system.
- *Title V: General Provisions.* Stipulates transition provisions from WIA to WIOA.

SUMMARY

Acknowledgment and treatment of disability have undergone massive transformation since the early 1900s. Through activism, individuals with disabilities have demanded legislation to be developed to protect them through a number of areas in life. Disability law overlaps with employment law, administrative law, consumer law, construction law, insurance law, education law, health law, social security law, and civil rights law. The U.S. Congress has passed many laws that support disability rights by addressing issues directly or recognizing and enforcing civil rights. Yet, even with legislation enacted to protect the civil rights of individuals with disabilities, it took many years before they were enforced. Education has also shown a tremendous amount of reform to address the needs of children with disabilities. During the 20th and 21st centuries, federal legislation was created and enacted to ensure the availability, rights, effectiveness, and funds for education services for children with disabilities. With continued advocacy, legislation was created and enacted to improve the results of educational services that are provided to children with disabilities. Quality of life includes mental and physical health, education, comfort, and employment opportunities. Continued advocacy led to the development of legislation that provided monetary support for various programs to include independent living, assistive technology, and vocational training.

Case Study: John

John Doe applies for a job with the accounting firm Howe, Billings, & Rowe. John has a hidden seizure disorder that is controlled with medication. After interviewing with the other partners, he has his last interview with the managing partner, Jeffery Smook. Mr. Smook asks John if there is anything that will keep him from doing the job. John says nothing at first but then discloses his condition. Mr. Smook then states that John should not even apply because he can live off of the government.

1. Has Mr. Smook done anything illegal? If so, what?
2. What would you advise John to do?

Discussion Questions

1. Compare and contrast the facts, arguments, and decisions of *Bartlett v. New York State Board of Examiners* and the *Petition of Rubenstein*.
2. Compare and contrast the Workforce Investment Act of 1998 and the Workforce Innovation and Opportunity Act of 2014. In addition to the employment of individuals with disabilities, how did these two acts help to advance the civil rights of individuals with disabilities?
3. Compare and contrast the Rehabilitation Act of 1973 with the Americans with Disabilities Act of 1990.
4. Compare the American with Disabilities Act of 1990 and The Individuals with Disabilities Education Act of 1975.

REFERENCES

ADA National Network. (n.d.). *Americans with Disabilities Act questions and answers.* https://adata.org/guide/americans-disabilities-act-questions-and-answers

Alpers, S., & Raharinirina, S. (2006). Assistive technology for individuals with disabilities: A review and synthesis of the literature. *Journal of Special Education Technology, 21*(2), 47–64.

Benfer, E. A. (2009). *The ADA Amendments Act: An overview of recent changes to the Americans with Disabilities Act.* American Constitution Society of Law and Policy. https://www.hivlawandpolicy.org/resources/ada-amendments-act-overview-recent-changes-americans-disabilities-act-emily-benfer

Colorado State University Disability Center. Disability Legislation History. Retrieved from: https://disabilitycenter.colostate.edu/awareness/disability-history/

Leahy, M. J., Chan, F., & Saunders, J. L. (2003). Job functions and knowledge requirements of certified rehabilitation counselors in the 21st century. *Rehabilitation Counseling Bulletin, 4*, 66–81.

Wallace, J. F., Flippo, K. F., Barcus, J. M., & Behrmann, M. M. (1995). Legislative foundation of assistive technology policy in the United States. In K. F. Flippo, K. J. Inge, & J. M. Barcus (Eds.), *Assistive technology: A resource for school, work, and community* (pp. 3–21). Brookes.

Wilcher, S. (2018). *The Rehabilitation Act of 1973: 45 years of activism and progress.* Insight Into Diversity. https://www.insightintodiversity.com/the-rehabilitation-act-of-1973-45-years-of-activism-and-progress/

Wright, B. A. (1983). *Physical disability: A psychosocial approach.* Harper & Row.

United States Access Board. (n.d.). *Rehabilitation Act of 1973.* https://www.access-board.gov/the-board/laws/rehabilitation-act-of-1973#502

U.S. Department of Justice. (2020). *A guide to disability rights laws.* https://www.ada.gov/cguide.htm#anchor65610

CHAPTER 3

A Global View of Disability and Social Justice

Franco Dispenza, PhD, LP, CRC

Learning Objectives

As a result of reading this chapter, the student will be able to:

- Identify key historic policies and efforts that have been drafted during the 21st century to improve the lives of persons with disabilities (PWD) around the globe.
- Describe unique sociocultural and vocational contexts impacting the lives of PWD living in countries throughout Africa, Asia, Europe, North America, South America, and Australia.
- Explain the utility of the *International Classification of Functioning, Disability, and Health* and the *International Classification of Functioning, Disability, and Health for Children and Youth* for purposes of clinical rehabilitation counseling with PWD from around the globe.
- Understand social justice advocacy models and recommendations that clinical rehabilitation counselors could utilize when working with international populations living with disabilities.

INTRODUCTION

On December 13, 2006, the United Nations (UN) adopted the Convention on the Rights of Persons with Disabilities, a human rights treaty made up of 50 articles that aimed to protect the lives and equality of persons with disabilities (PWD). The treaty calls on countries around the world to: (1) combat stereotypes, negative attitudes, prejudices, stigma, and prohibit discrimination on the basis of disability; (2) identify and strive to remove barriers so that PWD can access public transit, public facilities and services, communication technologies, housing, employment, and education; and (3) promote full participation in community, leisure, and cultural life, receive a wide array of habilitation and rehabilitation services, and have access to marriage and reproductive rights. More than 150 nations have ratified the treaty to date, including countries from North America (e.g., United States, Canada), Caribbean (e.g., Cuba, Haiti), Central and South America (e.g., Mexico, Brazil, Argentina), Europe (e.g., Spain, Italy, Romania), Africa (e.g., Republic of Congo, Ethiopia, South Africa), Central Asia (e.g., Uzbekistan, Afghanistan), Asia (e.g., China, Vietnam, Thailand), and Australia. However, the UN Department of Economic and Social Affairs on Disability (2019) reported that only 45 countries have antidiscrimination and disability-related laws. Further work is necessary to ensure that PWD are protected and afforded equal access to community, work, education, and living.

The World Health Organization (WHO, 2019) estimates that approximately one billion people are living with a disability around the globe and that disability rates will continue to rise because of increases in chronic illnesses and aging older adult populations. The *World Report on Disability* (WHO, 2011), one of the first documented initiatives to provide a global perspective on the needs, situations, and barriers facing PWD, clearly demonstrated that disability is a global human rights issue (Emerson, 2011). The report identified that PWD encounter considerable barriers when accessing community services. The report further identified that disability rates disproportionly affect women and children around the world and that PWD have worse health and socioeconomic outcomes than those not living with disabilities. Globally, children and youth with disabilities are either not enrolled in school, never complete their education, or are denied educational accommodations for their disabilities (Chun et al., 2016).

This chapter will first provide an overview of the impact that disability has across several different regions of the world, including Africa, Asia, Australia, Europe, North America, and South America. The chapter will then continue with a discussion on rehabilitation counseling practices with international populations, followed by a discussion on social justice advocacy with PWD from a global perspective. Clinical rehabilitation counselors and other rehabilitation professionals are committed to improving the lives of PWD across the life span and in their respective countries. Clinical rehabilitation counselors also advocate for the civil, sociopolitical, cultural, and economic rights of PWD and ensure that PWD have equitable access to these rights regardless of their nation of origin, culture, or language (Commission on Rehabilitation Counselor Certification [CRCC], 2017).

Disability Around the Globe

In this section, a broad overview of culture, psychosocial aspects of disability, and vocational implications of disability in different regions of the globe are provided. Although it is nearly impossible to conduct a review of every country in a brief chapter, a general survey still provides important perspectives that could help clinical rehabilitation counselors develop some initial multicultural knowledge with internationally diverse populations. Rich in diverse cultures, languages, histories, and religions, it proves difficult to succinctly summarize how disability functions in each of these different regions. It becomes more difficult when factoring significant variations that exist within groups across these regions. However, clinical rehabilitation counselors interested in international populations are encouraged to further explore the impact of disability in specific countries. This is especially important as there are cultural nuances and specificities in every cultural group or region within a country or continent that differ from one another.

Each region covered also has a brief case study for you to consider. There is no right or wrong way to approach each case study; they are provided as exercises to apply your understanding of disability and culture as a clinical rehabilitation counselor.

Africa

Africa consists of 54 countries, with an estimated 1.3 billion people living across five regions (i.e., northern, western, central, eastern, and southern) of the continent. Although not inclusive of all countries in Africa, Mitra and Sambamoorthi (2014) estimated that the average prevalence rate of disability among adults is approximately 15.4%. Researchers, scholars, and educators across many countries in Africa have been advancing disability scholarship and in 2012 initiated the open access journal *African Journal of Disability* (Swartz, 2018). Policy makers and governments in Africa have also worked diligently to promote issues of disability via politics and legislation, but PWD still experience sociocultural exclusion and stigma (Munsaka & Charnley, 2013; Reynolds, 2010; Stone-MacDonald & Butera, 2012).

Political, social, and spiritual contexts are important when considering disability across the continent of Africa. For instance, eastern and western regions of Africa have historically struggled with public health crises (e.g., HIV/AIDS, Ebola), high rates of poverty, droughts, famine, and wars, making it sometimes difficult to advance issues of disability equality or equity (Stone-MacDonald & Butera, 2012). Although people in different regions and countries of Africa acknowledge the role that medical and environmental factors have on the etiology of disabilities, there are still those who believe that disabilities have spiritual causes (Munsaka & Charnley, 2013; Reynolds, 2010). According to a review conducted by Stone-MacDonald and Butera (2012), Christian fatalism and supernatural occurrences (e.g., spirits or witchcraft) are still viewed as causes to disability in various regions.

Researchers have also focused on education and employment for PWD living across Africa. In a review of the literature, Engelbrecht and colleagues (2017) reported that barriers to education and employment begin during childhood, mainly as a result of not including children with disabilities in education and other learning, avocational, or vocational opportunities. As a result of not having adequate training or education during childhood, PWD encounter more barriers to employment as adults (Engelbrecht et al., 2017). PWD who do go on to pursue higher education also face obstacles. For instance, Morley and Croft (2011) found that PWD seeking higher education met considerable constraints, frustrations, exclusion, and danger in both Ghana and Tanzania. Women with disabilities may have an even more difficult time accessing higher education, but scholars have identified several psychosocial resiliencies that may help women with disabilities persist in higher education (Tuomi et al., 2015). In sub-Saharan Africa, Tuomi and colleagues (2015) interviewed six women with physical and sensory disabilities and found that family and teacher encouragement, financial support, and participating in student life helped the women in the study to persist in their educational pursuits.

Case Study: Aadila

Aadila Adimu is a 19-year-old woman with a visual-related disability attending a public university in Morogoro, Tanzania. She was raised in a rural part of Tanzania and was poor, but she grew up determined never to feel defeated. As a first-year college student, she has found it challenging to manage finances and activities of daily living without assistance (e.g., grooming, dressing, acquiring food, and cooking). She wants to do well in her studies, but she finds it difficult to focus given the stressors of managing her disability without help from her family.

1. What cultural aspects would you consider if you had the opportunity to help and work with Aadila Adimu?

Asia

Asia constitutes an expansive geographic region of the world that includes East Asia (e.g., China, Japan, South Korea), Southeast Asia (e.g., Philippines, Malaysia, Thailand), Central Asia (e.g., Uzbekistan, Turkmenistan, Kazakhstan), and the subcontinent of India. Approximately 4.62 billion people live across these regions. Although not inclusive of all countries in Asia, Mitra and Sambamoorthi (2014) estimate that the average prevalence rate of disability among adults is 10.75%.

Broadly, Asia is made up of *collectivist* cultures that prioritize family and community goals over the individual. This is in contrast to *individualistic* cultures (i.e., United States, Canada, Western European countries) that focus on achievements and competitive goals of the individual as a motivating priority. Many countries and diverse cultures across Asia place significant value on social order, harmony, peaceful interactions among members of society, family hierarchy, and respect (Chun et al., 2016; Yan et al., 2014). Many of these values are attributed to and informed by Eastern religions and philosophies such as Confucianism, Taoism, Hinduism, Islam, Sikhism, and Buddhism (Anees, 2014; Yan et al., 2014). Because of some of these worldviews and perspectives, disability is viewed as disharmonious and a challenge to family structure, and PWD are subjected to ridicule, prejudice, and marginalization (Yan et al., 2014). In South Korea and India, some people believe that supernatural forces cause disability or that disability is a punishment or atonement of sins from past lives (Anees, 2014; Yan et al., 2014).

Across the continent of Asia, occupational rehabilitation for injured workers has been a significant focus for policy makers. Occupational rehabilitation has shifted from a medical model and remediation focus to a biopsychosocial model that focuses on PWD in the workplace (Chan & Zhuo, 2011). Several different countries in Asia support infrastructure that helps compensate injured workers with the intention of getting them back to work (Chan & Zhuo, 2011; Chan et al., 2011; Tang et al., 2011). Given China's growing economy and large population, a three-tier medical and occupational rehabilitation model has been developed to help rehabilitate injured workers and return them to work safely. The goal of the three-tiered system is to provide the necessary services through occupational rehabilitation hospitals, healthcare settings, or rehabilitation centers at the national, provincial, city, or district level (Tang et al., 2011). In Japan, hospital-based vocational programs and sheltered workshops have been a popular avenue for vocational rehabilitation services for PWD (Oshima et al., 2014). Supported employment services, such as individual placement and support, have more recently been implemented and found to be successful among Japanese adults living with psychiatric disabilities (Oshima et al., 2014).

Case Study: Lee

Lee Park is a 15-year-old girl with a developmental disability. She lives with her mother, father, younger brother, and grandparents in Seoul, South Korea. As part of South Korea's initiative for inclusive education for students with disabilities, Lee takes inclusive classes with other students who do not live with disabilities. However, Lee struggles to understand the class material. She goes home every day crying and worried that she will be a failure for the rest of her life. Lee's parents are concerned that she is not receiving any vocational training and worry about her future.

1. How would you work with Lee and her family? In particular, what cultural aspects would you consider in your work?

Australia

Approximately 25 million people live in Australia, and an estimated 17.7% of Australians have some type of disability (Australian Bureau of Statistics, 2018). Like other countries, the Australian government has been diligent to implement legislation that provides PWD with inclusive access to mainstream society, such as public transportation and higher education (Stancliffe, 2014). However, PWD have struggled to access accommodations and still experience instances of sociopolitical exclusion (Stancliffe, 2014). Employment is another important focus in Australia (Buys et al., 2015; Stancliffe, 2014). There is an association between disability and unemployment, and the Australian government has made attempts to increase the entry of PWD into the Australian labor market (Buys et al., 2015). In addition to vocational rehabilitation services and other supports, employers are given extra funds to incentivize hiring PWD, including providing wage subsidies and funding for workplace modifications (Buys et al., 2015).

Clinical rehabilitation counselors also need to be mindful of Indigenous populations when considering diversity-related issues in Australia. Indigenous Australians have been oppressed, dehumanized, treated as inferior, and have high rates of impairment and disabilities when compared with non-Indigenous Australians (Hollinsworth, 2012). Hollinsworth (2012) called for "decolonizing disability" among Indigenous Australians and advocated for holistic and family-centered strategies to help Indigenous Australians adapt to and manage their health and well-being.

Case Study: Daniel

Daniel Benson is a 41-year-old Indigenous-Australian man with a psychiatric disability who lives in Brisbane, Australia. He has been unemployed for 8 months. He has been living with his sister and helping her care for her children while collecting disability benefits. He has worked previously in hospitality and tourism but recognizes that the stress of those industries negatively impacts his mental health. However, Daniel would like to get back to work and has decided to seek out vocational rehabilitation services.

1. How might you help provide vocational rehabilitation services to Daniel?

Europe

Europe consists of 44 countries. Although not inclusive of all countries in Europe, the average prevalence rate of disability among adults is estimated to be 9.04% (Mitra & Sambamoorthi, 2014). Prior to the 21st century, disability was viewed as a social security, welfare, or charity issue, whereby PWD were excluded from mainstream society (Vanhala, 2015). However, views have shifted from rehabilitation to political rights of PWD, social inclusion, and the removal of ecological barriers so that PWD can fully participate in society across Europe (Priestly et al., 2010). More than 30 European countries have some form of disability equality protection (Vanhala, 2015).

Many European countries have also focused on employment for PWD, utilizing an array of vocational rehabilitation practices, including sheltered workshops, supported employment, and individual placement and support for persons with severe psychiatric disabilities (Fioretti et al., 2014). Europe also has an aging workforce, which means that older adults living with disabilities are remaining in the workforce for extended periods of time (Pagán, 2013).

Case Study: Marco

Marco Loreto is a 26-year-old man with an intellectual disability living in Milan, Italy. He attends an employment training center for PWD and hopes that he can get a job in the near future. One day, Marco's father comes to the training center, requesting to speak with one of the counselors. Marco's father tells the administrator that he would prefer if his son stayed at home because it will be better for him to collect disability allowance checks from the government than to go to work. Marco hears about this while at the training center and becomes very upset at his father.

1. How might you approach Marco and his father if you were present at the employment training center?

North America

North America consists of 23 countries, inclusive of Canada, Mexico, the United States, and countries in Central America and the Caribbean. An estimated 579 million people live across North America. Although not inclusive of all countries in North America, but including Canada and the United States, the average prevalence rate of disability among adults is estimated to be 11.4% (Mitra & Sambamoorthi, 2014; United Nations, 2019). Canada, Mexico, and the United States all have progressive civil rights policies that promote, protect, and include PWD across social, educational, and vocational domains of life (Galer, 2018; Guzman & Salazar, 2014); however, PWD continue to encounter discrimination and stigma in education, employment, and their communities (Dispenza, 2019). Despite this, countries in North America have structured programs to help PWD access and maintain employment. Vocational and occupational rehabilitation services provide disability benefits, vocational or career counseling, training, and other employment-related services.

Health and socioeconomic inequities of PWD have been a topic of concern for many scholars and policy makers in North American countries. For instance, in the United States, PWD are less likely to receive preventive healthcare services, have higher rates of poor health outcomes (e.g., obesity, depression), and are more likely to engage in health risk behaviors such as tobacco use (U.S. Department of Health and Human Services, 2019). In a longitudinal study, Casey (2015) found that the rate of unmet healthcare needs was greater for Canadians living with disabilities than those not living with disabilities. Relatedly, Canadians living with disabilities encounter high poverty and unemployment rates when compared to those not living with disabilities (Galer, 2018). Similarly, in Mexico, PWD were less likely to have access to education and employment than persons not living with disabilities (Sandoval et al., 2017).

Case Study: Felix

Felix Romero is a 23-year-old man who came to the United States from Mexico with his family when he was 4 years old. After completing high school, he took a job as a construction worker. He became severely injured while on the job and acquired a mobility-related disability. He now relies on the use of a wheelchair. Felix identifies as Roman Catholic and is very close to his family. Since the accident he has been depressed and worries that he is a burden on his family. He has always considered himself a provider and is worried about how he will help support his family living with a disability.

1. What are some relevant cultural considerations you need to consider when helping Felix?

South America

South America consists of 12 countries, including Brazil, Argentina, and Venezuela. An estimated 429 million people live across South America. Although not inclusive of all countries in South America, Mitra and Sambamoorthi (2014) reported that the average prevalence rate of disability among adults is estimated to be 10.4%. Medical models of disability have remained widely popular across countries in South America (e.g., Argentina, Brazil, Chile, Colombia), although scholars have noted a recent shift towards adopting a social model of disability (Bampi et al., 2010; Kiarakosyan, 2015; Melo & Valdes, 2011; Schrader & Penillas, 2012). This means that the primary mode of attending to PWD has been by rehabilitating the medical or health aspects of their disability and focusing less on environmental and structural changes that are more socially inclusive of PWD.

Bravo-Valdiviseo and Muller (2001) note that learning and intellectual disability rates for children may be higher in countries in South America than those in North America or Europe because of poor nutrition, higher rates of poverty, unsanitary environments, and lower rates of cognitive-verbal development. Although there have been advances in the study and practice of special education and developmental psychology since the middle of the 20th century in countries across South America (Bravo-Valdiviseo & Muller, 2001), disability organizations and advocacy groups have been slow to develop in some countries, such as Brazil (Bampi, 2010; Kiarakosyan, 2015).

Case Study: Juliana

Juliana Andrade Silva is a 34-year-old-woman living in Rio de Janeiro, Brazil. She was born with a developmental disability and uses a manual wheelchair. Recently, she has chartered a national institute that advocates for the rights of people with disabilities in Brazil. Her main issue is that many of the sidewalks and streets are inaccessible to PWD because of potholes, manhole covers, and cracked asphalt. She states that she does not feel respected by her own country.

1. What are some social justice and advocacy considerations that you would consider if working with Juliana and her chartered organization?

Clinical Rehabilitation Practice on a Global Level

Rehabilitation Counseling With PWD

Clinical rehabilitation counselors should be familiar with the *International Classification of Functioning, Disability, and Health* (ICF; WHO, 2001) and the *International Classification of Functioning, Disability, and Health for Children and Youth* (ICF-CY; WHO, 2007) when providing rehabilitation counseling services to PWD across the life span. The ICF was endorsed by 191 countries in 2001, including Australia and countries in North America, South America, Asia, Africa, and Europe, providing a standardized framework that could be used when providing health and rehabilitation services to international populations living with disabilities. The ICF model provides a global conceptualization of body functioning and structure (i.e., psychology, physiology, and anatomy), activities and limitations, participation and restrictions, and environmental factors (e.g., social attitudes, laws, geographical terrain). Moreover, the ICF model employs a biopsychosocial framework, allowing practitioners, researchers, educators, and policy makers to examine the interplay of health, functioning, and disability in their respective environmental contexts (WHO, 2001).

Clinical rehabilitation counselors could use the ICF to assist in an array of rehabilitation counseling practices. The ICF could be particularly helpful with: (1) assessment and appraisal of functioning and participation of life activities; (2) treatment planning and case management, which includes formalizing goals and objectives for maximizing one's rehabilitation potential; (3) identification of psychosocial aspects of disability related to functioning, activities of daily living, quality of life, adaptation, and adjustment; (4) identification of possible accommodations, modifications, or assistive technologies for optimal functioning and integration into society; and (5) identification and collaboration with service providers to help address issues related to health and functioning. The ICF also has implications for vocational rehabilitation (Escorpizo et al., 2011), the core feature of practice for clinical rehabilitation counselors. By utilizing a biopsychosocial and ecological approach to vocational rehabilitation services and job placement, clinical rehabilitation counselors can identify systems and environmental factors that may hinder, impede, or facilitate employment for PWD (Homa, 2007). More specifically, the ICF model could be used to provide workplace accommodations based on a counselor's appraisal of functioning, strengths, and health (Johnson-Migalski & Drout, 2018).

Social Justice Advocacy for PWD

Clinical rehabilitation counselors engage in social justice and advocacy as part of their professional scope of practice (CRCC, 2017). Rehabilitation professionals engage in actions that help remove barriers (i.e., structural, sociopolitical, external, intrapsychic) so that PWD have opportunities to be engaged in their respective communities. Of course, this also includes ensuring that PWD have the autonomy of making personal decisions regarding their education, work, health, relationships, and well-being. Although many discussions of social justice and advocacy encourage counseling professionals to engage in activities *on behalf* of marginalized consumers (Brubaker & Goodman, 2012), clinical rehabilitation counselors participate in social justice advocacy "alongside marginalized and disempowered communities instead of *for* them" (Marshall-Lee et al., 2019). Rehabilitation professionals are mindful to be inclusive of PWD when they engage in social justice advocacy, for it is the historic exclusion of PWD that clinical rehabilitation counselors must actively prevent in their own practice.

Although beyond the scope of this chapter, clinical rehabilitation counselors can employ a variety of approaches and models of social justice advocacy when working with PWD. For example, clinical rehabilitation counselors may want to consider the model proposed by Goodman and colleagues (2004) that infuses multicultural and feminist theories. This model attends to the importance of self-examination, collaborative power dynamics, giving voice to marginalized persons and groups, critical consciousness raising, building on strengths, and meaningful engagement with communities when engaging in social justice advocacy with marginalized persons, groups, and communities (Marshall-Lee et al., 2019). As an extension of the scientist–practitioner–advocate model (Mallinckrodt et al., 2014), Ratts and Pedersen (2014) integrated the biopsychosocial approach with the counselor–advocate–scholar (CAS) model. This model contends that contextualized situations will dictate which role counselors will employ (i.e., counselor, advocate, scholar) to best help consumers. The model further aims to have counselors address systemic and oppressive barriers that may interfere with optimal functioning (Ratts & Greenleaf, 2018).

What should clinical rehabilitation counselors advocate for when considering international communities and cultures? The *World Report on Disability* (WHO, 2011) made nine specific recommendations to help improve practice and policies for PWD across the globe. Clinical rehabilitation counselors can use the recommendations made by the *World Report on Disability* (WHO & World Bank, 2011) to advocate for diverse PWD in their respective communities:

1. Advocate that policy makers, stakeholders, and community providers mainstream services and activities (e.g., education, health, employment) so that PWD can participate equally.
2. Advocate that policy makers and stakeholders invest in services and programs (e.g., vocational rehabilitation programs, assistive technologies) aimed at helping and supporting PWD transition and integrate in their respective communities.
3. Advocate that one's respective state or country develop national strategic plans that target the civil, social, cultural, and economic rights of PWD.
4. Advocate that PWD always are included in issues, concerns, and decisions pertaining to their own livelihood and well-being.

5.   Advocate that personnel in education, health care, rehabilitation, law and emergency services, journalism and media, technology, and other community institutions are appropriately trained to work with PWD.

6.   Advocate for adequate and sustainable funding for publicly available goods (e.g., assistive technologies) and services (e.g., health care).

7.   Advocate for inclusivity and campaigns to reduce stigma, prejudice, and negative attitudes toward diverse PWD.

8.   Advocate for improved national data collection efforts that gather comprehensive data on disability.

9.   Advocate for improved research efforts and methods across a variety of disciplines (e.g., rehabilitation, public health, special education, disability studies) to improve services for PWD.

SUMMARY

The United Nations adopted the Convention on the Rights of Persons with Disabilities in 2006, calling on countries to remove barriers so that PWD could fully participate in their communities. In 2011, the World Health Organization (WHO) released the *World Report on Disability*, demonstrating that disability is a global human rights issue. Approximately 15% of the world's population is living with a disability (WHO, 2019). Many countries around the world are working to advance social and legal issues of disability; however, PWD continue to encounter stigma, prejudice, and discrimination in education and work. Clinical rehabilitation counselors are encouraged to utilize the *International Classification of Functioning, Disability, and Health* and the *International Classification of Functioning, Disability, and Health for Children and Youth* for purposes of clinical rehabilitation counseling. Clinical rehabilitation counselors also are encouraged to consider social justice advocacy when working with international populations.

Discussion Questions

1. Reflect on some issues that continue to impact PWD around the globe. What are some similarities across the cultures and geographical regions discussed in this chapter? What are some differences?

2. Research two specific countries in different regions of the world (not including your own) and the ways in which PWD navigate their lives in those countries. Pay particular attention to the cultural nuances and specificities that disability takes on in those countries. Afterwards, compare and contrast how PWD live in those countries. What stands out the most to you?

3. Take some time to familiarize yourself with the World Health Organization's (2001) *International Classification of Functioning, Disability, and Health*, which you can easily access via the internet. What are some ways that you could use the classification system with international populations? How could the ICF help you identify psychosocial and vocational implications of disabilities when providing rehabilitation counseling services?

4. What additional efforts, if any, can rehabilitation professionals consider when advocating for PWD on a global level?

5. What strengths do you hold that could help facilitate competent rehabilitation counseling services with international populations? What are some growth edges that need to be further worked on?

REFERENCES

Anees, S. (2014). Disability in India: The role of gender, family, and religion. *Journal of Applied Rehabilitation Counseling, 45*(2), 32–28.

Australian Bureau of Statistics. (2018). *4430.0–Survey of Disability, Ageing and Carers 2018*. https://www.abs.gov.au/ausstats/abs@.nsf/mf/4430.0

Bampi, L. N. S., Guilhem, D., & Alves, D. E. (2010). Social model: A new approach of the disability theme. *Revista Latino-Americano de Enfermagem, 18*(4), 816–823. http://dx.doi.org/10.1590/S0104-11692010000400022

Bravo-Valdivieso, L., & Milicic, N. (2001). Learning disabilities studies in South America. In D. P. Hallahan, B. K. Keogh, & W. M. Cruickshank (Eds.), *Research and global perspectives in learning disabilities* (pp. 311–328). L. Erlbaum Associates.

Brubaker, M. D. & Goodman, R. D. (2012). Consumer Advocate: In Action. In. C. Y. Chang, C. A. B. Minton, A. L. Dixon, J. E. Myers, & T. J. Sweeney (Eds.), *Professional counseling excellence through leadership and advocacy* (pp. 141–161). Routledge/Taylor & Francis Group.

Buys, N., Matthews, L. R., & Randall, C. (2015). Contemporary vocational rehabilitation in Australia. *Disability and Rehabilitation, 37*(9), 820–824. https://doi:10.3109/09638288.2014.942001

Casey, R. (2015). Disability and unmet health care needs in Canada: A longitudinal analysis. *Disability and Health Journal, 8*(2), 173–181. https://doi.org/10.1016/j.dhjo.2014.09.010

Chan, C. C. H., & Zhuo, D. (2011). Occupational rehabilitation in twenty-first century Asia Pacific: Facilitating health and work: An introduction. *Journal of Occupational Rehabilitation, 21*(Suppl 1), S1–S4. https://doi.org/10.1007/s10926-011-9300-x

Chan, K.-F., Tan, C. W. C., Yeo, D. S. C., Tan, H. S. K., Tan, F. L., Tan, E. W., Szeto, G. P. Y., & Cheng, A. S. K. (2011). Occupational rehabilitation in Singapore and Malaysia. *Journal of Occupational Rehabilitation, 21*(Suppl 1), S69–S76. https://doi.org/10.1007/s10926-011-9289-1

Chun, J., Connor, A., Kociulek, J. F., Landon, T., & Park, J. (2016). Career development for youth with disabilities in South Korea: The intersection of culture, theory, and policy. *Global Education Review, 3*(3).

Commission on Rehabilitation Counselor Certification. (2017). *Code of professional ethics for rehabilitation counselors.* https://www.crccertification.com/code-of-ethics-3

Dispenza, F. (2019). Empowering the career development of persons with disabilities (PWD). *Journal of Career Development, 23,* 50–63. https://doi.org/10.1177/0894845319884636

Emerson, E. (2012). The World Report on Disability. *Journal of Applied Research in Intellectual Disabilities, 25*(6), 495–496. https://doi.org/10.1111/j.1468-3148.2012.00693.x

Engelbrecht, M., Shaw, L., & Van Niekerk, L. (2017). A literature review on work transitioning of youth with disabilities into competitive employment. *African Journal of Disability, 6,* 298. https://doi.org/10.4102/ajod.v6i0.298

Escorpizo, R., Reneman, M. F., Ekholm, J., Fritz, J., Krupa, T., Marnetoft, S.-U., Maroun, C. E., Guzman, J. R., Suzuki, Y., Stucki, G., & Chan, C. C. H. (2011). A conceptual definition of vocational rehabilitation based on the ICF: Building a shared global model. *Journal of Occupational Rehabilitation, 21*(2), 126–133. https://doi.org/10.1007/s10926-011-9292-6

Fioritti, A., Burns, T., Hilarion, P., van Weeghel, J., Cappa, C., Suñol, R., & Otto, E. (2014). Individual placement and support in Europe. *Psychiatric Rehabilitation Journal, 37*(2), 123–128. https://doi.org/10.1037/prj0000065

Galer, D. (2018). *Working towards equity: Disability rights activism and employment in late twentieth-century Canada.* University of Toronto Press.

Goodman, L. A., Liang, B, Helms, J. A., Latta, R., Sparks, E. & Weintraub, S. R. (2004). Training counseling psychologies as social justice agents. *The Counseling Psychologiest, 32*(6), 793–836. DOI: 10.1177/0011000004268802

Guzman, J. M., & Salazar, E. G. (2014). Disability and rehabilitation in Mexico. *American Journal of Physical Medicine & Rehabilitation, 93*(1), S36–S38.

Gerst-Emerson, K., Wong, R., Michaels-Obregon, A., & Palloni, A. (2015). Cross-national differences in disability among elders: Transitions in disability in Mexico and the United States. *The Journals of Gerontology: Series B, 70*(5), 759–768. https://doi.org/10.1093/geronb/gbu185

Hollinsworth, D. (2013). Decolonizing Indigenous disability in Australia. *Disability & Society, 28*(5), 601–615. https://doi:10.1080/09687599.2012.717879

Homa, D. B. (2007). Using the International Classification of Functioning, Disability and Health (ICF) in job placement. *Work: Journal of Prevention, Assessment & Rehabilitation, 29*(4), 277–286.

Johnson-Migalski, L., & Drout, M. O. (2018). Using the International Classification of Functioning, Disability, and Health (ICF) in Adlerian approaches. *The Journal of Individual Psychology, 74*(1), 38–54. https://doi.org/10.1353/jip.2018.0003

Kirakosyan, L. (2016). Promoting disability rights for a stronger democracy in Brazil: The role of NGOs. *Nonprofit and Voluntary Sector Quarterly, 45*(Suppl 1), 114S–130S. https://doi.org/10.1177/0899764015602129

Mallinckrodt, B., Miles, J. R., & Levy, J. J. (2014). The scientist practitioner advocate model: Addressing contemporary training needs for social justice advocacy. *Training and Education in Professional Psychology, 8*, 303–311. doi:10.1037/tep0000045

Marshall-Lee, E. D., Hinger, C., Popovic, R., Miller Roberts, T. C., & Prempeh, L. (2019). Social justice advocacy in mental health services: Consumer, community, training, and policy perspectives. *Psychological Services.* http://dx.doi.org/10.1037/ser0000349

Melo, P. Z., & Valdes, B.C. (2011). Socioeconomic determinants of disability in Chile. *Disability and Health Journal, 4*(4), 271–282. https://doi.org/10.1016/j.dhjo.2011.06.002

Mitra, S., & Sambamoorthi, U. (2014). Disability prevalence among adults: Estimates for 54 countries and progress toward a global estimate. *Disability and Rehabilitation, 36*(11), 940–947. https://doi:10.3109/09638288.2013.825333

Morley, L., & Croft, A. (2011). Agency and advocacy: Disabled students in higher education in Ghana and Tanzania. *Research in Comparative and International Education, 6*, 383–389.

Munsaka, E., & Charnley, H. (2013). "We do not have chiefs who are disabled": Disability, development and culture in a continuing complex emergency. *Disability & Society, 28*(6), 756–769. https://doi.org/10.1080/09687599.2013.802221

Oshima, I., Sono, T., Bond, G. R., Nishio, M., & Ito, J. (2014). A randomized controlled trial of individual placement and support in Japan. *Psychiatric Rehabilitation Journal, 37*(2), 137–143. https://doi.org/10.1037/prj0000085

Pagán, R. (2013). Job satisfaction and domains of job satisfaction for older workers with disabilities in Europe. *Journal of Happiness Studies: An Interdisciplinary Forum on Subjective Well-Being, 14*(3), 861–891. https://doi.org/10.1007/s10902-012-9359-x

Priestley, M., Waddington, L., & Bessozi, C. (2010). Towards an agenda for disability research in Europe: Learning from disabled people's organisations. *Disability & Society, 25*(6), 731–746. https://doi.org/10.1080/09687599.2010.505749

Ratts, M. J., & Greenleaf, A. T. (2018). Counselor–advocate–scholar model: Changing the dominant discourse in counseling. *Journal of Multicultural Counseling and Development, 46*(2), 78–96. https://doi:10/1002/jmcd.12094

Ratts, M. J., & Pedersen, P. B. (2014). *Counseling for multiculturalism and social justice: Integration, theory, and application* (4th ed.). American Counseling Association.

Reynolds, S. (2010). Disability culture in West Africa: Qualitative research indicating barriers and progress in the greater Accra region of Ghana. *Occupational Therapy International, 17*(4), 198–207. https://doi.org/10.1002/oti.303

Sandoval, H., Pérez-Neri, I., Martínez-Flores, F., del Valle-Cabrera, M. G., & Pineda, C. (2017). Disability in Mexico: A comparative analysis between descriptive models and historical periods using a timeline. *Salud Pública de México, 59*(4), 429–436. https://doi.org/10.21149/8048

Schrader, S. & Panillas, F. C. (2012). Crisis, class, and disability in Argentina: Red por los derechos de las personas con discapacidad. *Disability Studies Quarterly, 32*(3).

Stancliffe, R. J. (2014). Inclusion of adults with disability in Australia: Outcomes, legislation and issues. *International Journal of Inclusive Education, 18*(10), 1053–1063. https://doi.org/10.1080/13603116.2012.693395

Stone-MacDonald, A. & Butera, G. D. (2012). Cultural beliefs and attitudes about disability in East Africa. *Review of Disability Studies: An International Journal, 8*(1).

Swartz, L. (2018). Building capacity or enforcing normalcy? Engaging with disability scholarship in Africa. *Qualitative Research in Psychology, 15*(1), 116–130. https://doi.org/10.1080/14780887.2017.1416801

Tang, D., Chen, G., Xu, Y.-W., Hui-Lo, K. Y. L., Luo, X.-Y., & Chan, C. C. H. (2011). An emerging occupational rehabilitation system in the People's Republic of China. *Journal of Occupational Rehabilitation, 21*(Suppl 1), S35–S43. https://doi.org/10.1007/s10926-011-9299-z

Tuomi, M. T., Lehtomäki, E., & Matonya, M. (2015). As capable as other students: Tanzanian women with disabilities in higher education. *International Journal of Disability, Development and Education, 62*(2), 202–214. https://doi.org/10.1080/1034912X.2014.998178

United Nations. (2019). Department of Economic and Social Affairs on Disability. https://www.un.org/development/desa/disabilities/

U.S. Department of Health and Human Services, Office of Disease Prevention and Health Promotion. (2019). *Disability and Health.* In Healthy People 2020. https://www.healthypeople.gov/2020/topics-objectives/topic/disability-and-health

Vanhala, L. (2015). The diffusion of disability rights in Europe. *Human Rights Quarterly, 37*(4), 831–853.

World Health Organization. (2001). *International classification of functioning, disability and health (ICF).* Author.

World Health Organization. (2011). *World report on disability.* https://www.who.int/disabilities/world_report/2011/report.pdf

World Health Organization. (2019). *Disability.* https://www.who.int/disabilities/en/

Yan, K. K., Accordino, M. P., Boutin, D. L., & Wilson, K. B. (2014). Disability and the Asian culture. *Journal of Applied Rehabilitation Counseling, 45*(2), 4–8.

CHAPTER 4

Models of Disability

Bilal Urkmez, PhD, CRC
Chanda Pinkney, MA

Learning Objectives

As a result of reading this chapter, the student will be able to:

- Define models of disabilities.
- Describe the different models of disability.
- Explain the causes of disability through the lens of various models of disability.
- Understand societal views of disability and the relation to current social trends.
- Apply models of disability to case studies.

INTRODUCTION

The meaning and perception of disability is understood in a variety of ways, and today multiple models of disability that are used in the treatment of people with disabilities (PWD; Berghs et al., 2016; Fitzgerald, 2006). Examining these different models allows us to conceptualize the experience of disability. Smart (2004) defined models of disabilities in this way: "A model is a set of guiding assumptions, concerns, and propositions about the nature of phenomena or human experience. Models are often defined as human-made tools for understanding and human-made guidelines for action" (p. 33). Models of disability are abstractions or theories and do not exist in reality. However, they are not harmless abstractions (Smart, 2009a; Smart, 2009b). These models guide legislation and determine the service settings for PWD and where they live. Models also determine the theoretical approach of the professionals who assist PWD. Most of all, models determine the daily lived experience of having a disability. Furthermore, models of disability serve as the structure for rehabilitation services, providing the rationale for the funding for extensive studies (Smart, 2009a; Smart, 2009b).

The most common models of disability are the moral/religious model, the medical model, the sociopolitical model, and the identity model. Each of these models focuses on different aspects of the disability experience and brings its unique perspectives on disabilities. The various models of disability help clinical practitioners to provide better services to PWD (Tate & Pledger, 2003). Clinical rehabilitation counselors receive training in each of these models during their training program. Training on the various models of disability is essential for rehabilitation counselors because, as Smart (2004) points out, the different models of disability provide definitions of disability and explanations of causal attributions and responsibility attributions. The models also determine which professions serve PWD and which academic disciplines study, shape the self-identity of PWD, and guide the formulation and implementation of the policy. Finally, this preparation of various models of disability allows clinical rehabilitation counselors to shift within various models of disability to provide the consumer with disabilities with effective rehabilitation services. For these reasons, training in these models plays a vital role in their practice setting.

This chapter explores the different models of disability and describes the fundamental concepts of each while providing case vignettes to highlight the significance of each model. The models open with a case study describing scenarios that PWD encounter in their communities and throughout society. The strengths and limitations of each model of disability are discussed in detail. First, we start the chapter with the introduction of the case of Brian and then continue with presenting models of disability.

Case Study: Brian

Brian is a 14-year-old boy with a spinal cord injury as a result of a motor vehicle accident. Brian uses a wheelchair for mobility due to the accident, which happened 7 months prior. Brian suffered a crushed L2 vertebra, resulting in paraplegia. The American Spinal Injury Association (ASIA) classifies Brian's injury as a grade B, "incomplete" injury due to Brian having some sensory functions but no motor functions below the damaged vertebrae. While in high school, Brian and his family moved to a new city. The family's move resulted in Brian going to a new local high school. The new town has one high school dedicated to students in grades 9 through 12. On his first day of school, Brian finds out that not only are all his classes on the third floor in the school building, but there are no ramps, elevators, or lifts for him to utilize. Brian goes to the administrative office to inform the school administrators of the issue. The administrator informs Brian he is the only student with a wheelchair, and it is his problem he cannot get to class. Brian reports feeling isolated and depressed because of his inability to access his courses.

1. What are some of the considerations you can use to assist Brian?

Moral/Religious Model of Disability

Philosophical Approaches to Disability

The moral/religious model of disability is considered the oldest model and touches many religious traditions. In this model, disability is related to God's punishment for a particular sin by a person with a disability; it can also be related to sins committed by their family members (Henderson & Bryan, 2011). This model sometimes uses "evil spirits" to explain mental health issues such as schizophrenia. Henderson and Bryan (2011) define the moral/religious model of disability as follows:

> Some people, if not many, believe that some disabilities are the result of a lack of adherence to social morality and religious proclamations that warn against engaging in certain behaviors. To further explain the model, some beliefs are based upon the assumption that some disabilities are the result of punishment from an all-powerful entity. Furthermore, the belief is that the punishment is for act or acts of transgression against prevailing moral or religious edicts. (p. 7)

In the moral/religious model, a person's disability could be due to disobedient behavior or a family curse. A disability could also be a test of faith, with God selecting the individual and their family to endure the disability but allowing them the chance to rescue themselves through devotion, patience, and strength (Niemann, 2005). From this point of view, the individual sees their healing as a confirmation of their strong faith. If the individual is not healing from their disability, then they are regarded as having a lack of faith. In the case of Brian, the model views this accident as a test; Brian's family's faith and belief, along with his healing, depends on Brian and his family's strong relationship with God.

Another prominent aspect of the moral/religious model is the idea that the disability presents a person with the opportunity to mature and develop character. A person with a disability may have a chance of improving their patience, courage, and determination as a result of their disability. Consequently, PWD may have a chance to learn valuable life lessons that people without disabilities do not necessarily have an opportunity to learn.

Economic Approaches to Disability

Based on the moral/religious model, and depending on the religion, any financial hardship is a testimony of faith in waiting for a miracle or blessing. The individual or family is grateful for any "gifts" received from the community to supplement them in their time of need. Anything they get is a "blessing" and is "right on time." The individual may feel overwhelmed by growing medical and affiliated costs and do what they can and "let the Lord handle the rest." Based on this model, there could be two causes for Brian's accident. One possibility could be Brian's parents' previous sins resulted in the accident. The other blame is on Brian himself. Some people may see Brian as an unruly and "hard-headed" child who would never listen and gave his parents constant problems. So, the accident could be God's way of sitting Brian down and forcing him to listen to people.

Societal/Sociological Approaches to Disability

Although the moral/religious model of disability is not as standard as in the past, the underlying philosophy of the model is still used in society when presented with illness and disability (Henderson & Bryan, 2011; Rimmerman, 2013). Some cultures still use this model as a predominant view, especially societies dominated by religious ways of thinking (Dunn, 2015). In these cultures, the moral/religious model is the initial explanation when anything medically happens to a person. This model shaped societies' perceptions and opinions before people understood how science, genetics, and environmental factors affect the body and health. The person with the disability, and sometimes the family, would be considered outcasts by society because they had obviously lost God's favor.

Threat of Disability

The basis of the moral/religious model is that nothing happens unless a spiritual entity wants it to arrive (Retief & Letsosa, 2018). PWDs are noted in religious texts as people seeking the blessings of God as their only or last resort for healing. In this model, the PWD, or their family, may believe that renewed religious practice, incessant prayers, or "turning over a new leaf" will result in a miraculous recovery from the disability. If the PWD or family has a strong religious background, there is usually one "go-to" person all family members contact for spiritual guidance. If and when miracles happen, the individual with a disability recognizes the blessing and tries to live "right" going forward. In this model, attending religious activities, praying to their Higher Power, and showing unwavering faith are the only ways to heal the individual. Some individuals practice the art of "speaking it into existence" without acknowledging the disability as a testimony of being cured.

Medical Model of Disability

The medical model of disability has been in use for centuries. The medical model of disability is the most well-known of all the models of disability and has shaped the public's perception and attitude toward disability. The medical model of disability is rooted in the scientific method. This model defines disability in a fundamentally negative way by using the language of medicine (Thomas & Woods, 2003). Bickenbach (1993) defined the medical model of disability as:

> The most commonly held belief about (this model of) disablement is that it involves a defect, deficiency, dysfunctional, abnormality, failing, or medical "problem" located within the individual. Society may view a disablement as a defective characteristic. The person may be treated as functionally limited, anatomically abnormal, diseased, or pathoanatomical. The essence of disablement, in this view, is that there is something wrong with people with disabilities. (p. 61)

Philosophical Approaches to Disability

The medical model of disability has two main components. First, a disability must be present. Second, the pathology must be within the individual. Disability is viewed as a *pathology, disorder, or deformity* located within an individual (Carlson, 2010). In other words, the model sees disability as a consequence of some deviation from "normal" body function. The medical model of disability emphasizes individualization, privatization, and the medicalization of disability (Johnstone, 2012). In this model, PWDs are seen as victims of circumstances, misfortune, and pity. The medical model is not considered to be an interactional model because the definition of the problem exists entirely within the individual. Therefore, the medical model reinforces society's belief that "this is how the world is; take it or leave it." Thus, the person with a disability should "fix" themselves to fit into society (Smart, 2009a; Snart, 2008b; Tarvydas & Hartley, 2018). Based on this model, society has no obligation to make accommodations to ensure the individual's inclusion within the community. The model places all responsibilities on the individual diagnosed with the disability to "figure it out" if they desire to be a part of society. In summary, disability is an individual deficit/problem that has to be fixed, rehabilitated, or prevented (Solvang, 2000).

In the case of Brian, the medical model deems it Brian's responsibility to access the building and classroom because he is in the wheelchair rather than making the building more accessible. This perspective clearly shows that the medical model of disability does not notice the absence of accommodations and a lack of accessibility. Even more important, society often neglects to notice the presence of PWD. According to the medical model, a perfect world is a world without disabilities.

Economic Approaches to Disability

Based on the medical model of disability, the person with the disability is responsible for any financial aspects or services related to their disability. Again, the model's perspective is "their disability, their problem." According to the medical model, the individual pays for any medical-related travel, equipment/devices, and managed care costs. These costs also cover improvements in medical sciences that will increase the individual's functioning, extend their life span, and save their life (Llewellyn et al., 2008). In the case of Brian, he is financially responsible for his treatment. According to the medical model, Brian is the one that needs to make an effort to be a part of his new environment. People without disabilities may think "Why should I have to help if I did not cause the disability?" Besides economic responsibility, Brian is responsible for the necessary accommodations and arrangements to access his school building and classes on the third floor. If Brian needs ramps, lifts, or physical assistance, he should have the necessary people and devices available for use.

Societal/Sociological Approaches to Disability

The medical model of disability is well-known to the general public and carries with it the power and prestige of the well-established medical profession. The persistence of this model is based on two factors: (1) the public can easily understand it because of its precise definition and diagnostic system and (2) the long history of the model. Therefore, this model is influential in shaping the public's perceptions and attitudes toward disability. The medical model uses stigmatizing categories such as the blind, quads, or mentally ill; therefore, the general public views PWD as their categories.

As stated before, the location of the problem is within the individual. Therefore, PWD are responsible for their own treatment and care. Because the responsibility for the solution lies within the individual with the disability, the disability is a personal matter. The public bears no responsibility to accommodate or provide services to PWD (Smart, 2009a; Smart, 2009b). Society has no obligation to afford civil rights to individuals with disabilities. A disability is thought to be bad luck, but it is an individual's bad luck. The medical model of disability also claims that PWD should have done something to prevent disability. The model's perspective of disability causation results in prejudice, discrimination, and reduced opportunities for the individual (Smart, 2001). In the case of Brian, the community and school administrators are not responsible for assisting him in accessing the building or his classes. Based on the medical model of disability, Brian needs to work with the medical practitioner to have a plan to get around the barriers due to his disability. In this case, the rehabilitation counselor needs to work not only with Brian to assist with tackling the barriers but also help the community and school administrators to understand and possibly reduce the barriers.

Threat of Disability

The medical model of disability essentially treats all PWD with the same diagnosis with identical treatment plans. The medical model believes that disability can be quantified, measured, and standardized. In order to establish the presence of pathology and create a treatment plan for PWD, diagnostic testing and assessments are necessary (Smart, 2009a; Smart 2009b). This model uses a variety of classification systems, such as the International Classification of Impairment of Disabilities and Handicaps (ICIDH; World Health Organization, 1980), to standardize and evaluate the severity of disability or degree of impairment. However, many scholars argue against this rating system because there is no consideration about the degree of stigma and prejudice against the disability.

Given the continuous progress of science, the medical model focuses on advances in medicine and technology that can drastically reduce, or even cure, the signs or symptoms of a disability (Tarvydas & Hartley, 2018). The medical model views genetic testing, surgical procedures, physical therapy, experimental medications, prostheses, and other accessibility tools as aiding the individual's ability to become part of society (Tarvydas & Hartley, 2018). According to the medical model, these medical provisions allow the individual to become part of the community by "reducing" their disability. In some extreme cases, medical professionals have promoted the practice of eugenics as a "cure" to reduce and possibly eliminate the continuation of deficits in society.

Another particularly problematic assumption of the medical model is that the expertise of the doctor is more influential than that of the individual with the disability. The individual should follow doctors' orders, without exception, even though the individual has a better knowledge of how the disability affects them. The general public perceives doctors and other medical professionals as the authority in determining the presence of a disability based on their extensive education and training (Smart, 2009a, Smart, 2009b). The individual with the disability is not considered to be an active decision-maker because they do not have the knowledge and expertise on their disability. Another criticism of this model is PWD, depending on their economic status, have limited resources, without adding the ownership of accessibility, equipment, and managed care costs. The medical model does not consider external factors that may magnify an individual's physical disability.

Sociopolitical Model of Disability

Philosophical Approaches to Disability

The sociopolitical model, also referred to as the minority model of disability (Hahn, 1997), is a more recent model of disability. It represents a fundamental and radical change from the moral/religious and medical models of disability. Disability is commonly viewed as a problem that exists in a person's body that requires medical treatment. The sociopolitical model of disability requires a dramatic shift in thinking about disability, specifically with regards to the location of the "problem" or disability. In this model, the disability is not the "problem." Therefore, neither individuals nor their disabilities are the focus of intervention or treatment. PWD have "problems" because of the lack of civil rights and unequal opportunities (Barnes et al., 2010). Nothing in the disability prevents the individual from experiencing prejudice and discrimination. Laws and policies must focus on rehabilitating the environment rather than correcting or changing the individual with the disability. Because it is society that creates the difficulties of disability, PWD can be independent and equal in society, with choice and control over their own lives upon the removal of all barriers (Purtell, 2013).

The sociopolitical model of disability is interactional. In the sociopolitical model, policy makers, legislators, professional service providers, and the general public are considered part of the "problem" of disability, and therefore, teamwork is necessary for a response. To remove barriers and discrimination, society must respond to the "problem" collectively. The sociopolitical model asserts that prejudice and discrimination against individuals with disabilities are long-standing, systematic, and institutionalized in American life. The American Disabilities Act (ADA, 1990) states that the sociopolitical model is the most powerful model of disability. One of the strengths of the sociopolitical model is that it explains and describes more of the daily situations of PWD and puts them in control of their own lives. Social barriers are related to reduced opportunities, lowered expectations, and stigma. This model also has the power to mobilize people with all types of disabilities rather than to divide individuals with differing disabilities into rival factions. Accessing meaningful work is the primary part of the sociopolitical model of disability, along with rethinking disability in favorable terms (Barnes & Mercer, 2005).

Although several disability scholars believe in the power of the sociopolitical model of disability, Giddens (2006) notes several critiques of the approach. First, the sociopolitical model seemingly ignores the often painful realities of impairment. Second, medical sociologists are very skeptical of the model because they reject the sociopolitical model's distinction between impairment and disability. Medical sociologists claim that there is no clear answer to the question as to where impairment ends and disability starts.

So how might a rehabilitation counselor appropriately integrate the sociopolitical model into practice? In the case of Brian, the sociopolitical model of disability recognizes that the problem is with the building, not Brian, and thus, the rehabilitation counselor would suggest adding a ramp to the entrance. This model seeks to remove unnecessary barriers that prevent PWD from participating in society, accessing work, and living independently. In this case, this model asks what can be done for Brian to remove barriers so that he can have access to the building.

Societal/Sociological Approaches to Disability

In the sociopolitical model of disability, disability is not a product of bodily pathology but rather specific social and economic structures (Oliver, 1990). Disability scholars believe that the prejudice and discrimination found in the broader society are more of an obstacle than are medical impairments or functional limitations for most PWD. For example, Dembo, Leviton, and Wright (1975) noted that "handicapping conditions are between people rather than in people. … If the handicap is not in a person, then there are no handicapped persons. … Handicapped people exist only in the eyes of a viewer" (p. 131). Smart (2001) stated that individuals with disabilities mainly experience two problems: (1) the attitudes of people without disabilities toward people with disabilities and (2) potential environmental barriers. Moreover, Oliver (1981), a disabled activist and lecturer, emphasizes that people need to focus on the social aspect of disability, specifically how the social environment imposes limitations upon specific categories of people. Reviewing these scholars' ideas, disabilities are challenging issues for PWD, and society creates these challenges with environmental barriers.

In response to the medical model of disability, disability activists and scholars have offered a sociopolitical model of disability. The Union of the Physically Impaired against Segregation's (UPIAS) manifesto document, Fundamental Principles of Disability (1976), plays a crucial role in the development of this model. UPIAS (1976) emphasizes an essential conceptual distinction between the terms *impairment* and *disability*. In this model, there is a sharp distinction between impairment and disability (Barnes, 1991). Impairment is "lacking part of all of a limb, or having a defective limb, organ or mechanism of the body," whereas a disability is the disadvantage or restriction of activity caused by a contemporary social organization, which takes little account of people who have physical impairments, and thus excludes them from participation in the mainstream of social activities (UPIAS, 1976).

From this perspective, disability is defined as a social and civil construction, and the environment is the problem. In the sociopolitical model, PWD do not accept the inferior, dependent, and stigmatizing definition of disability. The sociopolitical model primarily focuses on addressing the barriers of participation experienced by PWD because of various ableist, social, and environmental factors in society (O'Connell et al., 2008). If society constructs disability, society can also deconstruct disability. Discrimination, inferiority, and prejudice are not inevitable, natural, or unavoidable consequences of disabilities. For many people with disabilities, social discrimination, hostility, ostracism, and exclusion are worse than the physical or mental impairment itself. According to this model, the definition of disability has three aspects: (1) the person with the disability must define the disability; (2) the person with the disability must refuse the definition of disability that was determined by experts or professionals; and (3) the person with the disability must refuse the "disabled role" of deviance and pathology (UPIAS, 1976).

Threat of Disability

The sociopolitical model refutes medical categorization based on a diagnosis because such grouping is the source of prejudice and discrimination. However, the medical classification system is often embedded in laws and statutes. According to the sociopolitical model, categorization has resulted in the following: (1) allowing the general public to avoid focusing on the universal problems of people with all types of disabilities; (2) leading society to believe that a person with a disability is inferior; and (3) teaching the community to think of some people as having disabilities or not having disabilities (Smart & Smart, 2006). Therefore, in the sociopolitical model, these categories affect the daily lives of PWD. Many PWD view themselves as a U.S. minority group who has been denied their rights, rather than as a group of people who are biologically inferior and deviant. Higgin (1992) states that Americans with disabilities are foreigners in their own country. This model includes self-definition, self-determination, elimination of prejudice and discrimination, rejection of medical categories, and achievement of full equality and civil rights under U.S. laws.

Identity Model of Disability

For the identity model of disability, we use the case study of Caroline to gain a better understanding of how PWD view themselves within society.

Case Study: Caroline

Caroline is a 23-year-old college junior studying computer programming. Caroline was born deaf and uses American Sign Language (ASL) to communicate. Caroline lives at home with her parents (both are deaf and use ASL) and younger brother (who can hear but knows ASL). Caroline takes college classes online in the evening and works during the day at the local grocery store. Caroline goes out with her friends every week and enjoys participating in local activities throughout her community. Caroline is engaged to Joseph, a 25-year-old chef at a local restaurant. Caroline is happy with her life and accomplishes all the goals she sets for herself. Caroline does not feel her deafness is a "disability" and loves the acceptance by other (deaf) people like her. When asked whether she would ever consider using a hearing aid or a cochlear implant, Caroline quickly signs, "NO!"

1. What are some of the considerations you can use to assist Caroline?

Philosophical Approaches to Disability

The identity model of disability looks at disability from a different angle. In this model, PWD view themselves as part of an inclusionary group, similar to race, ethnicity, or a religious group (Retief & Letsosa, 2018). PWD feel there is nothing wrong with them or their "disability," and they feel they have every right for inclusion in "normal" society. The individual with the disability accepts their disability, whether acquired or congenital (Forber-Pratt & Zape, 2017). With the identity model, the barriers society places before PWD are the cause of the "disability," not the person's inability to complete a task because of their deficit. Brewer and colleagues (2012) offer the following definition of the identity model of disability:

> Disability as a marker of membership in a minority identity, much like gender or race. Under an identity model, disability is primarily defined by a certain type of experience in the world—a social and political experience of the effects of a social system not designed with disabled people in mind. While the identity model owes much to the social model, it is less interested in the ways environments, policies and institutions disable people, and more interested in forging a positive definition of disability identity based on experiences and circumstances that have created a recognizable minority group called "people with disabilities." (p. 5)

The identity model of disability is similar to the sociopolitical model of disability in that it agrees that society "creates" disability for individuals. The model differs from the sociopolitical model because it sees disability as a positive experience. In this model, many PWD affirm their existence and abilities in society by advocating for equal rights and championing self-images that celebrate their "disability." PWD are annoyed and upset more by society's barriers that emphasize the disability. PWD link themselves with identifying groups advocating societal change to protect and promote their civil rights, manage everyday stressors, and gain equal opportunities (Forber-Pratt & Zape, 2017; Retief & Letsosa, 2018). In this model, PWD have a collective sense of disability pride composed of four parts: (1) professing the disability;

(2) understanding that disability is a natural part of being human; (3) that, despite society's perspective, having a disability is not a harmful predicament; and (4) having a disability creates an awareness of a minority group (Putnam, 2005).

The identity model is not without its critics. Some people feel this model promotes separation due to PWD associating with a particular group (Retief & Letsosa, 2018). Some critics point out that not only is there a separation between PWD and those without disabilities but that there are actually three subgroups within this model (Tarvydas & Hartley, 2018). One group is PWD with physical or noticeable disabilities (blind, use of prosthetics). The second subgroup is the Deaf community. The Deaf community is not subjected to society's reaction to their disability because it is not immediately detectable. Instead, communication is the main factor separating the Deaf and hearing communities because not all hearing individuals are fluent in ASL. The third subgroup is individuals with a current or prior mental health diagnosis. The majority of individuals with a mental health diagnosis encounter stigma and discrimination of having a mental diagnosis at one point in their life. Because PWD do not seek society's acceptance, it may give "regular" society a basis to discriminate against PWD in the form of pay, housing, and employment. Other critics believe that this model works against the sociopolitical model of disability because the individual will not allow society to limit their access to places.

Human Rights Model of Disability

According to the human rights model of disability, society creates limitations and barriers for PWD. In this model, society must address social barriers to ensure that all people have the same rights, dignity, and respect. This model views PWD the same as those without disabilities and that all people are entitled to the same human rights. This model is an improvement of the sociopolitical model of disability, implementing the Treaty of the Convention on the Rights of Persons with Disabilities in 2006. In the human rights model, PWD are the primary decision makers on all things affecting them. Similar to the sociopolitical model, this model perceives the disability as within society and not within the individual. The model focuses on the human being's inherent dignity and medical characteristics, if necessary (Degener, 2016).

Even though the human rights model of disability is very similar to the sociopolitical model of disability, Degener (2017) identified six differences separating these two models. First, the sociopolitical model assists people in comprehending the social factors shaping society's perception of disability, whereas the human rights model enlists a theoretical framework stressing dignity in disability policies for PWD. Second, this model includes both first- and second-generation human rights, such as civil, political, socioeconomic, and cultural rights. Third, the sociopolitical model of disability neglects to acknowledge the existence of pain and suffering in the lives of PWD, whereas the human rights model argues that the life challenges confronted by PWD should be respected and considered when creating social justice theories. Fourth, whereas the sociopolitical model rarely acknowledges the necessity of identity politics, the human rights model allows PWD to co-identify with minority and other cultural groups. Fifth, whereas the sociopolitical model is critical of public health policies recommending impairment prevention, the human rights model endorses the well-developed policies protecting PWD. Lastly, whereas the social model of disability is beneficial in bringing to light why so many PWD experience financial hardships, the human rights model suggests practical recommendations for improving the quality of life for PWD.

Cultural Model of Disability

The cultural model of disability emerged from disability studies in the United States (Waldschmidt et al., 2017). This model emphasizes how PWD and individuals without disabilities function within the same environment (Retief & Letsosa, 2018). Compared to the sociopolitical model, in which disability is evidence of discrimination practices, the cultural model of disability offers a philosophical perspective of focus on society and culture. In the medical model, disability is an unforeseen event, and in the sociopolitical model, disability is a result of rejection and discrimination. The cultural model questions society's perception of "normal" and what defines a person as "disabled" (Waldschmidt et al., 2017). The medical and sociopolitical models each concentrate on one factor regarding disability; the cultural model considers several cultural factors (Retief & Letsosa, 2018). Based on the model, Harrison & Kahn (2003) defines disability as being shared by PWD, as social experiences, due to impairments that limit their function within mainstream society.

In this model, it is crucial how people in the culture, both able-bodied and PWD, are discussed and represented. These acknowledgments result in the morals, beliefs, and values in that culture and its identity. According to Waldschmidt et al. (2017), four distinct practices within society result in classifying disability:

1. Academia, media, and society define what is normal, disabled, and impairments. For the individual, the disability is only experience or situation, not a fact.
2. The perception of "disability" does not designate a feature but accentuates a difference. The disability is as an actual and naturalized fact. The word *disability* refers to the physical characteristics of a person and is used to describe the health of a person.
3. Defining disability and ability is another way of declaring what is normal and abnormal in society.
4. Society defines PWD's problems and decides on how to resolve those obstacles. Society creates and defines the balance of normalcy and deviance, inclusions or excluded, and designs and forms identity.

Some critics of the model (Snyder & Mitchell, 2006) think that some of the "cultures" created for PWD are no more than involuntary stays at facilities such as group homes, government institutions, research facilities, and supervised workshops (Retief & Letsosa, 2018). By placing PWD in supervised residences, critics believe that these individuals are labeled and classified because of their disabilities. This alienation creates more social stigma for PWD. They note that there is a difference between involuntary and "genuine" cultures, such as the Deaf community of independent living movements. The cultural model of disability offers the perspective of understanding disabilities, the disability rights movement and culture, and the formation of various independent living resources for PWD in a "genuine" culture (Retief & Letsosa, 2018).

Advocates of the cultural model of disability believe in the importance of collaborating between ability and disability (Waldschmidt et al., 2017). PWD encourage the media to focus more on the individual instead of the disability, as in the medical model. This means changing the language used in the media and increasing the employment of PWD within media through the use of policies and codes of practices and encouraging the change of language in media globally (Harrison, 2003).

Economic Model of Disability

The economic model of disability is also known as the functional model of disability because the individual cannot complete any work functions or roles (Smart, 2009a; Smart, 2009b). The economic model looks at disability in terms of how much PWD can participate in the workforce (Retief & Letsosa, 2018). This model defines disability as the inability to work and also views disability as a deficit or flaw. Compared to the medical model, which defines disability in terms of biology, the economic model simplifies disability from an economic standpoint (Riggar & Maki, 2004).

In the economic model, the severity of an individual's disability depends on the medical professional's diagnosis and prognosis (Tarvydas & Hartley, 2018). The diagnosis and prognosis then determine if the individual is disabled or capable of obtaining and maintaining employment. This model, used mostly by policy makers, determines a person's eligibility for government assistance, such as Social Security Disability Insurance (SSDI), Supplemental Security Income (SSI), Medicaid, and Medicare, based on the medical professional's determination (Amponsah-Bediako, 2013). In the economic model of disability, PWD are a growing consumer market with unaddressed needs and wants. In this model, PWD are the same as individuals without a disability: they travel, have families and friends, spend money, and like the more luxurious things in life (Tarvydas & Hartley, 2018). This model believes in meeting the buying power and demands of PWD. Many people feel this model also helps businesses grow because they answer the needs of their consumers, PWD. Disability scholars believe this model reduces isolation of PWD from society by supplying products and goods that encourage inclusivity (Tardyvas & Hartley, 2018).

Critics of this model feel it can result in discrimination and prejudice toward PWD because of possible limitations caused by the disability. First, the inability to "work" is the only function considered in the model; critics point out that PWD's participation in recreational and community activities are not addressed. (Riggar & Maki, 2004). Second, critics argue the interchangeable label of the "functional" model to the "labor-market" model because it only focuses on an individual's work and earning abilities. Lastly, the model is unable to keep up with the changing definition of work disability in the labor market because of the revolution and evolution of assistive/adaptive technology affording many PWD the opportunity to work.

Charity Model of Disability

The charity model of disability came into existence in response to the government ignoring the needs of PWD (Tsai & Ho, 2010). Religious and philanthropic agencies assumed the function of service providers for PWD, thus creating the foundation of the model. The charity model of disability views PWD as victims of circumstance who need constant assistance throughout life. In this model, disability is an unfortunate incident thrust upon the individual, who can overcome their situation by the kindness and mercy of others (Tsai & Ho, 2010). Similarly, this model coincides with the medical model in that the disability is a problem inherited by the person, who is thus the victim of a deficit. The individual is categorized in three ways: (1) sad, passive, and tragic; (2) aggressive, bitter, and twisted; and (3) courageous, brave, and inspirational

(Amponsah-Bediako, 2013). Based on the model, a disability is a tragic situation in which the individual becomes a victim of the impairment and is suffering (Retief & Letsosa, 2018).

According to the charity model of disability, charitable organizations should organize donations and fundraisers to help care for PWD. The model's purpose is to promote better treatment towards PWD (Henderson & Bryan, 2011). As a result, many nonprofit organizations and agencies use the charity model as the foundation for creating such businesses. In this model, employers or community agencies see PWD's issues as charitable causes for action (Lim & Chia, 2017). For example, instead of employers focusing on real issues like creating a workplace that is accessible for people with disabilities, the employer may think of fundraising events to meet the social and economic obligations of PWD. As a result, this model does not focus on employment and placement issues of people with disabilities.

The charity model is often criticized for depicting PWD as helpless, dependent, depressed, and needing the protection and constant care of nondisabled people (Retief & Letsosa, 2018). Another criticism of the model is the negative impacts on PWD's self-esteem because donors may be expecting a level of gratitude from PWD for their donations (Lim & Chia, 2017). This model perceives PWD as pitiful and unable to care for themselves, personally or economically, which leads to discrimination at the societal level (Amponsah-Bediako, 2013). Consequently, the individual may become institutionalized and stigmatized by society (Lim & Chia, 2017). In order to address the negative societal beliefs of disability, disability scholars believe more education and employment opportunities are needed to promote the treatment of PWD with respect.

Limitation of Models of Disability

No single model of disability has the power to explain every aspect of the disability experience because of the complexity of disability (Tate & Pledger, 2003). All models of disability seek to answer the question, "What is a disability?" (Berkowitz, 1987). Each model provides a different answer to this question, and their answers for disability affects society's views. For example, the moral/religious model emphasizes that disability is related to God's punishment and influences the interactions of society with PWD. Models of disability also determine the needs of disability differently. No one model can completely define and discuss disability and address all of the needs of PWD, nor can a single academic discipline respond to all these needs. Therefore, it is vital to train practitioners, including physicians, clinical rehabilitation counselors, social workers, and clinical mental health counselors, in all models of disability. Providing training on all models of disability is an opportunity for human service practitioners to see the limitations and the strength of each model. Specifically, rehabilitation counselors must have training in all models of disability to have better understating for different professions as a part of the treatment team. Other important questions that these models seek to address are "Who is responsible for disability" and "Who is responsible for the solution?" Each model of disability brings a different answer to these questions. For example, based on the medical model, PWD are responsible for their disability and solution. On the other hand, the sociopolitical model of disability emphasizes that social barriers are the cause of disability, and society is responsible for the solutions. Although each model describes responsibilities differently, all models of disability have something to contribute to understanding disability (Blustein, 2012). Lastly, society contributes to the progression of PWD's efforts to gain genuine acceptance and independence within their communities, despite perceived disabilities.

SUMMARY

In this chapter, we provided an overview of different models of disability discourse and case studies. Models of disability are guidelines utilized throughout the world to define a person's disability, the expectation of the person with a disability, and societal and governmental responses regarding the disability. A model of disability can measure the severity of the disability, the source of the disability, expectations of managing the disability, and society's and PWD's perspectives of the disability. The utilization of a model of disability can influence laws, policies, medical research, technology, communities, architecture, and the media (Smart, 2009a; Smart, 2009b). Each model has a significant impact on society's perception of PWD within their community.

Discussion Questions

1. Select the model of disability that best matches your own thinking and explain five reasons why.
2. What are the main differences between the medical model of disability and the sociopolitical model of disability?
3. What are the advantages and disadvantages of the medical model of disability?
4. What are the advantages and disadvantages of the sociopolitical model of disability?
5. How does the economic model of disability explain high unemployment rates for people with disabilities?
6. Besides some employment difficulties by PWD, what other current issues could the charity model of disability address?
7. Could the role of spirituality in health care, mainly when a person receives a diagnosis of a life-changing circumstance, be a possible resurgence of the moral/religious model of disability?

REFERENCES

Amponsah-Bediako, K. (2013). Relevance of disability models from the perspective of a developing country: An analysis. *Developing Country Studies*, *3*(11), 121–132.

Barnes, C. (1991). *Disabled people in Britain and discrimination: A case for anti-discrimination legislation.* C. Hurst & Company.

Barnes, C., & Mercer, G. (2005). Disability, work, and welfare: Challenging the social exclusion of disabled people. *Work, Employment and Society, 19*(3), 527–545.

Barnes, C., Mercer, G., & Shakespeare, T. (2010). The social model of disability. In A. Giddens & P. Sutton (Eds.), *Sociology: Introductory readings* (3rd ed.; pp. 161–166). Polity Press.

Berghs, M., Atkin, K., Graham, H., Hatton, C., & Thomas, C. (2016). Implications for public health research of models and theories of disability: A scoping study and evidence synthesis. *Public Health Research, 4.8*.

Berkowitz, E. D. (1987). *Disabled Policy: America's Programs for the Handicapped.* Cambridge University Press.

Bickenbach, J. E. (1993). *Physical disability and social policy.* University of Toronto.

Blustein, J. (2012). Philosophical and ethical issues in disability. *Journal of Moral Philosophy, 9*, 573–587.

Brewer, E., Brueggemann, B., Hetrick, N. & Yergeau, M. (2012). Introduction, background, and history. In B. Brueggemann (ed.), *Arts and humanities* (pp. 1–62). SAGE.

Carlson, L. (2010). *The faces of intellectual disability*. Indiana University Press.

Degener, T. (2017). A human rights model of disability. In P. Blancke & E. Flynn, *Routledge handbook of disability law and human rights* (pp. 31–49). Routledge.

Dembo, T., Leviton, G. L. & Wright, B. A. (1975). Adjustment to misfortune: A problem of social-psychological rehabilitation. *Rehabilitation Psychology, 22*(1), 1–100.

Dunn, D. (2015). *The social psychology of disability*. Oxford University Press.

Fitzgerald, H. (2006). Disability and physical education. In D. Kirk, D. MacDonald, & M. O'Sullivan (Eds.), *The handbook of physical education* (pp. 752–766). SAGE.

Forber-Pratt, A. J., & Zape, M. P. (2017). Disability identity development model: Voices from the ADA-generation. *Disability and Health Journal, 10*, 350–355.

Harrison, T. C., & Kahn, D. L. (2003). Disability: The cultural shift following impairment. *Family & Community Health, 27*(1), 86–93.

Hahn, H. (1997). Advertising the acceptable employment image: Disability and capitalism. In L. J. Davis (Ed), *The disabilities studies reader* (pp. 172–186). Routledge.

Henderson, G., & Bryan, W. (2011). *Psychosocial aspects of disability*. Charles C. Thomas.

Higgin, P. C. (1992). *Making disability: Exploring the social transformation of human variation*. Charles C. Thomas.

Johnstone, D. (2012*). An introduction to disability studies*. Taylor and Francis.

Lim, B. H., & Chia, K. H. (2017). Conceptualizing the special needs community therapy from the main ecosystemic models. *European Journal of Special Education Research, 2*(3), 107–124.

Llewellyn, A., Agu, L., & Mercer, D. (2008). *Sociology for social workers*. Polity Press.

Niemann, S. (2005). Persons with disabilities. In M. Burke, J. Chauvin, & J. Miranti (Eds.), *Religious and spiritual issues in counseling: Applications across diverse populations* (pp. 105–134). Brunner-Routledge.

O'Connell, C., Finnerty, J., & Egan, O. (2008). *Hidden voices: An exploratory study of young careers in Cork*. Combat Poverty Agency.

Oliver, M. (1981). A new model of the social work role in relation to disability. In J. Campling (Ed.), *The handicapped person: A new perspective for social workers* (pp. 19–32). RADAR.

Oliver, M. (1990). *The politics of disablement*. Macmillan.

Purtell, R. (2013). Music and the social model of disability. In J. Williams (Ed.), *Music and the social model: An occupational therapist's approach to music with people labelled as having learning disabilities* (pp. 26–32). Jessica Kingsley.

Putnam, M. (2005). Conceptualizing disability developing a framework for political disability identity. *Journal of Disability Policy Studies, 16*(3), 188-198. https://doi.org/10.1177/10442073050160030601

Retief, M., & Letsosa, R. (2018). Models of disability: A brief overview. *HTS Theologies Studies/Theological Studies, 74*(1), 1–8.

Riggar, T., & Maki, D. (2004). *Handbook of rehabilitation counseling*. Springer Publishing.

Rimmerman, A. (2013). *Social inclusion of people with disabilities*. Cambridge University Press.

Smart, J. (2004). Models of disability: The juxtaposition of biology and social construction. In T. Riggar & D. Maki (Eds.), *Handbook of rehabilitation counseling* (pp. 25–49). Springer Publishing.

Smart, J. F. (2009a). *Disability, society, and the individual* (2nd ed.). PRO-ED.

Smart, J. F. (2009b). The power of models of disability. *Journal of Rehabilitation, 75*(2), 3–11.

Smart, J. F., & Smart, D. W. (2006). Models of disability: Implications for the counseling profession. *Journal of Counseling and Development, 84*, 29–40.

Sharon L. & Snyder, D. T. (2006). *Mitchell cultural locations of disability*. Retrieved from: https://press.uchicago.edu/ucp/books/book/chicago/C/bo3533856.html

Solvang, P. (2000). The emergence of an us and them discourse in disability theory. *Scandinavian Journal of Disability Research, 2*, 3–20.

Tarvydas, V. M., & Hartley, M. T. (2018). *The professional practice of rehabilitation counseling* (2nd ed.). Springer Publishing.

Tate, D. G., & Pledger, D. C. (2003). An integrative conceptual framework of disability: New directions for research. *American Psychologist, 58*, 289–295.

Thomas, D., & Woods, H. (2003). *Working with people with learning disabilities*. Jessica Kingsley.

Tsai, I.-I., & Ho, M.-S. (2010). An institutionalist explanation of the evolution of Taiwan's disability movement: From the charity model to the social model. *Journal of Current Chinese Affairs, 39*(3), 87–123.

Union of the Physically Impaired against Segregation. (1976). *Fundamental principles of disability*. Author.

Waldschmidt, A., Berressem, H., & Ingwersen, M. (2017). *Culture–theory–disability: Encounters between disability studies and cultural studies*. Transcript-Verlag.

World Health Organization. (1980). International Classification of Impairments, Disabilities and Handicaps (ICIDH), WHO, Geneva. Retrieved from: https://apps.who.int/iris/bitstream/handle/10665/41003/9241541261_eng.pdf?sequenc

CHAPTER 5

People With Disabilities

Ajasha M. Long, MS
Louvisia Conley, MEd, EdS
Juwanna Kindred, MS
Sharon Brown, PhD, CRC
Chrisann Schiro-Geist, PhD, CRC, D/ABVE

Learning Objectives

As a result of reading this chapter, the student will be able to:

- Define disability.
- Differentiate between acute and chronic disabilities.
- Differentiate between congenital and acquired disabilities.
- Describe some psychosocial components of adjustment to disability.
- Explain the role of family and social support with regards to disability.
- Describe the difference between interdisciplinary and multidisciplinary teams.
- Describe common disabilities.

Defining Disability

The word *disability* is a broad term that can be used to refer to an array of conditions and impairments. Due to this conceptual variability, the definition of disability has undergone several changes over the past few decades. Currently, the *International Classification of Functioning, Disability, and Health* (ICF) conceptualizes the term *disability* as a multidimensional and dynamic interaction between an individual's health conditions and contextual factors (personal factors and environmental factors; World Health Organization [WHO], 2001). According to the ICF, problems with human functioning are categorized into three areas: impairments, activity limitations, and participation restrictions (Centers for Disease Control and Prevention [CDC], 2001). *Impairments* are problems in bodily functions or structures. This category can include conditions such as blindness and paralysis. *Activity limitations* are challenges in executing activities. This category can include difficulties such as walking or eating. *Participation restrictions* are difficulties in involvement in any area of life. This category can include, but is not limited to, accessibility challenges and discrimination in public spaces (CDC, 2001). Disability refers to difficulties in one or all of these aforementioned areas.

When conceptualizing the term *disability*, it is important to keep in mind that an individual's environment has a substantial impact on their experience and extent of disability. Environments that are unsafe or inaccessible can create or exacerbate disabilities by creating barriers to optimal health and functioning. Examples of these potential environmental barriers include:

- An individual who uses a wheelchair and lives in a town or area where there are no sidewalks or ramps.
- An individual who has a speaking impairment who does not have an assistive technology device to help with communication.
- An individual living with chronic lower back pain who works in a building without an elevator.

With environmental factors having a substantial impact on the inclusion and participation of individuals living with disabilities, this chapter will focus largely on the various roles in which social support, community, and the environment play in the lives of individuals living with disabilities.

Chronic Versus Acute

It would be remiss to present a chapter on disability without noting that not all disabilities are created equal. In the healthcare system, disabilities are typically labeled as either chronic or acute. Historically, the term *chronic disability* referred to conditions that were serious and irreversible (Varekamp et al., 2013). However, the term now refers to conditions that persist longer than a 3-month time span. Chronic disabilities are conditions that will typically require a lifetime of care because they typically cannot be cured, only managed. Chronic disabilities typically develop and worsen over time. As such, individuals living with chronic disabilities may need to make lifestyle changes (dietary modifications, physical activity changes, etc.) to manage their conditions. Chronic disabilities/illnesses may include, but are not limited to, cancer, multiple sclerosis, muscular dystrophy, cardiac conditions, cerebral palsy, scoliosis, chronic pain, lupus, seizure disorder, intellectual disability, mental health conditions, acquired brain injury, and so on.

Acute disabilities typically have rapid onset and are short in duration. The symptoms often appear suddenly and may begin to change and worsen very rapidly (Vorvick, 2019). Although acute disabilities may cause disruptions in an individual's lifestyle, these conditions typically resolve themselves within a standard amount of time, if the appropriate care is given. However, in some cases acute disabilities can lead to chronic conditions. Acute disabilities/illnesses may include, but are not limited to, cardiac conditions, appendicitis, pneumonia, acute respiratory distress, asthma attacks, and so on.

Congenital Versus Acquired

Another notable distinction in the overall disability literature is the experience of individuals living with congenital disabilities versus acquired disabilities (Bogart, 2014). A *congenital disability* is a medical condition that was present at or before birth. These disabilities may be physical, intellectual, or developmental and may range from mild to severe. Congenital disabilities can be caused by genetic or environmental factors, and an individual living with a congenital disability may experience health concerns throughout the duration of their life. Examples of congenital disabilities are cerebral palsy, Down syndrome, spina bifida, fetal alcohol syndrome, and cystic fibrosis.

In contrast, an *acquired disability* is a disability that has developed over a person's lifetime and was not present at birth. These types of disabilities are typically the result of an accident or illness rather than a congenital disorder (Employer Disability Information, 2019). Acquired disabilities can be visible or invisible. Some examples of acquired disabilities include loss of hearing/vision, spinal injuries, multiple sclerosis, head/brain trauma, injury/loss of limbs, stroke, and mental health concerns. Individuals living with acquired disabilities may face unique challenges both physically and psychologically because they may be forced to adjust to a lifestyle that is starkly different from the one they were living before acquiring a disability.

Currently, there appears to be a dearth of research on the psychosocial impact of congenital disabilities. Rehabilitation professionals have suggested that this scarcity can be attributed to an implicit assumption that society has about individuals living with congenital disabilities (Bogart, 2014). For instance, some people may assume that individuals living with a congenital disability may not face as much difficulty with adjustment because they have never known a life without disability. Although individuals with congenital disabilities face their own unique challenges, comparison studies of congenital versus acquired disabilities have found that individuals living with congenital disabilities had greater acceptance of their disability and were better adapted than those living with an acquired disability (Bogart et al., 2012; Li & Moore, 1998). Furthermore, due to the nature of their origin, congenital and acquired disabilities may have different consequences physically, emotionally, and psychologically.

Adjustment to Disability

Adjustment to disability has been the subject of keen interests for many rehabilitation counselors and psychologists. This dynamic process involves an interaction between the affective, cognitive, and behavioral changes that will eventually enable an individual to reach an optimal state of physical and psychological functioning (Bogart, 2014). Many disability- and nondisability-related factors can impact an individual's adjustment to disability.

Self-Concept

Although each person's disability experience is unique, one key component in adjustment is a person's ability to incorporate their disability into their self-concept (Bramble & Cukr, 1998; McDaniel, 1976; Smart, 2008). In the disability literature, *self-concept* has been defined as the collection of an individual's self-esteem, group identity, and self-efficacy (Smart, 2008). For individuals living with a disability, self-concept may be negatively skewed due to social interactions, stigma, and societal beliefs about individuals with disabilities. Therefore, in order for an individual to achieve an optimal self-concept, they must be able to create meaning from their experience and use it to build a positive self-image.

Stigma

Although individuals with disabilities comprise one of the largest minority groups in the world, a substantial amount of societal stigma and prejudice around people with disabilities continues to exist. It is important to note that the conceptualization of stigma varies depending upon culture and environment because society determines what is considered normal and abnormal. In a broader sense, stigma refers to an attribute or characteristic that is deeply discrediting and reduces the status of an individual in the eyes of society (Goffman, 1963). Individuals living with disabilities, especially conditions that are visible, may face considerable rejection and bias from society. These negative societal attitudes can erode one's self-concept and impact an individual's ability to adjust to a disability (Marini & Stebnicki, 2012).

Social Support

Researchers have consistently cited social support as a major factor in an individual's adjustment to disability (Marini & Stebnicki, 2012; Schulz & Decker, 1985; Wilson et al., 2006). *Social support* refers to how much an individual feels as though they are loved and cared about by others (Jenson et al., 2014). Although its effects may vary by age, social support is an important resource for individuals with disabilities because it can act as a buffer against disability-related stressors. Additionally, social support is a perceived concept, meaning that what may be considered "supportive" for one individual, may not be for the next individual. Overall, the concept has been shown to be a potent predictor of adjustment to disability.

The aforementioned components are those frequently cited in the literature as being key indicators of adjustment to disability. However, adjustment may vary depending upon the individual, and there are many other physical, psychological, and environmental factors that can also impact adjustment.

Disability and Family

Families are typically the primary caregivers for individuals living with disabilities (Miller et al., 2012). However, the role of caregiving often extends outside of the typical family nucleus (mom, dad, etc.), with grandparents and other extended family stepping in to provide support. Moreover, social support has consistently been shown to moderate the emotional and psychological effects of living with a disability. In particular, stress-buffering models have suggested that the emotional impact of living with a disability is diminished if an individual has specific coping resources like social support (Carr et al., 2019; Pearlin, 1999). Caring for an individual with a disability can be a particularly challenging experience; however, families can exhibit incredible resiliency if paired with the appropriate resources and support.

Parenting a Child With a Disability

Although some parents are able to extract meaning from their experience as caregivers, caring for a child with a disability can present physical, financial, and emotional difficulties. Parents of children with disabilities may struggle with feelings of anger, resentment, and denial at the time of their child's diagnosis. Additionally, parents may struggle with ongoing questions regarding their child's diagnosis and may face difficulty when making decisions about the child's future. These feelings can persist as the child ages. Parents and caregivers may feel that they must conceal their emotions in order to remain positive for their children. It is also common for parents and caregivers to experience feelings of grief and loss, as parents often develop expectations and aspirations for children even before they are born. Feelings of grief and loss may occur if that child does not represent the "ideal" expectation. Parents need the opportunity to grieve the loss of these expectations in order to create new dreams and hopes for their children (Klein & Shive, 2001).

In addition to the psychological components of caring for a child with a disability, parents and caregivers may also have to sacrifice their plans and dreams in order to meet the unique needs of the child. Career aspirations and other endeavors may need to be modified or put on hold to benefit the child. Some parents may even be forced to relocate to be closer to family members or relatives who can offer support.

Additionally, having a child with a disability can be a trigger for family conflict because other siblings or family members can feel invisible or unacknowledged due to the amount of attention that the child with a disability might be receiving (Miller et al., 2012). Feelings of jealousy or possessiveness may emerge as a result of this perceived imbalance.

Despite the many challenges that parents of children with disabilities may face, family researchers have identified specific processes that can foster resilience among families of children with disabilities (Bayat, 2007). Meaning making, collaboration of resources, and affirmation of strengths are just a few of these processes (Bayat, 2007; Miller et al., 2012).

Marriage/Romantic Partnership

Marriage involving individuals with disabilities has been a subject of long-standing debate because attitudes regarding sexuality and marriage of individuals with disabilities has been historically negative (Pan & Ye, 2012). Depending upon the type of disability, many individuals may face more challenges in the area of marriage and romantic partnership than people without disabilities because physical and emotional impairments often require extra attention and effort. Financial concerns, unstable employment patterns, and ongoing health concerns can present unique challenges for individuals living with disabilities.

Role Transition

One of the potential challenges that individuals who are in romantic relationships and living with a disability may face is role shift/transition. Individuals living with a disability may face various shifts and transitions in their career options, independence, relational status, and so on (Parker, 1993; Tepper, 1999). This may place strain and tension on a marriage or relationship, specifically for individuals who have a high need for assistance. This narrative may be even more salient for individuals living with an acquired disability because they may face distinct adjustment difficulty due to feelings of grief and other psychological challenges that accompany an acquired disability.

Financial Concerns

Another set of challenges that partnered individuals with disabilities may face are financial concerns. Individuals with disabilities are more than twice as likely to be unemployed than individuals without disabilities (Bureau of Labor Statistics, 2019). Things like physical challenges, doctor's appointments, transportation, and mobility can all present barriers to employment for individuals living with disabilities. As such, some individuals with disabilities may be forced to depend on family members or other social support for financial help. This may lead to psychological and emotional concerns such as feelings of guilt, remorse, and resentment.

Sexuality

Although the sexual relationship is an essential portion of marriage or partnership, sexuality among individuals with disabilities has long been a subject of contingency. Many couples report a change in their sexual relationship when one of the partners has or has acquired a disability (Parker, 1993). Both pain and physical impairments can present barriers to exploring sexuality among individuals with disabilities. Rehabilitation counselors are in a unique position to work with individuals with sexuality concerns. They can collaborate with consumers in normalizing fears and concerns about sexuality, educating consumers on the impact of physical impairments, and assisting with developing alternative methods for sexual expression.

Interdisciplinary Teams

In rehabilitation, interdisciplinary teams have been effective in improving patient treatment outcomes. Interdisciplinary teams are an essential partnership, bringing together different healthcare and welfare services workers to support the individual in their return to self before sickness or illness. Interdisciplinary rehabilitation collaboration consists of a group of professionals from different specialties coming together to discuss treatment for the patient collectively and deciding on the best outcome of treatment. According to Korner (2010), interdisciplinary team members meet regularly in order to discuss and collaboratively set treatment goals for the patients and then jointly carry out the treatment plan. Interdisciplinary rehabilitation teams apply an evidence-based approach in the implementation of their collaboration to ensure competent and capable services and delivery of patient care.

The term *multidisciplinary* refers to a team or collaborative process where members of different disciplines assess or treat patients independently and then share the information. According to McCallin (2001), *interdisciplinary* describes a deeper level of collaboration in which processes such as evaluation or development of a plan of care is done jointly, with professionals of different disciplines pooling their knowledge in an independent matter. The difference between the multidisciplinary and interdisciplinary approaches is that multidisciplinary team members appear to focus on the professional tasks in the individual's work, whereas an interdisciplinary team is a group of professionals working on goals that will result in positive change and outcomes. According to McCallin (2001), the different focus may mirror the change in a society that recognizes the importance of integrating tasks and processes in synergistic human interactions.

The conceptual framework of interdisciplinary practice consists of four phases: (1) sensitization, (2) exploration, (3) implementation, and (4) evaluation in facilitating the professional collaboration roles of the team member. The sensitization phase focuses on discussing power imbalances and differing values and exploring the meaning of roles and decision-making processes for creating awareness of everyone's practice constructs. The exploration phase seeks to clarify that everyone in the group values the other members' knowledge and contributions to the team. During the implementation phase, trusting relationships among the group are developed and members trust the knowledge, decision-making capacity, and ethics of each team member and exhibit a willingness to engage in joint power-sharing within the group, regardless of educational or professional preparation. During the intervention phase, the professional collaborative team works with the patient to gain an understanding of how powers can be shared and each member's role can be valued. The final phase is evaluation, whereby the professionals assess the impact of their collaboration on the patient's satisfaction, as well as their own (Orchard, 2005). During each of these phases, the team also focuses on the barriers and deals with conflicts and attitude differences among group members.

Interdisciplinary teams in rehabilitation are the heartbeat of successful interprofessional collaboration. The interdisciplinary team focuses on patient goals, the participation of each team member, successful collaboration, respecting differences in perspective, and determining what the data are saying in the results of the patient's assessment and test (White et al., 2013). The keys to practice in interdisciplinary teams are (1) recognizing that a strong relationship between team members is required to provide effective patient care, (2) that communication can be both a barrier and facilitator for team effectiveness, (3) that education and experience levels of team members are factors in interdisciplinary teams, and (4) that an understanding of the roles and responsibilities of the other team members is essential for optimal team functioning (White et al., 2013).

Disability and Community

Community involvement can be inspirational, supportive, and empowering in the lives of individuals with disabilities, whether physical, sensory, intellectual, or emotional. Community and disability create a collaboration of social inclusion, which allows individuals with disabilities to develop self-assurance, self-determination, independent living skills, and social interconnection with resources from their community. The social model of disability stands in contrast with the medical model, whereby a person presents with a series of medical complaints rather than as a whole person. Disability and community intertwine interpersonal and intrapersonal interactions in how the relationship is connected and communicated on a domestic and social level in one's life, having the ability to choose and have control over one's own life. Cawthon and Garberoglio (2017) report that community and social networks serve as threads that interweave between multiple contexts and environments through leveraging the power of relationships. Community is a collaboration network designed to deliver intervention through community participation, which enhances the quality of people's lives for the better (Cawthon & Garberoglio, 2017). Community participation brings together people, information, resources, and connections, which allows for sharing ideas through social interactions, which then generates and builds supportive relationships that can assist with one's interest for the common good and purpose.

Characteristics of Community Involvement

Community participation and social engagement have been described as representing both the physical presence and the meaningful network of relationships that create mutual support while building mutual respect. *Community engagement* has been defined as an individual engaging in and participating in activities of the same interest and ideas by which to create a sense of belonging to a social group that empowers one's ability to self-advocate and exercise independence in an inclusive environment. According to Lee and Morningstar (2019), the community provides opportunities for building mutual respect, as well as engaging in reciprocal personal relationships sustained by formal and informal supports. In sum, research suggests several indicators of the depth and quality of community participation, including frequency of community visits (i.e., community presence), type of involvement in adult activities (i.e., community involvement), and sense of belonging to social networks (i.e., social engagement; Lee & Morningstar, 2019).

Benefits of Community Involvement

The increasing amounts of change in our society continue to restructure our approach to broader, more community-based resources that are needed for individuals with disabilities. Engagement with social activities is crucial to meeting and attaining individual goals. Community involvement for individuals with disabilities is the avenue that will lead not only to engagement in necessary rehabilitation services but also contribute to an improved quality of life. An exploration of the most efficient community resources requires an understanding of the needed supports, ongoing necessary interventions, and rehabilitation services. It is also critical that people with disabilities learn how to self-advocate through the social system. This enables the necessary motivation, which will improve well-being. The benefit to the community is the establishment of institutionalized empowerment for the disenfranchised that is systemic and self-maintaining. With this engagement, a decrease in attitudinal and communication barriers is expected.

Greater engagement with the community creates a more robust social network that will connect individuals with employment and educational resources. According to Cawthon and Garberoglio (2017), without social interconnection, individuals experience reduced community engagement, resulting in fewer social strengths. Further, they indicate that a decrease in community involvement correlates with a decrease in psychosocial development. This approach is person-centered, whereby the individual determines what is uniquely needed for them in community.

Community Involvement Creates a Sense of Social Interconnection

Community engagement enables social interconnection that encourages high motivation and increased self-esteem for persons with disabilities. Through the development of social connections, individuals with disabilities can begin to engage in identity exploration, assessing their purpose and ultimately determining what type of engagement they need within the community. In this way, individuals are exposed to predictive extracurricular activities that are significant to living independently. Universal interconnection creates a refreshing network with likeminded individuals in an interdisciplinary framework. According to Cawthon and Garberoglio (2017), participating in extracurricular activities may offer opportunities to build connections to community networks, gain experience in navigating the social situation, and strengthen soft skills that are often part and parcel of community interconnection.

One approach to understanding community is the six principles for engaging people and communities (People and Communities Board, 2016). In this model, the community becomes the system, surrounding the person with a variety of subsystems. Providing person-centered care, partnering with the community, narrowing inequality, encouraging family engagement and support, volunteering, and intersecting with economic partners is an ideal model to enable the best quality of life. The goal is to achieve homeostasis and improve the quality with a person-centered perspective and provide for full inclusion into the community. Any weak subsystem is survivable by developing competency skills in the other subsystems. Seeing the community from this perspective provides a holistic approach and develops a community-focused theoretical base.

To conclude, community involvement increases our ability to build community-based resources. This allows us to create a robust social network to empower persons with disabilities. The journey toward self-exploration enables the person to recognize that they can accomplish more than what they expected of themselves. Building strong relationships within the community at the micro-level can deepen participation for the persons with disability and create a sense of togetherness to support everyone's development.

Types of Disabilities

It is estimated that there are more than one billion people living with some form of disability. Of these individuals, nearly 200 million report experiencing considerable difficulty with functioning (World Report on Disability, 2011). As the prevalence of disabilities continues to rise, it is imperative that rehabilitation counselors are aware of the unique role that they play in helping manage this increase (World Report on Disability, 2011).

Physical Disabilities

A physical disability is a condition that limits one or more basic physical activities, such as walking, climbing stairs, reaching, lifting, or carrying (CDC, 2019). A physical disability can be either congenital or acquired. In 2019, the CDC reported that approximately 13.7% of Americans had a serious mobility disability. The two most common types of physical disabilities are musculoskeletal disabilities and neuromuscular disabilities. A neuromuscular disorder affects the nerves that control the muscles. An example of a neuromuscular disorder is muscular dystrophy. Musculoskeletal disorders are injuries, loss, or pain that affects the joints, ligaments, muscles, nerves, tendons, and structures that support the neck and back. An example of a musculoskeletal disorder is spina bifida.

Muscular Dystrophy

The CDC (2019) describes muscular dystrophy (MD) as a group of inherited muscle diseases caused by mutations in a person's genes. Muscular dystrophy affects specific muscle groups and is known to cause muscle weakness and loss of muscle tissue. There are several different types of muscular dystrophy, and the symptoms can vary from person to person. Muscular dystrophies are known to run in families, but it is possible for a person to be the first in their family to have muscular dystrophy. There is no known cure for muscular dystrophy. Early interventions and treatments, such as physical therapy, orthopedic devices, surgery, speech therapy, and medication, can help the symptoms and prevent complications.

Spina Bifida

Spina bifida is one of the most common nervous system birth defects in the United States. According to the National Institute of Neurological Disorders and Stroke (NINDS), spina bifida (cleft spine) is characterized by the incomplete development of the brain, spinal cord, and or meninges (the protective covering around the brain and spinal cord). Approximately 1,500 to 2,000 babies are born with spina bifida each year in the United States (National Institute of Neurological Disorders and Stroke [NINDS], 2020). Spina bifida happens when the spinal column does not close all the way, causing damage to the nerves and spinal cord. The symptoms of spina bifida vary from person to person, and in some cases it can cause physical and intellectual complications. Spina bifida is diagnosed before birth and, in mild cases, after birth. The causes of spina bifida are unknown. Like most congenital disorders, spina bifida has no cure. Treatment for spina bifida depends on the severity of the disorder, and this includes ongoing surgery, medications, and physical and/or behavioral therapy.

Sensory Disabilities

A sensory disability is an impairment related to any of the five senses: hearing, taste, smell, sight, and touch. Sensory disabilities can be congenital or acquired. Two of the most well-known sensory disabilities are blindness/visual impairment and deafness/hard of hearing.

Low Vision/Blindness

According to the CDC (2017), 6.8% of children younger than 18 years in the United States have a diagnosed eye and vision condition. Nearly 3% of children are blind or visually impaired. Blindness or visual impairment means that a person has trouble seeing or the inability to see anything even when wearing glasses or any type of visual corrections. The leading causes of blindness and low vision in the United States are primarily age-related eye diseases (CDC, 2017). Treatment for visual impairment or partial blindness may involve surgery or medication. Those who become completely blind over time may eventually need to learn new skills and a new way of life, such as learning how to read Braille and using a guide dog or a walking cane.

Deafness/Hard of Hearing

Approximately 2 to 3 out of every 1,000 children in the United States are born with a detectable level of hearing loss in one or both ears. According to the National Institute on Aging (NIA, 2018), deafness is a hearing impairment or a complete loss of hearing in one or both ears. A hearing loss can develop at any age, affecting a person's ability to communicate and develop social and language skills. Treatment and intervention for the deaf and/or hard of hearing vary by person. In some cases, surgery, hearing aids, hearing implants, and cochlear implants can be effective treatments for persons who are hard of hearing. Intervention programs are helpful for those who have completely lost their ability to hear or who are deaf. These programs are designed to help build a person's social skills, language skills, and other important skills they may need to live a successful and independent life.

Developmental/Intellectual Disabilities

In the United States, about 1 in 6, or 17%, of children aged 3 through 17 have one or more intellectual disabilities (CDC, 2019). Intellectual disabilities typically develop before the age of 18 and are characterized by limitations in intellectual functioning as well as difficulties in social and practical skills. A child with an intellectual disability tends to learn at a slower rate than other children. Some of the more commonly known intellectual disabilities include fetal alcohol syndrome and genetic and chromosomal conditions such as Down syndrome and fragile X syndrome.

Down Syndrome

Down syndrome is a chromosomal genetic condition in which a person is born with an extra chromosome (Martin et al., 2009). Down syndrome is typically detected during pregnancy and is found in approximately 400 in 1,500 live births in the United States, affecting all ages, races, and economic levels (Kazemi et al., 2016). Children with Down syndrome usually have a low IQ and usually experience some developmental and physical delays (Adams et al., 1981). Most individuals with Down syndrome have additional health issues, including heart defects and early onset Alzheimer disease (Kazemi et al., 2016). However, in some cases of Down syndrome, individuals have the facial features associated with the syndrome (i.e., a flattened face, a short neck, and an oversized tongue) but no other medical conditions (CDC, 2018). Because it is a chromosomal condition, there is no treatment for Down syndrome. Positive support from family and friends or early interventions in life will often help persons with Down syndrome to improve their physical and intellectual abilities and enable them to live a fulfilling life.

Fragile X Syndrome

Out of all of the inherited genetic disorders, fragile X syndrome (FXS) is the most common cause of intellectual disabilities. FXS is a genetic condition that causes a range of developmental problems that can result in learning disabilities and/or cognitive impairment. FXS is caused by changes in the fragile X mental retardation 1 (*FMR1*) gene. *FMR1* is the gene that makes a protein needed for normal brain development, which is called fragile X mental retardation protein (FMRP). FXS is found in both males and females, but it appears to be more severe in males. Affected females tend to have mild mental retardation and variable associated physical features (Sherman et al., 2005). Approximately 1.4 per 10,000 men and .09 per 10,000 women have FXS (Hunter et al., 2014). There is no cure for FXS. However, treatment and early intervention services can help children as early as 0 months to 3 years old learn vital skills.

Learning Disabilities

According to the *Diagnostic and Statistical Manual of Mental Disorders* (DSM-5; American Psychiatric Association [APA], 2013), a learning disability is a neurological disorder that affects a child's ability to learn, retain, and process information. Learning disabilities are often diagnosed during the early school years. In 2009, approximately 2.5 million, or 5%, of public school students were diagnosed with a learning disability (Mahrezi et al., 2016). A specific learning disability does not play a role in a child's intelligence, but it does affect a child's ability to acquire and apply reading, writing, and math skills. Dyslexia and attention deficit/hyperactivity disorder (ADHD) are the two most common learning disorders.

Dyslexia

Dyslexia is the most common neurocognitive disorder. *Neurocognitive disorder* is a general term used to refer to a group of conditions that frequently lead to impaired mental function (Grohol, 2020). These conditions are typically not caused by psychiatric illness. According to the Yale Center for Dyslexia and Creativity (2017), dyslexia is a learning disorder that affects 20% of the population and represents 80% to 90% of those with learning disabilities. Dyslexia affects a person's ability to read, write, spell, and learn a second language. Although often diagnosed early in life, dyslexia can also emerge in adulthood as a result of a brain injury or in the context of dementia (National Institute of Neurological Disorders and Stroke, 2019). Dyslexia is not in any way related to a person's intelligence quotient (IQ), and it can be identified by the age of 5. Early identification and intervention can prevent reading or learning difficulties.

Attention Deficit/Hyperactivity Disorder

According to the National Institute of Mental Health (NIMH, 2019), attention deficit/hyperactivity disorder (ADHD) is a condition that makes it difficult for a person to maintain focus or to control impulsive behaviors. ADHD is one of the most common childhood disorders, and it can continue through adolescence and into adulthood. According to the CDC (2020), 11% of all children in the United States aged 4 to 17 years have been diagnosed with ADHD. Researchers at the National Institute of Mental Health (NIMH, 2019) suggested that ADHD is caused by interactions between genes and environmental or nongenetic factors. Persons with ADHD experience symptoms of inattentiveness, over activity, and impulsivity. Although there is no cure for ADHD, medication and therapy will help reduce symptoms and improve functioning.

Psychiatric Disabilities/Mental Health

Disabilities that are not apparent or visible to others are considered invisible disabilities. Approximately 10% of the U.S. population has an invisible disability. Mental disorders are some of the most common invisible disabilities. Mental disorders are common in the United States, affecting millions of people each year. According to the National Alliance on Mental Illness (NAMI), 19.1%, or 47.6 million, U.S. adults experience mental illness each year. Mental illness ranges from mild to severe and should never be ignored or left untreated. One in 24 (4.1%) Americans has a serious mental illness. The most common severe mental disorders are schizophrenia, depressive disorder, and bipolar disorder.

Schizophrenia

Schizophrenia is perhaps the most severe and disabling of the psychiatric disorders. According to the National Institute of Mental Health (NIMH, 2020), schizophrenia can be characterized as disruptions in thought processes, perceptions, emotional responsiveness, and social interactions. Schizophrenia is a chronic lifelong brain disorder that affects 1.1% of the U.S. population . Signs of schizophrenia can occur in anyone at any age, but it typically emerges in the late teens or early adulthood. According to the NIMH (2020), the symptoms of schizophrenia can be divided into three categories: positive, negative, and disorganized/cognitive symptoms. Persons with positive symptoms of schizophrenia may lose touch with reality. They may experience symptoms of hallucinations, delusions, jumbled thoughts, trouble concentrating, and movement disorders. Negative symptoms are similar to thinking deficiencies and cognitive failing. In negative symptoms of schizophrenia, a person may experience a decrease in motivation, poor judgment, antisocial behavior, emotional withdrawal, and monotone and monosyllabic speech. Persons with schizophrenia may have a hard time retaining and understanding information. Cognitive symptoms include memory loss or forgetfulness and trouble focusing.

Depression

Depression is one of the most common psychological disorders, affecting approximately 17.3 million U.S. adults (NIMH, 2017). Depression, which is categorized as a mood disorder, can occur at any age but most often emerges in late adolescence and early adulthood. Approximately 17% of people will experience depression during their lifetime. Women are twice as likely as men to suffer from depression. More than 24% of women and 12% of men will experience a major depressive disorder during their lifetime (Ettinger, 2017). Assessing a major depressive disorder can be challenging because symptoms are subjective and are based on a person's personal beliefs, feelings, and emotions. According to the DSM-5 (APA, 2013), a person with a major depressive disorder must experience at least five of the following symptoms during a 2-week period: a depressed mood, loss of interest or pleasure in daily activities, a change in appetite or weight, problems with sleeping, difficulty with concentrating, feelings of worthlessness, and suicidal thoughts.

Bipolar Disorder

Similar to depression, bipolar disorder is also classified as a mood disorder. Bipolar disorder alters a person's mood, thinking, and energy. Persons with bipolar experience extreme mood swings that cause emotions to be extremely high (mania or hypomania) or extremely low (depression). Bipolar disorder presents in both men and women equally and typically emerges in late adolescence and early adulthood. More than 6 million Americans are diagnosed with bipolar disorder each year (Ettinger, 2017; NIMH, 2017). There is no cure for bipolar disorder, but proper treatment and a healthy lifestyle can help reduce symptoms.

SUMMARY

The purpose of this chapter was to describe various types of disabilities, their causes, symptoms, and treatment implications. Although this chapter provided a thorough synopsis of different types of disabilities, it does not represent or detail all disability/illness experiences. To provide adequate service to a consumer, one must have a thorough understanding of an individual's disability. As such, this chapter seeks to assist rehabilitation professionals in understanding the many types of disabilities and how they can assist consumers in daily living.

Discussion Questions

1. At what age can a person be tested for an intellectual disability?
2. Is there a difference between bipolar disorder and depression?
3. List the positive and negative symptoms of schizophrenia. How do these symptoms differ?
4. Explain the value and values connected to community participation for persons with disabilities and their families. Who determines what values are the most important in a community of persons with disabilities?
5. Describe the issues related to community relationships and partnerships for persons with disabilities, from a systems approach. Does systems theory support the movement toward higher utilization of community action for persons with disabilities, especially from a person-centered model?
6. Explain the interdisciplinary team's approach in rehabilitation and its crucial teamwork in the patient's treatment.
7. How do the practices of interdisciplinary teams facilitate professional roles? How do these roles work in a rehabilitation collaboration team?
8. How do the multidisciplinary model and the interdisciplinary model differ?

Case Study: James

James is a 35-year-old construction worker who recently experienced a C6–C7 spinal cord injury from a motor cycle accident. He was the sole financial provider for his household, but he can no longer continue his job as a construction worker due to his physical limitations. James's wife, Barbara, has never worked outside of the home. However, due to the recent turn of events, Barbara has taken a job as a cashier at the local supermarket. During his rehabilitation appointment, James expresses frustration and anger about his physical limitations and states that he feels like "less of a man" because he cannot provide financially for his family in the way that he is used to. Additionally, James reports feeling disheartened by changes in his sexual function and response, noting that he has not been able to achieve the level of intimacy that he had with his wife prior to the accident.

1. Identify the challenges that James is currently experiencing.
2. As a rehabilitation counselor, what steps would you take to help James?

REFERENCES

Adams M. M., Erickson J. D., Layde P. M., Oakley G. P. (1981, August 14). Down's syndrome. Recent trends in the United States. *JAMA, 246*(7), 758–60. doi: 10.1001/jama.246.7.758. PMID: 6454794.

Al-Mahrezi, A., Al-Futaisi, A., & Al-Mamari, W. (2016). Learning Disabilities: Opportunities and challenges in Oman. *Sultan Qaboos University Medical Journal, 16*(2), e129–e131. https://doi.org/10.18295/squmj.2016.16.02.001

American Psychiatric Association. (2013). *Diagnostic and statistical manual of mental disorders* (5th ed.). Author.

Andersson, J., Ahgren, B., Axelsson, S. B., Eriksson, A., & Axelsson, R. (2011). Organizational approaches to collaboration in the vocational rehabilitation: An international literature review. *International Journal of Integrated Care, 11*, 137. https://doi:10.5334/ijic.670

Andrew, J., & Andrew, M. J. (Eds.). (2017). *The disability handbook.* Aspen Professional.

Anastasiou, D., & Kauffman, J. M. (2011). A social constructivist approach to disability: Implications for special education. *Exceptional Children, 77*, 367–384.

Bayat, M. (2007). Evidence of resilience in families of children with autism. *Journal of Intellectual Disability Research, 51*(9), 702–714.

Behm, J., & Gray, N. (2011). *Interdisciplinary rehabilitation team.* Jones & Bartlett Learning.

Bogart, K. (2014). The role of disability self-concept in adaptation to congenital or acquired disability. *Rehabilitation Psychology, 59*(1), 107–115. https://doi.org/10.1037/a0035800

Bogart, K. R., Tickle-Degnen, L., & Ambady, N. (2012). Compensatory expressive behavior for facial paralysis: Adaptation to congenital or acquired disability. *Rehabilitation Psychology, 57*, 43–51. https://doi:10.1037/a0026904

Bramble, K., & Cukr, P. (1998). Body image. In I. M. Lubkin (Ed.), *Chronic illness: Impact and interventions* (4th ed.; pp. 283–298). Jones and Bartlett Learning.

Brault, M. W. (2012). American with disabilities: 2010. *Current Populations Reports,* P70-131. U.S. Bureau of the Census. https://www.census.gov/library/publications/2012/demo/p70-131.html

Bureau of Labor Statistics. (2019). Persons with a disability: Labor force characteristics. [News release]. https://www.bls.gov/news.release/pdf/disabl.pdf

Carr, D., Cornman, J., & Freedman, V. (2019). Do family relationships buffer the impact of disability on older adults' daily mood? An exploration of gender and marital status differences. *Journal of Marriage and the Family, 81*(3), 729–746. https://doi.org/10.1111/jomf.12557

Cawthon, S. W., & Garberoglio, C. L. (2017). *Shifting the dialog, shifting the culture: Pathways to successful postsecondary outcomes for Deaf individuals.* Gallaudet University Press.

Centers for Disease Control and Prevention. (2001). *The ICF: An overview.* https://www.cdc.gov/nchs/data/icd/icfoverview_finalforwho10sept.pdf

Centers for Disease Control and Prevention. (2017). *Fast facts of common eye disease.* https://www.cdc.gov/visionhealth/basics/ced/fastfacts.htm#:~:text=Approximately%206.8%25%20of%20children%20younger,wearing%20glasses%20or%20contact%20lenses.

Centers for Disease Control and Prevention. (2019a). *Definition of disability.* Retrieved from: https://www.cdc.gov/nchs/data/hpdata2010/focusareas/fa06_definitions.pdf

Centers for Disease Control and Prevention. (2019b). *What is muscular dystrophy?* Retrieved from: https://www.cdc.gov/ncbddd/musculardystrophy/facts.html

Centers for Disease Control and Prevention. (2020). *Data and statistics about ADHD.* Retrieved from: https://www.cdc.gov/ncbddd/adhd/data.html

Centers for Disease Control and Prevention. (2019, December 05). *Facts about Down Syndrome.* Retrieved October 24, 2020, from https://www.cdc.gov/ncbddd/birthdefects/downsyndrome.html

Chappell, P., & Johannsmeier, C. (2009). The impact of community-based rehabilitation as implemented by community rehabilitation facilitators on people with disabilities, their families, and communities within South Africa. *Disability and Rehabilitation, 31*(1), 7–13.

Crishna, B. (1998). What is community-based rehabilitation? A view from experience. *Child: Care, Health, and Development, 35*(1), 27–35.

Curtis, R. S. (1998). Values and valuing in rehabilitation. *Journal of Rehabilitation, 64*(1), 42–47.

Deepak, S., Biggeri, M., Mauro, V., Kumar, J., & Griffo, G. (2013). Impact of community-based rehabilitation on persons with different disabilities. *Disability, CBR & Inclusive Development, 24*(4), 5–23.

Dougherty, A. M. (2014). *Psychological consultation and collaboration in school and community settings* (6th ed.). Brooks/Cole.

Dzau, V. J., Lurie, N., & Tuckson, R. V. (2018). After Harvey, Irma, and Maria, an opportunity for better health: Rebuilding our communities as we want them. *American Journal of Public Health, 108*(1), 32–33. http://dx.doi.org/10.2105/AJPH.2017.304194

Employer Disability Information. (2019). *Acquired disabilities.* http://www.employerdisabilityinfo.ie/advice-and-information/what-is-disability/acquired-disabilities

Ettinger, R. H. (2017). Psychopharmacology (2nd ed.). Psychology press.

Falvo, D., & Holland, B. (2018). *Medical and psychosocial aspects of chronic illness and disability* (6th ed.). Jones & Bartlett Learning.

Geist, C. S., & Calzaretta, W. A. (1982). *A placement handbook for counseling persons with disabilities.* Charles C. Thomas.

Goffman, E. (1963). *Stigma: Notes on the management of spoiled identity.* Prentice Hall.

Gonzales, L., Yanos, P. T., Stefancic, A., Alexander, M. J., & Harney-Delehanty, B. (2018). The role of neighborhood factors and community stigma in predicting community participation among persons with psychiatric disabilities. *Psychiatric Services, 69*(1), 76.

Grohol, J. M. (2020). *Symptoms of major neurocognitive disorder.* Psych Central. https://psychcentral.com/disorders/symptoms-of-major-neurocognitive-disorder/

Hultén, M. A., Patel, S. D., Westgren, M., Papadogiannakis, N., Jonsson, A. M., Jonasson, J., & Iwarsson, E. (2010). On the paternal origin of trisomy 21 Down syndrome. *Molecular cytogenetics, 3*, 4. https://doi.org/10.1186/1755-8166-3-4

Hunter, J., Rivero-Arias, O., Angelov, A., Kim, E., Fotheringham, I., & Leal, J. (2014). Epidemiology of fragile X syndrome: a systematic review and meta-analysis. *Am J Med Genet A., 164A*(7), 1648–58. doi: 10.1002/ajmg.a.36511. Epub 2014 Apr 3. PMID: 24700618.

Jensen, M. P., Smith, A. E., Bombardier, C. H., Yorkston, K. M., Miró, J., & Molton, I. R. (2014). Social support, depression, and physical disability: Age and diagnostic group effects. *Disability and Health Journal, 7*(2), 164–172.

Kazemi, M., Salehi, M., & Kheirollahi, M. (2016). Down Syndrome: Current Status, Challenges and Future Perspectives. *International journal of molecular and cellular medicine, 5*(3), 125–133.

Keith, R. A. (1991). The comprehensive treatment team in rehabilitation. *Archives of Physical Medicine and Rehabilitation, 72*(5), 269–274.

Kendall, E., Buys, N., & Larner, J. (2000). Community-based service delivery in rehabilitation: The promise and the paradox. *Disability and Rehabilitation, 22*(10), 435–445.

Klein, S., & Shive, K. (2001). *You will dream new dreams.* Kensington Books.

Koch, L. C., & Rumrill, P. D. (2016). *Rehabilitation counseling and emerging disabilities: Medical, psychosocial and vocational aspects.* Springer Publishing.

Korner, M. (2010). Interprofessional teamwork in medical rehabilitation: A comparison of multidisciplinary and interdisciplinary team approach. *Clinical Rehabilitation, 24*(8), 745–755. https://doi.org/10.1177/0269215510367538

Knudsen, M. E., & Bethune, K. S. (2018). Manifestation determinations: An interdisciplinary guide to best practices. *Teaching Exceptional Children, 50*(3), 153–160.

Laursen, B. K. (2018). What is collaborative, interdisciplinary reasoning? The heart of interdisciplinary team research. *Informing Science, 21*, 75–106. https://doi.org/10.28945/4010

Lee, H., & Morningstar, M. E. (2019). Exploring predictors of community participation among young adults with severe disabilities. *Research & Practice for Persons with Severe Disabilities, 44*(3), 186–199. https://doi.org/10.1177/1540796919863650

Li, L., & Moore, D. (1998). Acceptance of disability and its correlates. *Journal of Social Psychology, 138*, 13–25. https://doi:10.1080/00224549809600349

Loisel, P., Durand, M. J., Baril, R., Gervais, J., & Falardeau, M. (2005). Interorganizational collaboration in occupational rehabilitation: perceptions of an interdisciplinary rehabilitation team. *Journal of Occupational Rehabilitation, 15*(4), 581–590.

Long, A. F., Kneafsey, R., & Ryan, J. (2003). Rehabilitation practice: Challenges to effective team working. *International Journal of Nursing Studies, 40*(6), 663–673. https://doi.org/10.1016/S0020-7489(03)00015-4

Marini, I., & Stebnicki, M. (2012). *The psychological and social impact of illness and disability* (6th ed). Springer Publishing.

McCallin, A. (2001). Interdisciplinary practice—a matter of teamwork; an integrated literature review. *Journal of Clinical Nursing, 10*, 419–428.

McDaniel, J. W. (1976). *Physical disability and human behavior* (2nd ed.). Pergamon Press.

Miller, E., Buys, L., Woodbridge, S. (2012). Impact of disability on families: Grandparents' perspectives. *Journal of Intellectual Disability Research, 56*(1), 102–110.

Millington, M. J., & Marini, I. (Eds.). (2015). *Families in rehabilitation counseling: A community-based rehabilitation approach.* Springer Publishing.

Millner, U. C., Woods, T., Furlong, N. K., Rogers, E. S., Rice, D., & Russinova, Z. (2019). Socially valued roles, self-determination, and community participation among individuals living with serious mental illnesses. *American Journal of Community Psychology, 63*(1/2), 32–45. https://doi.org/10.1002/ajcp.12301

Morisse, F., Vandemaele, E., Claes, C., Claes, L., & Vandevelde, S. (2013). Quality of life in persons with intellectual disabilities and mental health problems: An explorative study. *The Scientific World Journal, 2013*, Article ID 491918. https://doi.org/10.1155/2013/491918

National Institute of Neurological Disorders and Stroke. (2020). *Spina bifida fact sheet.* Retrieved from: https://www.ninds.nih.gov/Disorders/Patient-Caregiver-Education/Fact-Sheets/Spina-Bifida-Fact-Sheet

National Alliance on Mental Illness. (2020). *Mental health by the numbers.* Retrieved from: https://www.nami.org/mhstats#:~:text=19.1%25%20of%20U.S.%20adults%20experienced,represents%201%20in%2025%20adults.

National Institute of Mental Health. (2019). *Attention-deficit/hyperactivity disorder (ADHD): The basics.* https://www.nimh.nih.gov/health/publications/attention-deficit-hyperactivity-disorder-adhd-the-basics/index.shtml

National Institute of Mental Health. (2020a). *Schizophrenia definition.* Retrieved from: https://www.nimh.nih.gov/health/statistics/schizophrenia.shtml

National Institute of Mental Health. (2020b). *Depression overview.* Retrieved from: https://www.nimh.nih.gov/health/topics/depression/index.shtml

National Institute on Aging. (2018). *Hearing loss: A common problem for older adults.* https://www.nia.nih.gov/health/hearing-loss-common-problem-older-adults

National Institute of Neurological Disorders and Stroke. (2019, March 27). *Dyslexia Information Page.* Retrieved October 24, 2020, from https://www.ninds.nih.gov/disorders/all-disorders/dyslexia-information-page

Orchard, C. A., Curran, V., & Kabene, S. (2005). Creating a culture for interdisciplinary collaborative professional practice. *Medical Education Online, 10*, 11. https://doi:10.3402/meo.v10i.4387

Pan, L., & Ye, J. (2012). Sexuality and marriage of women with intellectual disability in male-squeezed rural China. *Sexuality and Disability, 30*(2), 149–160.

Parker, G. (1993). Disability, caring and marriage: The experience of younger couples when a partner is disabled after marriage. *Journal of Social Work, 23*, 565–580.

Parson, R., & Zhang, N. (2016). Role of social justice in counseling. In C. Duan & C. Brown (Eds.), *Becoming a multiculturally competent counselor* (pp. 329–352). SAGE.

Patterson, C. H. (1958). The interdisciplinary nature of rehabilitation counselor training. *Personnel & Guidance Journal, 36*(5), 310–313. https://doi.org/10.1002/j.2164-4918.1958.tb01052.x

Pearlin, L. I. (1999). The stress process revisited: Reflections on concepts and their interrelationships. In C. S. Aneshensel & J. C. Phelan (Eds.), *Handbook of sociology of mental health* (pp. 395–415). Kluwer.

People and Communities Board, with support from National Voices. (2016). *Six principles for engaging people and communities: Putting them into practice.* National Health Service. https://www.nationalvoices.org.uk/sites/default/files/public/publications/six_principles_-_putting_into_practice_-_web_hi_res_-_updated_nov_2016.pdf

Roessler, R. T., Rubin, S. E., & Rumrill, P. D. (2016). *Foundations of the vocational rehabilitation process* (7th ed.). PRO-ED.

Schulz, R., & Decker, S. (1985). Long-term adjustment to physical disability: The role of social support, perceived control, and self-blame. *Journal of Personality and Social Psychology, 48*(5), 1162–1172. https://doi-org.proxy.bsu.edu/10.1037/0022-3514.48.5.1162

Shapio, D. R., & Sayers, L. K. (2003). Who does what on the interdisciplinary team: Regarding physical education for student with disabilities. *Teaching Exceptional Children, 35*(6), 3. https://doi.org/10.1177/004005990303500605

Sherman, S., Pletcher, B. A., & Driscoll, D. A. (2005). Fragile X syndrome: Diagnostic and carrier testing. *Genetics in medicine: official journal of the American College of Medical Genetics, 7*(8), 584–587. https://doi.org/10.1097/01.gim.0000182468.22666.dd

Simplican, S. C., Leader, G., Kosciulek, J., & Leahy, M. (2015). Defining social inclusion of people with intellectual and developmental disabilities: An ecological model of social networks and community participation. *Research in Developmental Disabilities, 38*, 18–29. https://doi.org/10.1016/j.ridd.2014.10.008

Smart, J. (2008). *Disability, society, and the individual* (2nd ed.). PRO-ED.

Strasser, D. C., Falconer, J. A., Herrin, J. S., Bowen, S. E., Stevens, A. B., & Uomoto, J. (2005). Team functioning and patient outcome in stroke rehabilitation. *Archives of Physical Medicine and Rehabilitation, 86*(3), 403–409. https://doi.org/10.1016/j.apmr.2004.04.046

Strasser, D. C., Uomoto, J. M., & Smits, S. J. (2008). The interdisciplinary team and polytrauma rehabilitation: A prescription for partnership. *Archives of Physical Medicine and Rehabilitation, 89*(1), 179–181. https://doi.org/10.1016/j.apmr.2007.06.774

Tepper, M. (1999). Letting go of restrictive notions of manhood: Male sexuality, disability, and chronic illness. *Sexuality and Disability, 17*(3), 37–52.

Varekamp, I., van Dijk, F., & Kroll, L. E. (2013). Workers with a chronic diseases and work disability. *Bundesgesundheitsbl, 56*, 406. https://doi-org.proxy.bsu.edu/10.1007/s00103-012-1621-1

Verdonschot, M. M. L., de Witte, L. P, Reichrath, E., Buntinx, W. H. E., & Curfs, L. M. G. (2009). Community participation of people with an intellectual disability: A review of empirical findings. *Journal of Intellectual Disability Research, 53*(4), 303–318.

Vorvick, L. (2019). *Acute vs. chronic conditions.* MedLine Plus. https://medlineplus.gov/ency/imagepages/18126.htm

White, M. J., Gutierrez, A., McLaughlin, C., Eziakonwa, C., Stephens Newman, L., White, M., Thayer, B., Davis, K., Williams, M., & Asselin, G. (2013). A pilot for understanding interdisciplinary teams in rehabilitation practice. *Association of Rehabilitation Nursing, 38*, 142–152. https://doi.org/10.1002/rnj.75

Wilson, S., Washington, L. A., Engel, J. M., Ciol, M. A., & Jensen, M. P. (2006). Perceived social support, psychological adjustment, and functional ability in youths with physical disabilities. *Rehabilitation Psychology, 51*(4), 322–330. https://doi-org.proxy.bsu.edu/10.1037/0090-5550.51.4.32

World Health Organization. (2001). *International classification of functioning, disability, and health.* Author.

Yale Center for Dyslexia and Creativity. (2017). *What is Dyslexia?* Retrieved October 24, 2020, from https://dyslexia.yale.edu/dyslexia/what-is-dyslexia/

World Report on Disability. (2011). *World report on disability.* Retrieved from: https://www.who.int/disabilities/world_report/2011/report.pdf

The Duplicity of Disability and Abuse

Building Bridges

Dr. Brian L. Bethel, PhD, LPCC-S, LCDC III, RPT-S

Learning Objectives

As a result of reading this chapter, the student will be able to:

- Identify specific risks and vulnerabilities of abuse/neglect for persons with disabilities.
- Discuss the known prevalence of maltreatment for individuals with disabilities.
- Identify specific forms of abuse and exploitation.
- Articulate various hypotheses regarding causal factors of abuse for people with disabilities.
- Describe specific strategies to better advocate for individuals with disabilities who are survivors of abuse.

INTRODUCTION

Although most of us recognize that change is an inevitable part of life, many people rely upon the predictability and certainty that comes from their daily routines. In fact, the stability of these consistent experiences is often paramount in meeting our fundamental needs for safety, security, and an overall sense of well-being. As a result, individuals who experience severe disruptions in their physical or psychological functioning often confront challenges as a result of their disability. While many of us can adapt to certain adversities, persons with disabilities must assimilate into a world of continuous change. Unfortunately, this process of adaption for persons with disabilities often creates significant risks and vulnerabilities. This chapter will explore the intersectionality of disability and maltreatment. In particular, this chapter highlights the unfortunate vulnerabilities for persons with disabilities specific to various types of abuse and exploitation. Moreover, various forms of abuse and exploitation will be defined to assist clinicians who advocate for these vulnerable populations.

Disability and Victimization Across the Life Span

For decades scholars have attempted to identify, explore, and report the phenomenon of disability adaptation. Without question, it has been well established that a chronic illness, traumatic injury, and/or disability triggers a series of psychological reactions (Dembo et al., 1956; Kendall & Buys, 1998; Linkowski, 1971; Livnah & Atonak, 1997; Olkin, 1999; Smart, 2008). In addition, the psychological challenges that are associated with the adaptation process are often exacerbated by the many pervasive attitudes, biases, and stereotypes that stigmatize individuals with disabilities (Beaudry, 2016; Marini, 2012). Although legislative actions have offered some protections for people with disabilities in recent years, the unfortunate reality is that persons with disabilities continue to confront attitudinal barriers and discrimination (Rubin & Roessler, 2001; Smart, 2008). As such, the vulnerabilities for individuals with disabilities are encompassed within all physical, social, occupational, and psychological domains of their life.

Among the many injustices that persons with disabilities encounter is the increased vulnerability for abuse and exploitation. However, only in recent years have researchers started to acknowledge the toxic relationship between individuals with disabilities and abuse (Palusci et al., 2017). In fact, only within the last 25 years has the professional literature recognized the higher rates of victimization for persons with disability compared to the general population (McCabe et al., 1994). Without question, abuse and exploitation present insidious and complex challenges that often precipitate many negative outcomes for individuals with disabilities. Given that abuse and exploitation have no socioeconomic, demographic, religious, or cultural boundaries, these tragedies are common for individuals with disabilities across the life span (Casteel et al., 2008).

The disheartening reality is that abuse and exploitation are a ubiquitous phenomenon for people with disabilities. Although there is some variation, the rate of abuse for children with disabilities at the turn of the millennium ranged from 22% to as high as 70% (National Research Council, 2003). However, research across the last 2 decades has provided a broad consensus among professionals that children with disabilities have an even greater vulnerability of becoming victims of child abuse and neglect (Mandell et al., 2005; Shannon, 2006; Sullivan & Knutson, 2000). One of the most widely cited studies indicated that children with disabilities were 3.4 times more likely to be abused than children without disabilities (Sullivan & Knutson, 2000). This translates into 31% of children with disabilities having been abused compared with a prevalence rate of 9% among children without disabilities. Although individuals with disabilities experience oppression and domination in various domains of their daily lives (Shannon, 2006), these statistics certainly illuminate the risk for children with disabilities specific to child maltreatment.

A multitude of studies have asserted that women who are diagnosed with multiple disabilities confront an increased risk of violence and a longer duration of victimization compared to women without disabilities (Wilczynski et al., 2015). It has also been noted that adolescent females with disabilities have a higher propensity for sexual victimization (Lund, 2011; Randall et al., 2000). Additional studies have proposed that women with disabilities are 4 times more likely to experience sexual assault compared to the general population (Martin et al., 2006). Intimate partner violence has also been reported to be more prevalent for individuals with disabilities. Women and men who identified as having a psychiatric or physical disability were more likely to report intimate partner violence within the last year compared to the general population (Hahn et al., 2014).

Because the term *disability* represents a broad spectrum of physical and psychiatric conditions, a multitude of factors contribute to the increased risk for abuse and exploitation. Although there is no one factor that can be identified as the root cause of maltreatment for persons with disabilities, it has been suggested that it is likely a combination and interaction of factors that correlates with the increased rate of abuse and exploitation for people with disabilities (Gore & Janssen, 2007). Specific types of disabilities present individualized risks due to the nature of the individual's diagnosis. For example, individuals with disabilities may not have the competencies needed to protect themselves from abuse or neglect and may lack the knowledge of the resources they need for protection (Wilczynski et al., 2015). Likewise, people with communication-related disabilities would likely have difficulty reporting their abusive experience(s) (Bryen et al., 2003). Individuals with intellectual disabilities are not always familiar with skills to protect themselves from abuse (Khemka et al., 2009).

The American Academy of Pediatrics (AAP) declared that there are a number of causal factors that often contribute to the abuse of children with disabilities (Council on Environmental Health, 2016). As noted earlier, disability is a broad term that is used to describe various types of conditions. As a result, the disability spectrum presents a great diversity of challenges for parents and caregivers. Unfortunately, this creates enormous obstacles for children and families because each child with a disability presents differing stressors and challenges for their entire family (Hibbard & Desch, 2007). Not surprisingly, parental stress has been cited as one of the most frequent factors in child abuse for children with disabilities (Sullivan & Knutson, 2000). A child's disability is likely to require changes for family members. These changes in family routine typically affect the entire family unit, creating significant adjustment issues and increased tension within the familial system. Similarly, family isolation, irrational parental expectations for their child, as well as the parental belief that the child exhibits difficult behavior all place the child in a vulnerable environment (Gore & Janssen, 2007).

Types of Abuse and Exploitation

Unfortunately, a variety of behaviors, actions, and inactions can be used as tactics to gain power and control over persons with disabilities. As such, there are many forms of abuse that perpetrators may utilize. However, the most frequently recognized forms of abuse are physical abuse, emotional abuse or deprivation, and sexual abuse (Child Welfare Information Gateway, 2011).

The National Center on Elder Abuse (NCEA, 2020) has offered the following definitions to delineate various forms of abuse and exploitation:

- *Physical abuse:* Physical abuse is defined as the use of physical force that may result in bodily injury, physical pain, or impairment. Physical abuse may include, but is not limited to, such acts of violence as striking (with or without an object), hitting, beating, pushing, shoving, shaking, slapping, kicking, pinching, and burning. In addition, inappropriate use of drugs and physical restraints, force-feeding, and physical punishment of any kind also are examples of physical abuse.
- *Sexual abuse:* Sexual abuse is defined as nonconsensual sexual contact of any kind with an elderly person. Sexual contact with any person incapable of giving consent is also considered sexual abuse. It includes, but is not limited to, unwanted touching and all types of sexual assault or battery, such as rape, sodomy, coerced nudity, and sexually explicit photographing.
- *Emotional or psychological abuse:* Emotional or psychological abuse is defined as the infliction of anguish, pain, or distress through verbal or nonverbal acts. Emotional/psychological abuse includes, but is not limited to, verbal assaults, insults, threats, intimidation, humiliation, and harassment. In addition, treating

National Center on Elder Abuse, Selections from "Types of Abuse," https://ncea.acl.gov/Suspect-Abuse/Abuse-Types.aspx, U.S. Department of Health and Human Services.

an older person like an infant; isolating an elderly person from their family, friends, or regular activities; giving an older person the "silent treatment"; and enforced social isolation are examples of emotional/psychological abuse.

- *Neglect:* Neglect is defined as the refusal or failure to fulfill any part of a person's obligations or duties to an elder. Neglect may also include failure of a person who has fiduciary responsibilities to provide care for an elder (e.g., pay for necessary home care services) or the failure on the part of an in-home service provider to provide necessary care.

Neglect typically means the refusal or failure to provide an elderly person with such life necessities as food, water, clothing, shelter, personal hygiene, medicine, comfort, personal safety, and other essentials included in an implied or agreed-upon responsibility to an elder.

- *Self-neglect:* Self-neglect is characterized as the behavior of an elderly person that threatens their own health or safety. Self-neglect generally manifests itself in an older person as a refusal or failure to provide themselves with adequate food, water, clothing, shelter, personal hygiene, medication (when indicated), and safety precautions. The definition of self-neglect excludes a situation in which a mentally competent older person, who understands the consequences of their decisions, makes a conscious and voluntary decision to engage in acts that threaten their health or safety as a matter of personal choice.
- *Abandonment:* Abandonment is defined as the desertion of an elderly person by an individual who has assumed responsibility for providing care for an elder or by a person with physical custody of an elder.
- *Financial or material exploitation:* Financial or material exploitation is defined as the illegal or improper use of an elder's funds, property, or assets. Examples include, but are not limited to, cashing an elderly person's checks without authorization or permission; forging an older person's signature; misusing or stealing an older person's money or possessions; coercing or deceiving an older person into signing any document (e.g., contracts or will); and the improper use of conservatorship, guardianship, or power of attorney (NCEA, 2020).

Similarly, the Child Welfare League of America (CWLA) Standards for Services for Abused or Neglected Children and Their Families has provided generally accepted broad definitions of child abuse and child maltreatment. Specifically, the federal Child Abuse Prevention and Treatment Act (CAPTA) defines *child maltreatment* as "any recent act, or failure to act on the part of a parent or caretaker which results in death, serious physical or emotional harm, sexual abuse, or exploitation" or "an act or failure to act which presents an imminent risk of serious harm" (U.S. Department of Health and Human Services, 2020). This definition also delineates four subtypes of abuse:

- *Physical abuse:* Physical acts by parents or caregivers that cause or could have caused physical injury to the child.
- *Neglect:* Failure of parents or other caregivers, for reasons not solely due to poverty, to provide the child with needed, age-appropriate care, including food, clothing, shelter, protection from harm, supervision appropriate to the child's development, hygiene, education, and medical care.
- *Sexual abuse:* Sexual activity, by a parent or other caregiver, with a child, including but not limited to any kind of sexual contact through persuasion, physical force, or other coercive means; exploitation through sexual activity that is allowed, encouraged, or coerced; and child prostitution or pornography.
- *Emotional maltreatment:* Parental or other caregiver acts or omissions, such as cause the child serious impairment of their physical, social, mental, or emotional capacities (CAPTA, 2011).

The Impact of Abuse

Robust research outlines the numerous effects of abuse on the lives of survivors (Barfield et al., 2012). In recent years there has been an increasing focus on the examination and impact of traumatic events in the lives of survivors. According to the National Child Traumatic Stress Network (NCTSN, 2012), childhood traumatic events include physical and sexual abuse, neglect, emotional abuse, death or separation from loved ones, exposure to intimate partner violence, community violence, bullying, and exposure to disasters. Although these are shocking to most, research has found that traumatic experiences, unfortunately, are common. Researchers have documented that most people will experience at least one traumatic event in their lifetime (Kilpatrick et al., 2013).

The impact of the traumatic experience of abuse in combination with a person's disability increase the complexity of their psychological reactions (Perry, 2000). Although all persons might be susceptible to mental health issues, individuals with disabilities confront a number of complex psychological and emotional challenges, as well as an increased vulnerability of abuse. Specifically, people with disabilities often experience a variety of stress reactions and frustrations that are associated with the difficulties in trying to manage their disability (Lyons et al., 2012). In addition, individuals with disabilities affected by maltreatment frequently face challenges of negative behavioral, emotional, and social experiences (Shannon, 2006). Bethel (2005) asserted that children who are survivors of abuse commonly feel betrayed, overwhelmed, and helpless, which may further complicate the child's healing process. Consistent with earlier research, Henderson and Thompson (2014) reported that survivors of abuse often have feelings of isolation, a great sense of fear, as well as an inability to trust.

Abuse, in and of itself, robs its survivors of attachment and security. This is more complex for individuals with disabilities because they are often dependent upon their abusers for medically necessary care and protection. Based upon the dependency that is required by people with disabilities, many have been taught compliance and oftentimes feel the need to obey those in authority (Orange & Brodwin, 2005). So even when abuse occurs, some persons with disabilities may not report it because of the belief that the caretaker knows what is best (Sobsey, 1994). Moreover, individuals with cognitive delays may not possess the verbal capacity or neurological processing abilities necessary to gain mastery over the trauma from abuse. Therefore, persons with cognitive and physical disabilities may be perceived as "easy targets" of abuse because their disability may prevent them from defending themselves or escaping the abusive situation (Orange & Brodwin, 2005).

Intervention and Treatment

Despite the alarming statistics specific to persons with disabilities who are victims of abuse and exploitation, there remains a paucity of research that addresses specific interventions to empower this population (Wilczynski et al., 2015). However, some professionals have proposed empirically supported models of trauma-based interventions to assist persons with disabilities in gaining mastery over their abusive experiences. In particular, trauma-focused cognitive behavioral therapy has been offered as an effective model for working with individuals with disabilities who are survivors of abuse. This structured form of therapy includes the following components: affective-identification and modulation skills, adaptive stress management skills, emphasis on the cognitive triad, a creation of the child's trauma narrative, promoting cognitive processing of the death experience, psycho-educational material specific to trauma and grief, safety planning for the future, and joint sessions with the child and caregiver (Cohen et al., 2004).

A limited number of other counseling paradigms have been offered in the research to assist counselors who work with persons with disabilities who have experienced abuse. Specifically, cognitive behavioral counseling has been reported as a beneficial model for exploring an individual's irrational ideations, negative self-perceptions, as well as behavior modification (Thurneck et al., 2007). Henderson and Thompson (2014) suggested group counseling as a means for persons with disabilities to increase their relationship skills while simultaneously offering a supportive and nurturing environment. Considering that many persons with disabilities may have communication impairments, counselors should also explore nontraditional counseling paradigms. Although traditional counseling theories have remained dependent upon the verbal exchanges between a child and clinician, creative therapies also offer a unique approach that is not as dependent on a child's communication skills. These can include play therapy, art therapy, bibliotherapy, and sand play (Bethel, 2005; Thurneck et al., 2007).

Although the nature of counseling services offers survivors with disabilities and their families specialized services to address the multitude of clinical symptoms that are associated with abuse, clinicians must maintain competencies in serving these populations. In considering the aforementioned cited effects of abuse for persons with disabilities, professional counselors face a host of features that represent the uniqueness of this population. Accordingly, counseling professionals must be flexible in adapting traditional counseling services for individuals with disabilities. Furthermore, professional counselors must maintain competencies related to specific disabilities for the consumers that they serve, as well as achieving professional competencies related to addressing the effects of abuse and neglect.

Recommendations for Counseling Professionals

Among the various recommendations for counseling professionals who work with individuals with disabilities is the continual examination of one's values, attitudes, and beliefs. Henderson and Thompson (2014) discussed the importance of self-evaluation for professionals. They suggested that one of the greatest challenges associated with counseling people with disabilities is largely related to a clinician's preconceived ideas regarding an individual's specific diagnosis. This categorization of persons with disabilities has often led to professionals overlooking individual strengths. Counselors who view people with disabilities simply as a label or as a victim can greatly minimize a person's strengths and capabilities (Henderson & Thompson, 2014). Regrettably, these further create therapeutic roadblocks for people with disabilities in their pursuit toward resilience.

The ability to establish a therapeutic rapport is an essential skill for counseling professionals. However, when serving people with disabilities who are survivors of maltreatment, the importance of a strong therapeutic relationship cannot be overemphasized. Individuals with disabilities frequently encounter feelings of anxiety, shame, as well as other negative feelings surrounding their disability (Henderson & Thompson, 2014). The abuse experience itself exacerbates these affective responses as it robs survivors of the basic ability to trust others. Therefore, clinicians must work diligently to foster a nurturing and supportive environment for people with disabilities who are impacted by the abuse experience.

Collaboration is also an essential element for counselors who work with individuals with disabilities. A person's disability may require specialized services from a diversity of healthcare professionals. Henderson and Thompson (2014) reported that it was paramount for counselors who work with these populations to work closely with all agencies who serve the survivor as well as the individual's family members. Hibbard and Desch (2007) echoed this recommendation by stating that medical professionals need to collaborate with other treatment providers who work with survivors with disabilities. Counselors who serve persons with disabilities may also find themselves in an advocacy role. Professional counselors are in a unique position to not only serve as a therapeutic agent of change but also provide support for the best interest of individuals via advocacy efforts. These responsibilities can include working to ensure that appropriate referrals are being initiated, as well as follow-up recommendations (Gore & Janssen, 2007).

Additionally, it is important that rehabilitation counselors know the indicators of abuse and be able to differentiate the symptoms of the disability from potential signs of abuse (Hibbard & Desch, 2007). Hibbard and Desch (2007) found that professionals who serve people with disabilities have attributed cardinal signs of abuse to a disability. Hibbard and Desch (2007) outlined specific disorders that mimic signs of abuse. Consequently, rehabilitation counselors should educate the individual, family members, educators, mental health professionals, and others about the specific disability and key factors to distinguish between the condition and characteristics of abuse. It is also necessary for rehabilitation counselors to educate families and school professionals about the risk factors associated with disability and abuse. Gaining a better understanding of these risk factors may aid professionals in delivering appropriate and quality services for people with disabilities.

Case Study: Dylan

School personnel were the first to raise concern regarding 7-year-old Dylan. The staff from Dylan's school contacted Child Protective Services (CPS) due to bruising on the child's face and arms. The child had been diagnosed with cognitive disabilities, attention deficit hyperactivity disorder (ADHD), and a visual disability. Although Dylan told his teacher that he walked into his bedroom door, the bruising on his arms appeared to come from fingers, according to the initial report. School officials had also reported that Dylan's mother had continually described her child as "out of control" during conferences and openly expressed her frustration about the child's behavior.

CPS staff and the school nurse found additional bruising on the child's lower back upon further examination. Documentation from the CPS report noted that Dylan told the child welfare investigator that "I get spanked because I am bad." The bruising on the child's lower back was also described as "significant," according to the investigative report. The child told officials that his mother uses a belt to spank him, but the law enforcement report noted wide bruises on the child's back that would not be consistent with a belt. When contacted, Dylan's mother stated, "I spank my child and that is my right as his parent."

1. What specific factors associated with Dylan's disabilities increase his risk for future abuse?
2. What specific factors regarding the child's disabilities create challenges for the development of protective capacities?
3. What specific strategies can counseling professionals utilize to advocate for the child?

Case Study: Joseph

Joseph is a 5-year-old child who was referred to services as the result of an autism spectrum diagnosis. Joseph had lived with his mother and stepfather until 4 weeks ago when Joseph began to exhibit sexually acting out behaviors. Specifically, the child would often expose himself to family members at home and classmates at school and was found by his grandmother trying to insert toys into his rectum. Information from the child's diagnostic assessment supported the diagnosis of autism spectrum disorder because Joseph was described to have difficulty socializing with his peers, often stayed isolated in the home, and enjoyed engaging in solitary activities. Although Joseph had adequate competencies with communication, he had difficulty interpreting social cues. The child, like many children with autism, was fascinated with Spiderman, which consumed most of his conversations.

CPS referred Joseph for an evaluation at a local child advocacy center. The child participated in a forensic evaluation and medical assessment. It was during the child's forensic interview that Joseph disclosed that he and his stepfather played the "secret game." The child was reluctant to provide detailed information but ultimately reported that the game involved "putting things there," as he pointed to his rectum. Joseph went on to say that he and his stepfather played this game during their "special time" when his mother was at work, and this is what Spiderman does. When directly asked about "safe people," Joseph identified his mother, stepfather, and grandparents.

1. What specific factors associated with Joseph's disabilities increase his risk for future abuse?
2. Are there specific services that can be offered to provide the child with psycho-educational information specific to body safety?
3. How could a counseling professional work to empower Joseph and his mother?

Case Study: Sharon

Adult Protective Services first became involved with Sharon when they received a report that the 67-year-old female was home alone and unable to care for herself. According to the report, Sharon was found in her bed when the investigator arrived, and she reported that she cannot leave her bed without assistance. As the result of an automobile accident 5 years earlier, Sharon is dependent upon others to assist her with mobility. Although she has a wheelchair available, she is unable to transfer herself from her bed securely to her wheelchair. When investigators met with Sharon, they noted her bedding was soiled and she had an empty glass beside her bed.

(Continued)

Case Study: Sharon (*Continued*)

The report notes that Sharon lives with her 40-year-old daughter, but Sharon reported that she works a lot. Sharon stated that her daughter had left the home around eight that morning and would be home after five in the afternoon. Investigators found several bottles of Sharon's medication that were limited or had missing pills based on the dates on the prescription bottles. Sharon reported that her daughter dispenses her medications. Investigators also noted Sharon's home was dirty and infested with roaches. There was limited food in the home, and none was accessible to Sharon. A review of Sharon's finances also found limited funds, as several cash withdrawals had been made from her bank account.

1. What specific measures should be taken to ensure Sharon's safety?
2. What services could be recommended to strengthen Sharon's protective capacities?
3. How could counseling professionals work to empower Sharon?

Case Study: Levi

Levi was a 7-year-old child who was found walking along a busy street without parental supervision. Law enforcement responded to investigate after a neighbor called expressing that the child appeared to be lost. When law enforcement made contact with Levi, the child could not tell them his address but did say he lived "in a white house." After law enforcement drove several blocks, Levi was eventually able to point out his house. Officers made contact with Levi's mother, who yelled profanities at the child for leaving the house. The responding officer reported that the child's mother referred to Levi as "a damn retard." The child's mother told officers that her son was diagnosed with intellectual developmental disorder and he's too "stupid to know better."

As the child's mother was repeatedly scolding him, Levi became tearful. It was noted that Levi's siblings, who were older, also began to belittle the child. The officer reported that the child was told, "If you're that dumb you deserve to be kidnapped" and "People love to kidnap retards." When officers attempted to address the lack of supervision, Levi's mother was extremely defensive and projected blame onto the child. Levi's mother was quick to point out that her other children do not have behavior problems.

1. What are the specific factors that are likely to increase the child's risk for future abuse?
2. How could counseling professionals work with Levi to develop safety and protective capacities?
3. What services and strategies could be offered to the family to potentially decrease the likelihood of abuse?

SUMMARY

In conclusion, it has been well established that there is a significant prevalence of abuse for individuals with disabilities (Baladerian, 1994; Gore & Janssen, 2007; Hibbard & Desch, 2007; Sullivan & Knutson, 2000). While this presents a heartbreaking reality, it is clear that interdisciplinary collaboration is necessary to combat this problem. While this chapter has provided a general framework, clinical counselors, rehabilitation counselors, and social service professionals must take an active role to address the epidemic of abuse, neglect, and exploitation of individuals with disabilities. Through efforts of awareness, advocacy, education, and collaboration, clinical and rehabilitation counselors can be a guiding force in addressing the pervasive issue of maltreatment for persons with disabilities. This author proposes that we all have a role to play to ameliorate the abuse of people with disabilities if we all take steps toward building bridges.

Discussion Questions

1. What are the key causal factors that are likely to increase the vulnerabilities of abuse for individuals with disabilities?
2. What impact does abuse have for survivors with disabilities?
3. Identify and discuss specific research-supported models and therapeutic paradigms that are recommended for persons with disabilities who are survivors of abuse.
4. Why do you believe children with disabilities are at an increased risk for child maltreatment?
5. How does a person's specific disability contribute to an increased risk of abuse? Discuss specific types of disabilities and the unique characteristics associated with the disability that may increase a greater propensity for abuse.

REFERENCES

Baladerian, N. J. (1994). Abuse and neglect of children with disabilities. *Arch Factsheet, 36.*

Barfield, S., Dobson, C., Gaskill, R., & Perry, B. D. (2012). Neurosequential model of therapeutics in a therapeutic preschool: Implications for work with children with complex neuropsychiatric problems. *International Journal of Play Therapy, 21*(1), 30–44.

Beaudry, J. S. (2016). Beyond (models of) disability? *Journal of Medicine and Philosophy, 41*(2), 210–228. https://doi.org/10.1093/jmp/jhv063

Bethel, B. (2005). Play therapy techniques for sexually abused children. In S. Brooke (Ed.), *Creative therapies cases: Art, play, dance, music, and drama therapies with sexual abuse survivors.* C. Thomas.

Bryen, D. N., Carey, A., & Frantz, B. (2003). Ending the silence: Adults who use augmentative communication and their experiences as victims of crimes. *Augmentative and Alternative Communication, 19*(2), 125–134.

Casteel, C., Martin, S. L., Smith, J. B., Gurka, K. K., & Kupper, L. L. (2008). National study of physical and sexual assault among women with disabilities. *Injury Prevention, 14*, 87–90.

Child Welfare Information Gateway. (2011). *Definitions of child abuse and neglect in federal law.* https://www.childwelfare.gov/systemwide/laws_policies/statutes/define.pdf

Cohen, J. A., Goodman, R. F., Brown, E. J., & Mannarino, A. P. (2004). Treatment of childhood traumatic grief: contributing to a newly emerging condition in the wake of community trauma. *Harvard Review Psychiatry, 12*, 213–216.

Council on Environmental Health. (2016). Prevention of childhood lead toxicity. *Pediatrics, 138*(1) e20161493; DOI: https://doi.org/10.1542/peds.2016-1493

Dembo, T., Leviton, G. L., & Wright, B. A. (1956). Adjustment to misfortune: A problem of social-psychological rehabilitation. *Artificial Limbs, 3*, 4–62.

Gore, M. T., & Janssen, K. G. (2007). What educators need to know about abused children with disabilities. *Preventing School Failure, 52*(1), 49–55.

Hahn, J. W., McCormick, M. C., Silverman, J. G., Robinson, E. B., & Koenen, K. C. (2014). Examining the impact of disability status on intimate partner violence victimization in a population sample. *Journal of Interpersonal Violence, 29*(17), 3063–3085.

Henderson, D. A., & Thompson, C. L. (2014). *Counseling children* (9th ed.). Brooks Cole.

Hibbard, R. A., & Desch, L. W. (2007). Maltreatment of children with disabilities. *Pediatrics, 119*(5), 1018–1025.

Kendall, E., & Buys, N. (1998). An integrated model of psychosocial adjustment following acquired disability. *Journal of Rehabilitation, 64*(3), 16–20.

Khemka, I., Hickson, L., Casella, M., Accetturi, N., & Rooney, M. E. (2009). Impact of coercive tactics on the decision-making of adolescents with intellectual disabilities. *Journal of Intellectual Disability Research, 53*(4), 353–362.

Kilpatrick, D., Resnick, H., Milanak, M., Miller, M., Keyes, K., & Friedman, M. (2013). National estimates of exposure to traumatic events and PTSD prevalence using DSM-IV and DSM-5 criteria. *Journal of Traumatic Stress, 26*, 537–547.

Linkowski, D. C. (1971). A scale to measure acceptance to disability. *Rehabilitation Counseling Bulletin, 4*, 236–244.

Livneh, H., & Antonak, R. F. (1997). *Psychosocial adjustment to chronic illness and disability.* Aspen Publishers.

Lund, E. M. (2011). Community-based services and interventions for adults with disabilities who have experienced interpersonal violence: A review of the literature. *Trauma, Violence, & Abuse, 12*, 171–182. http://doi:10.1177/152483801141637

Lyons, A. M., Leon, S. C., Roecker, Phelps, C. E., & Dunleavy, A. M. (2010). The impact of child symptom severity on stress among parents of children with ASD: The 27 moderating role of coping styles. *Journal of Child and Family Studies, 19*, 516–524. http://doi:10.1007/s10826-009-9323-5

Mandell, D. S., Novak, M. M., & Zubritsky, C. D. (2005). Factors associated with age of diagnosis among children with autism spectrum disorders. *Pediatrics, 116*, 1480–1486. 1632217410.1542/peds.2005-0185. http://dx.doi.org.libalasu.idm.oclc.org/10.1542/peds.2005-0185 .

Marini, I. (2012). The historical treatment of persons with disabilities. In I. Marini, N. M. Glover-Graf, & J. Millington (Eds.), *Psychosocial aspects of disability insider perspectives and counseling strategies* (pp. 3–32). Springer Publishing.

Martin, S. L., Ray, N., Sotres-Alvarez, D., Kupper, L. L., Moracco, K. E., Dickens, P. A., & Gizlice, Z. (2006). Physical and sexual assault of women with disabilities. *Violence Against Women, 12*, 823–837.

McCabe, M. P., Cummins, R. A., & Reid, S. B. (1994). An empirical study of sexual abuse of people with intellectual disabilities. *Sexuality and Disability, 12*, 297–306.

National Center on Elder Abuse. (2020). *Types of abuse.* http://ncea.acl.gov/Suspect-Abuse/Abuse-Types.aspx

National Child Traumatic Stress Network. (2012). *The 12 core concepts: Concepts for understanding traumatic stress responses in children and families.* https://www.nctsn.org/resources/12-core-concepts-concepts-understanding-traumatic-stress-responses-children-and-families

National Research Council. (2003). *Elder mistreatment: Abuse, neglect, and exploitation in an aging America.* National Academies Press.

Olkin, R. (1999). *What psychotherapists should know about disability.* Guilford Press.

Orange, L., & Brodwin, M. (2005). Childhood sexual abuse: What rehabilitation counselors need to know. *Journal of Rehabilitation, 71*(4), 5–11.

Paluscil, V. J., Nazer D., Greydanus, D. E., & Merrick, J. (2017). Children disability and abuse. *International Journal of Child Health Human Development, 10*(3), 205–214.

Perry, B. D. (2000). *The neuroarcheology of childhood maltreatment: The neurodevelopmental costs of adverse childhood events.* Child Trauma Academy. http://www.juconicomparte.org/recursos/Neuroarcheology%20of%20childhood%20maltreatment_zmH8.pdf

Randall, W., Parilla, R., & Sobsey, D. (2000). Gender, disability status and risk for sexual abuse in children. *Journal on Developmental Disability, 7*, 1–15.

Rubin, S. E., & Roessler, R. T. (2008) *Foundations of the vocational rehabilitation process* (6th ed.). PRO-ED.

Shannon, P. (2006). Children with disabilities in child welfare: Empowering the disenfranchised. In N. B. Webb (Ed.), *Working with traumatized youth in child welfare* (pp. 155–170). Guilford Press.

Smart, J. (2008). *Disability, society, and the individual* (2nd ed.). PRO-ED.

Sobsey, D. (1994). *Violence and abuse in the lives of people with disabilities.* Paul H. Brookes Publishing.

Sullivan, P. M., & Knutson, J. F. (1998). The association between child maltreatment and disabilities in a hospital-based epidemiological study. *Child Abuse & Neglect, 22*(4), 271–188.

Thurneck, D. A., Warner, P. J., & Cobb, H. C. (2007). Children and adolescents with disabilities and health care needs: Implications for intervention. In H. T. Prout & D. T. Brown (Eds.), *Counseling and psychotherapy with children and adolescents: Theory and practice for school and clinical settings* (4th ed.; pp. 419–453). John Wiley & Sons.

United States. (1994). Child Abuse Prevention and Treatment Act, as amended: November 4, 1992. [Washington, D.C.]: National Center on Child Abuse and Neglect.

United States Department of Health & Human Services (2020). *What is child abuse or neglect? What is the definition of child abuse and neglect?* Retrieved from: https://www.hhs.gov/answers/programs-for-families-and-children/what-is-child-abuse/index.html#:~:text=What%20is%20the%20definition%20of%20child%20abuse%20and%20neglect%3F,-Just%20as%20there&text=%22Any%20recent%20act%20or%20failure,imminent%20risk%20of%20serious%20harm.%22

Wilczynski, S. M., Connolly, S., DuBard, M., Henderson, A., & McIntosh, D. (2015). Assessment prevention, and intervention for abuse among individuals with disabilities. *Psychology in the Schools, 52*, 9–21.

CHAPTER 7

Legal and Ethical Issues in Counseling

Mona Robinson, PhD, LPCC-S, LSW, CRC
Mary-Anne M. Joseph, PhD, LPC, CRC

Learning Objectives

As a result of reading this chapter, the student will be able to:

- Explain the role and processes needed for clinical rehabilitation counselors to ethically advocate on behalf of their consumers in a culturally responsible manner.
- Discuss the ethical standards and guiding principles of professional conduct.
- Understand the difference between legal and ethical standards.
- Apply ethical decision-making models to counseling practice.

INTRODUCTION

Ethics is at the heart of what we do as clinical rehabilitation counselors. From intake to closure we are responsible for making legal and ethical decisions that will not harm our consumers. Not only must our decisions be ethical, but we are also required to ensure that our actions, behaviors, service provision, dissemination of resources, and so on are all conducted in a legal and ethical manner. Ethics and ethical behavior are rooted in our morals and values, beginning on a very basic level. As children we learn the concepts of right and wrong, and as we age and grow we assess the value of right as we incorporate it into our daily lives. This is the quintessential start of the development of our ethical and moral compass. This compass is significantly impacted by one's family, community, cultural upbringing, and/or religion.

Defining Ethics

Merriam-Webster's Dictionary (2020) broadly defines ethics as a code of moral values that guides a person's behavior. Others have provided similar but more specific definitions. Neulicht and colleagues (2010) describe ethics as a term that refers to particular characteristics. Weston (2008) notes that ethics is solely focused on a person's actions and values related to the things that they believe in that results in their behavior. Ethics has also been referred to as one's professional behavior and interactions. Remley and Herlihy (2016) posit that although the terms *morals*, *values*, and *ethics* are often used interchangeably because of their focus on human conduct and relationships, they are in fact distinct terms. The American Counseling Association (ACA, 2014) defines ethics as "a discipline within the philosophy that is concerned with human conduct and moral decision making."

It is important to note that ethics varies from the law in that the law is enforced by the government and ethics are enforced by professional organizations such as the Commission on Rehabilitation Counseling and the American Counseling Association. More important, it is vital to note that one's code of professional ethics is always superseded by the law. Simply put, "laws are created by elected officials, enforced by police, and interpreted by judges. Ethics are created by members of the counseling profession and are interpreted and enforced by ethics committees and licensure and certification boards" (Remley & Herlihy, 2007, p. 7).

The two primary ethical governing bodies for clinical rehabilitation counselors are the Commission on Rehabilitation Counseling Certification (CRCC) and the American Counseling Association (ACA). The CRCC "is the world's largest rehabilitation counseling organization responsible for certifying rehabilitation counselors" and "is dedicated to improving the lives of individuals with disabilities" (CRCC, 2017). This organization "sets the standard for competent delivery of quality rehabilitation counseling services through its nationally accredited and internationally recognized certification program" (CRCC, 2019). The ACA's mission is intended "to enhance the quality of life in society by promoting the development of professional counselors, advancing the counseling profession, and using the profession and practice of counseling to promote respect for human dignity and diversity" (ACA Code of Ethics, 2014).

We will begin our discussion with the concept of ethics and then explore the law later in the chapter. Prior to discussing the varying types of ethics, it is first necessary to discuss the ethical principles presented by the CRCC's Code of Professional Ethics and the ACA's Code of Ethics.

Ethical Principles

Now that we have defined ethics and identified our ethical governing bodies, let us now turn our attention to the six ethical principles that are at the core of our ethical codes of conduct. Ethical principles can be thought of as professional values. These values are considered the foundation for ethical behavior and decision making (ACA, 2014; CRCC, 2017). Both the CRCC and the ACA codes of professional ethics discuss the essential nature of autonomy, beneficence, nonmaleficence, justice, fidelity, and veracity.

The ethical principle of autonomy calls for clinical rehabilitation counselors to respect the right of their consumers to make their own decisions (ACA, 2014; CRCC, 2017). For instance, a consumer has the right to select their own vocational goal. The clinical rehabilitation counselor is responsible for working with the consumer to explore their options and make an informed decision; however, the consumer has the right to make the final decision. Additionally, consider the consumer who is experiencing depressive symptoms; the clinical rehabilitation counselor may believe that it is in the consumer's best interest to take antidepressant medications (as prescribed by a psychiatrist), but the consumer may prefer to seek out herbal remedies. Again, the final decision rests in the hands of the consumer, so long as the consumer is not a danger to themselves or others.

The ethical principle of beneficence calls for rehabilitation and counseling professionals to do good to their consumers (ACA, 2014; CRCC, 2017). The clinical rehabilitation counselor is responsible for helping the consumer explore all their vocational options so the consumer can make an informed choice when selecting their vocational goal. This is a clear example of the clinical rehabilitation counselor practicing beneficence and promoting good for their consumer. In the case of the consumer who is experiencing depressive symptoms, the counselor could provide the consumer with resources for professionals who are well trained in the use of prescription of herbal remedies for depression.

The ethical principle of nonmaleficence calls for counseling and rehabilitation professionals to do no harm to their consumers (ACA, 2014; CRCC, 2017). For instance, when a clinical rehabilitation counselor is working to assist a consumer in selecting an appropriate vocational goal, they do not withhold information from the consumer that could help them to select an appropriate vocational goal. For instance, if the clinical rehabilitation counselor knows that the consumer will experience significant difficulty acquiring a position in their chosen field of study, the clinical rehabilitation counselor has a responsibility to make the consumer aware of such challenges and recommend potential solutions for the consumer to consider before moving forward. Failure to take such action is potential maleficence. Likewise, if the counselor working with the consumer who is experiencing depressive symptoms fails to refer their consumer to a reputable practitioner to explore herbal remedies, the counselor could be engaging in maleficence.

The ethical principle of justice calls for clinical rehabilitation counselors to be fair to their consumers (ACA, 2014; CRCC, 2017). In so doing, the rehabilitation counselor has a responsibility to provide all consumers with the same opportunities for vocational services and goal achievement. Historically, research has shown that minorities have received lower levels of vocational counseling and clinical mental health services compared to their White counterparts (Leung et al., 2007). Such actions would not be in line with the ethical principle of justice. It should be clear that providing more effective services to one group because of their ethnic or racial makeup is unfair discriminatory treatment and, as such, unethical behavior.

The ethical principle of fidelity calls for clinical rehabilitation counselors to be faithful to their consumers (ACA, 2014; CRCC, 2017). Whether one serves as a rehabilitation counselor or a clinical rehabilitation counselor, these professionals have a responsibility to show dedication to their consumer. This requires professionals to exhibit unconditional positive regard and acceptance to their consumers. Unconditional positive regard and acceptance is best described by Corey (2016) as communicating "a deep and genuine caring for the consumer as a person. … The caring is non-possessive and it is not contaminated by evaluation or judgment of the consumer's feelings, thoughts, and behavior as good or bad" (p. 174). Consider for instance, the clinical rehabilitation counselor who willingly and enthusiastically continues to work with their consumer even though the consumer did not succeed in their first on-the-job training experience. The rehabilitation counselor is faithful to the consumer and will continue to work with the consumer until they achieve their vocational goal. Likewise, the clinical rehabilitation counselor working with their consumer who fails to follow up on a referral to an herbalist will continue to assist them.

The ethical principle of veracity calls for clinical rehabilitation counselors to be truthful to their consumers (ACA, 2014; CRCC, 2017). While this may appear to be a straightforward concept, at times it may be appealing for professionals to be facetious to their consumers. Note that even white lies may result in detrimental consequences. Clinical rehabilitation counselors have an ethical obligation to tell the truth about confidentiality. They must inform their consumers that although they are required to keep the consumer's information private, there are limits to confidentiality and that the counselor has an obligation to share the consumer's information in instances of duty to warn or when being subpoenaed.

Confidentiality

The need for confidentiality arises out of the concept of privacy. Privacy is the right of a person to select what, if any, of their personal information should and should not be shared with others (Remley & Herlihy, 2007). Confidentiality is more of an ethical concept that is specific to the relationship between the consumer and the professional serving the consumer. This concept of confidentiality stipulates that the professional must first acquire the consumer's permission prior to sharing their information with others. This brings us to privileged communication, which is a legal concept that protects consumers from having the confidential information they shared with their counselor shared in court of law without their consent (Remley & Herlihy, 2007; Shuman & Weiner, 1987).

When considering the concepts of confidentiality and privileged communication, it is essential to note the exceptions to these concepts. Such exceptions include the following:

- The consumer waives their right to privileged communication.
- The consumer dies.
- The counselor may be required to share information with subordinates or fellow professionals.
- The counselor may need to protect someone who is in danger.
- The counselor may encounter confidentiality issues when counseling multiple consumers such as couples, families, and groups.
- The counselor is working with a consumer who is a minor.

The counselor will also encounter exceptions to confidentiality that are mandated by law (Glosoff et al., 2000; Remley & Herlihy, 2007).

Case Study: Sam

Sam is a new clinical rehabilitation counselor providing vocational and mental health services at an elementary school. His previous counseling experience was at a school in another district, where he was one of three counselors for the entire school. Budget limitations in this new district require that Sam share his time between two different elementary schools, serving half-time in each, as the only clinical rehabilitation counselor. Sam currently shares space with the school psychologist, a full-time employee of the district who rotates her time among all of the schools in the district. Sam generally has difficulty finding a space to meet privately with his students because the psychologist usually occupies the office for testing and administration. Sam often does not have access to student files prior to his meetings with students, so he carries them around and reads them whenever he can. Since the school is very small and Sam has difficulty

(continued)

Case Study: Sam *(continued)*

finding a private space elsewhere in the building, he often finds that he can utilize a corner of the cafeteria to meet with students individually. Although the space is loud and not particularly private, he does the best he can with the space provided.

1. What confidentiality concerns may arise with Sam's approach? And how could these concerns be addressed in an ethical manner?

Duty to Warn

Most counselors are familiar with the *Tarasoff* case (1976), commonly referred to as the "duty to warn," wherein the Tarasoff family sued the Regents of the University of California. The landmark case was the result of a lawsuit filed against a therapist who failed to inform a woman and her parents of a consumer's intent to cause harm. Although the ruling in the case obligates therapists to inform individuals and law enforcement of specific threats, they should not discuss specific details of the consumer's personal history that is not relevant to the threat (American Psychological Association [APA], 2020).

Case Study: Martha

Martha is a clinical rehabilitation counselor at a residential facility that serves adolescents with substance abuse disorders. Many of her students have come to this school as a last resort. Martha is working with a 16-year-old named Susan, who had been falling through the cracks in the system until she finally arrived at Martha's office door. Susan has been involved with drugs and alcohol, truancy, and is in danger of failing school. Susan discloses that she started using drugs 6 years ago when her stepfather began sexually abusing her. Susan began crying one day and informed Martha that she plans to kill her stepfather if she has to return to the home. Susan said her mother refuses to believe her stepfather is abusing her. Susan is scheduled to return home in 3 weeks. Martha is having doubts about Susan's safety and readiness, despite the confidences expressed by the other members of Susan's treatment team who believe she is lying and attribute it to her drug use and as a way to prevent returning to her home.

1. What steps should Matha take in this situation? Outline steps and potential outcomes for this case.

Types of Ethics

Three specific types of ethics have been discussed in recent decades: mandatory ethics, aspirational ethics, and positive ethics. This section explores these three types of ethics and elaborates upon their implementation with reference to the CRCC and ACA codes of ethics. First, we present section A.1.b of the CRCC Code of Professional Ethics, which discusses the establishment of a rehabilitation plan, followed by section A.4.b. of the ACA Code of Ethics, which discusses personal values:

> Clinical rehabilitation counselors and consumers work together to develop integrated, individual, mutually agreed-upon, written rehabilitation plans that offer a reasonable promise of success and are consistent with the abilities and circumstances of consumers. Clinical rehabilitation counselors and consumers regularly review rehabilitation plans to assess their continued viability and effectiveness and to revise them as needed. (CRCC, 2017, p. 4)

> Counselors are aware of—and avoid imposing—their own values, attitudes, beliefs, and behaviors. Counselors respect the diversity of consumers, trainees, and research participants and seek training in areas in which they are at risk of imposing their values onto consumers, especially when the counselor's values are inconsistent with the consumer's goals or are discriminatory in nature. (ACA, 2014, p. 5).

The use of mandatory ethics requires the professional to focus on the minimal level of professional practice. A clinical rehabilitation counselor practicing mandatory ethics who abides by the section A.1.b of the CRCC Code of Ethics may simply ensure that the vocational goal was selected and agreed upon by the consumer. This action meets the minimum requirements of section A.1.b.

Regarding section A.4.b of the ACA Code of Ethics, the counselor may recognize that they hold values, attitudes, or beliefs that vary from that of their consumer, and they may simply decide not to discuss this matter with the consumer or let the consumer know that they disagree with the consumer's values, beliefs, or attitudes. This eliminates the potential for the counselor to directly impose their values, beliefs, attitudes, or actions onto the consumer or to offend their consumer. However, such actions are indicative of a counselor who is practicing mandatory ethics.

Aspirational ethics are considered a higher level of ethical practice than mandatory ethics. Aspirational ethics entails an understanding of the spirit behind the code and the principles on which the code rests (Corey et al., 2003). In this case, a clinical rehabilitation counselor practicing aspirational ethics who abides by section A.1.b of the CRCC Code of Ethics would ensure that the vocational goal was selected by and agreed upon by the consumer and that the clinical rehabilitation counselor also discussed the potential assets and limitations of the selected vocational goal with the consumer. The clinical rehabilitation counselor would take this action in consideration of ethical principles and in conjunction with following section A.1.b of the code. For instance, the clinical rehabilitation counselor avoids doing harm by ensuring that the consumer participates in the selection of the goal. However, the clinical rehabilitation counselor would also be promoting beneficence as they explore the assets and limitations of the vocational goal with the consumer. In taking this additional step, the clinical rehabilitation counselor further empowers their consumer.

Regarding section A.4.b of the ACA Code of Ethics, the counselor may recognize that they hold a value, attitude, or belief that varies from that of their consumer. The counselor may also take some time to identify the origins of their consumer's values, beliefs, or attitudes so the counselor can gain a better understanding of the consumer's culture and worldview. Such action would also be in line with the ethical principles that encourage counselors to do no harm, promote good, and to be fair to their consumers. In exploring the consumer's worldview, the counselor is going beyond the basic requirements of the code, as they attempt to understand and potentially respect their consumer's values, beliefs, or attitudes, therefore allowing the counselor to practice aspirational ethics.

Last, but certainly not least, is positive ethics, which is an approach taken by practitioners who want to do all they can to assist their consumers as opposed to simply doing the minimum requirements of their job in an effort to stay out of trouble (Corey, 2016). For instance, a clinical rehabilitation counselor practicing positive ethics who abides by section A.1.b of the CRCC Code of Ethics may ensure that the vocational goal was selected and agreed upon by the consumer and may also discuss the assets and limitations of the vocational goal with the consumer. However, in this case the clinical rehabilitation counselor may also present the consumer with other potential options for vocational goals and perhaps provide the consumer with some opportunities for vocational exploration such as job shadowing or an internship. In offering such opportunities, the clinical rehabilitation counselor is going beyond both mandatory and aspiration ethics as they attempt to do all they can to assist their consumer.

Regarding section A.4.b of the ACA Code of Ethics, the counselor may recognize that they hold a value, attitude, or belief that varies from that of their consumer and take some time to identify the origins of their consumer's values, beliefs, or attitudes. In an effort to embody positive ethics, the counselor may also take some time to explore the origins of their own values, beliefs, and attitudes. Once they have gained new perspective on the matter at hand, the counselor may even review relevant literature related to the value differences they identified between themselves and their consumer. This range of activities not only ensures the counselor does not impose their values on their consumer or violate ethical principles; it also assists the counselor in becoming more culturally competent.

Ethical Codes of Conduct

Now that you have a better understanding of the concept of ethics and the principles of the profession's codes of ethics, let's now venture into a brief description of the CRCC's and the ACA's codes of ethics. A code of professional ethics guides the professional behavior of those serving in a field or profession (ACA, 2014; Corey et al., 2007; Tarvydas & Cottone, 2000). Developed by a profession's governing body, codes of professional ethics are intended to minimize harm to consumers and the general public through the establishment of professional norms and expectations. Thus, it is essential that clinical rehabilitation counselors ensure that they are well-versed in the ethical codes.

Codes of ethics can be viewed as having six purposes. First and foremost, as previously mentioned, professional codes of ethics guide professional conduct. Second, codes of ethics ensure the accountability of practitioners. Third, they serve as catalysts for improving practice and service provision to consumers. Fourth, codes of ethics aid practitioners in working autonomously and effectively, engaging in appropriate self-regulation and evaluation. Fifth, the implementation of codes of ethics supports and enhances internal stability of service organizations. Sixth, they serve as a means of protection for practitioners.

The CRCC Code of Professional Ethics consists of 12 sections (A–L) that address a variety of areas: the counseling relationship (section A); confidentiality and privileged communication (section B); privacy, advocacy, and accessibility (section C); professional responsibility (section D), relationships with other professionals and employers (section E); forensic services (section F); assessment and evaluation (section G); supervision, training, and teaching (section H); research and publication (section I); technology, social media, and distance counseling (section J); business practices (section K); and resolving ethical issues (section L). The CRCC Code of Ethics and the ACA Code of Ethics have many commonalities. The ACA Code of Ethics is divided into nine sections. These sections address the following areas: the counseling relationship (section A); confidentiality and privacy (section B); professional responsibility (section C); relationships with other professionals (section D); evaluation, assessment, and interpretation (section E); supervision, training, and teaching (section F); research and publication (section G); distance counseling, technology, and social media (section H); and resolving ethical issues (section I). The ACA and CRCC codes of ethics have a multitude of similarities and often mirror one another in the spirit and presentation of many of their respective ethical codes.

Ethical Issues

Clinical rehabilitation counselors and other counselors should be on the lookout for the following ethical issues when engaged in active service provision:

- Issues related to consumer rights
- Issues related to professional responsibility
- Issues related to professional boundaries
- Issues related to confidentiality and the limits of confidentiality
- Issues related to record keeping
- Issues related to the use of technology
- Issues related to professional competence
- Issues related to serving minors
- Issues related to serving vulnerable populations
- Issues related to serving groups and families
- Issues related to diagnosis
- Issues related to testing
- Issues related to varying types of discrimination and prejudice (Remley & Herlihy, 2007)

When working to address such ethical issues, clinical rehabilitation counselors would do well to utilize appropriate ethical decision-making models (EDMs). Both the CRCC and the ACA emphasize the importance of ethical decision-making and present steps to help clinical rehabilitation counselors navigate the ethical decision-making process.

Ethical Decision-Making Models

The ACA states that "when counselors are faced with ethical dilemmas that are difficult to resolve, they are expected to engage in a carefully considered ethical decision making process, consulting available resources as needed" (ACA, 2014, p. 3). Likewise, the CRCC Code of Professional Ethics states that "Rehabilitation counselors are expected to use a credible model of ethical decision-making that can bear public scrutiny of its application. Through a chosen ethical decision making process and evaluation of the context of the situation, rehabilitation counselors work to resolve any ethical dilemmas that may arise" (2017, p. 3). Practitioners should be aware that ethical decision making is not a purely cognitive or linear process. The process involves the feelings and interpretations made by practitioners, and it influences future behavior with consumers. Note that ethical decision making should always involve consultation. Clinical rehabilitation counselors would do well to consult with supervisors, colleagues, and/or seasoned professionals when engaging in ethical decision-making activities.

Four main types of ethical decision-making models have been presented over recent decades: the social constructivist ethical decision-making model (Cottone, 2001), the integrative ethical decision-making model (Tarvydas, 1998), the feminist ethical decision-making model (Hill et al., 1995), and the transcultural integrative ethical decision-making model (Garcia et al., 2003).

Brief Descriptions of the Models

Table 7.1 highlights the steps of the four ethical decision-making models.

TABLE 7.1 Ethical Decision-Making Models

Social Constructivist	Integrative	Feminist	Transcultural Integrative
Interpersonal: • Negotiate • Consensualize • Arbitrate	Interpret the situation through awareness and fact-finding: • Sensitivity and awareness • Stakeholders and their claims • Fact-finding	Recognize the problem	Interpret the situation through awareness and fact-finding
Place the decision in social context vs. the decision of the counselor	Formulate an ethical decision: • Problem • Standards/codes/laws/policies • Consultation	Form a collaborative definition of the problem	Formulate an ethical decision
Decisions made in interactions	Select an action: • Weigh competing values • Personal and contextual influences	Develop solutions	Weigh competing, nonmoral values and affirm the course of action
Multiple "competitive truths" (no distinct right/wrong)	Plan and execute the selected course of action: • Sequence • Barriers • Evaluation	Choose a solution	Plan and execute the selected course of action
Use consensus as basis (ethical codes)	Reflection, context, balance, collaboration	Review the process and choice of solution	
A truth vs. the truth	Combine virtue and principle ethics	Implement and evaluate solution with consumer	
		Continued reflection consumer	

In an effort to develop a more comprehensive approach to ethical decision making, Wheeler and Bertram (2015) developed an eight-step process:

1. Define the problem.
2. Identify the relevant variables.
3. Review ethical codes.
4. Examine institutional policy and the law.
5. Be aware of personal influences.
6. Engage in professional consultation.
7. Enumerate options and consequences.
8. Decide and take action.

Once practitioners have progressed through these eight steps, it is vital that they document their decision.

Case Study: Loretta

Loretta is a counselor in a community mental health agency that sponsors workshops aimed at preventing the spread of HIV/AIDS. The agency has attempted to involve the local churches and religious organizations in these workshops. One church withdrew its support because the workshops encouraged "safer" sexual practices, including the use of condoms, as a way of preventing HIV/AIDS. A church official contended that the use of condoms is contrary to church teachings. Loretta, who is member of this church, finds herself struggling with her own value conflicts. She believes in the teachings of her church and thinks the official had a right to withdraw, but she is also aware that many people in the community she serves are at high risk for contracting HIV/AIDS because of drug use and/or sexual practices.

1. How would you address Loretta dilemma with the use of one of the ethical decision-making models? Consider the exploration of the decision-making model provided.

Table 7.2 shows how Loretta can use Wheeler and Bertram's (2015) ethical decision-making steps in determining how to respond to her dilemma.

TABLE 7.2 Wheeler and Bertram's Ethical Decision-Making Steps

Step	Practical Application
1. Define the problem.	Loretta's church withdrew support for a workshop that promotes safer sex due to their religious beliefs regarding the use of condoms as a way to prevent HIV/AIDS.
2. Identify the relevant variables.	The withdrawal of vital community services is based upon religious beliefs.
3. Review ethical codes.	ACA: A.1 and A.1.a, Consumer Welfare and Primary Responsibility; A.4.a and A.4.b, Avoiding Harm and Imposing Personal Values on Consumers CRCC: A.1 and A.1.a, Welfare of Those Served and Primary Responsibility; A.2, Respecting Diversity; A.2.a and A.2.b, Respecting Culture and Nondiscrimination
4. Examine institutional policy and the law.	Discrimination on the basis of religion is prohibited.
5. Be aware of personal influences.	Loretta is struggling with her own value conflict because she is aware that many people in the community she serves are at high risk for contracting HIV/AIDS.
6. Engage in professional consultation.	Loretta decides to consult with colleagues.
7. Enumerate options and consequences.	Educate her church on how withdrawing involvement can be viewed as discriminatory and discuss how their decision impacts the people she serves. Reflect on how her own personal values could impact the people she serves and ponder whether she should find another venue in which to hold the workshop.
8. Decide and take action.	Loretta decides to educate her church members and proceed with holding the workshop at a different venue.

After going through the ethical decision-making process, some practitioners may ask themselves if they have made the right decision regarding the ethical dilemma. Van Hoose and Paradise (1979) encouraged practitioners to consider four key issues. First, practitioners should consider whether they maintained personal and professional honesty during the ethical decision-making process. Second, the practitioners should ask themselves if they have focused on their consumers' best interests. Third, practitioners should determine whether the decision(s) they made were done so without malicious intent or personal gain. And last, but certainly not least, practitioners should be able to justify actions as best judgment considering the current state of the profession.

SUMMARY

The profession of counseling occurs in a variety of settings, and as such, legal, ethical, and professional standards for clinical rehabilitation counselors must be addressed as they apply to counseling and related settings. Ethical principles, codes, and statutory and case laws are often used as a basis for determining the most appropriate professional behavior for counselors providing services. Professional standards are used to identify critical issues and propose options for responsible professional behavior. Ethical and legal issues should include considerations within the context of cultural variables, including race, ethnicity, gender, age, religion, and sexual orientation. Professional standards of counseling provide an opportunity for counselors to reflect upon their own values and how they impact the counseling process. This chapter provided a context for gaining an understanding of and the application of legal, ethical, and professional standards by utilizing ethical decision-making models. A discussion of ethics, ethical principles, and ethical decision-making models were explored. Lastly, case studies were utilized to assist the student in applying the concepts.

Discussion Questions

1. What is ethics?
2. What is the purpose of an ethical code?
3. What is the difference between legal standards and ethical standards?
4. What is duty to warn?
5. Describe the concepts of confidentiality and privileged communication.

Case Study: Evelyn

Use an ethical decision-making model to respond to the following case studies.

Evelyn is a counselor in private practice. She has been working with Donna for about 6 weeks on issues in her relationship, career, and general self-esteem. From the beginning, Evelyn felt a connection with Donna different from that with her other consumers. They are both feminists, share similar backgrounds, and have a great deal in common. Evelyn finds that she and Donna relate more as friends than as counselor–consumer in most of their discussions. When Donna begins to talk about her struggles with how to approach her family of origin and the difficult issues that she is facing with them, Evelyn shared her personal story that had eerily similar circumstances. Donna listens intently but does not seem to fully agree as she usually does with Evelyn's suggestions. Evelyn is further noticing that Donna is making great strides in her self-esteem. Evelyn looks forward to her weekly sessions with Donna and therefore does not bring up the issues of her own self-disclosure, Donna's progress, or the future direction of their work together.

Case Study: Anthony

Use an ethical decision-making model to respond to the following case studies.

Anthony is working in a vocational rehabilitation agency with individuals attempting to reenter the workforce. The agency has been primarily successful in placing most of their consumers in appropriate work settings. Anthony has been with the agency since his master's practicum and has been employed full time following his graduation 3 months ago. Anthony was hired, in part, because of his success with job placements and the high evaluations his consumers have given him. Anthony comes to work one day and sees that his second appointment is with one of the first individuals he helped to place in a secretarial position, who has just lost her job due to complications with job fulfillment due to her physical limitations. When she enters for her appointment, the consumer is quite agitated and blames Anthony for placing her in such an awful work environment. She states that he should have known better about her abilities and limitations and the work that would be required at this site. She threatens to contact Anthony's supervisor and file a formal complaint about his incompetence as a rehabilitation counselor.

REFERENCES

American Counseling Association. (2014). ACA code of ethics. Author.

American Psychological Association. *Ethical principles of psychologists and code of conduct.* https://www. apa.org/ethics/code

Commission on Rehabilitation Counselor Certification. (2019). *About CRCC.* https://www.crccertification. com/about-crcc

Commission on Rehabilitation Counselor Certification. (2017). *Code of professional ethics for rehabilitation counselors.* https://www.crccertification.com/code-of-ethics-3

Corey, G. (2016). *Theory and practice of counseling and psychotherapy* (10th ed.). Thomson Brooks/Cole.

Corey, G., Corey, M. S., & Callanan, P. (2003). *Issues and ethics in the helping professions* (6th ed.). Thomson Brooks/Cole.

Corey, G., Schneider, Corey, M., & Callanan, P. (2007). *Issues and ethics in the helping professions* (7th ed.). Thomson Higher Education.

Cottone, R. R. (2001). A social constructivism model of ethical decision-making in counseling. *Journal of Counseling & Development, 79,* 39–45.

Edwards, G. S. (2010). Database of state *Tarasoff* laws. *SSRN.* http://dx.doi.org/10.2139/ssrn.1551505

Garcia, J. G., Cartwright, B., Winston, S. M., Borzuchowska, B. (2003). A Transcultural integrative model for ethical decision making in counseling. *Journal of Counseling & Development.* 81(3), 268–278. DOI: 10.1002/j.1556-6678.2003.tb00253.x.

Glosoff, H. L., Herlihy, B., & Spence, B. (2000). Privileged communication in the counselor–consumer relationship. *Journal of Counseling & Development, 78,* 454–462.

Hill, M., Glaser, K., & Harden, J. (1995). A feminist model for ethical decision making. In E. J. Rave & C. C. Larsen (Eds.), *Ethical decision making in therapy: Feminist perspectives* (pp. 18–37). Guilford.

Leung, P., Flowers, C., Talley, W., & Sanderson, P. (2007). *Multicultural issues in rehabilitation and allied health.* Aspen Professional Services.

Merriam-Webster. (2020). Ethics. Retrieved from: https://www.merriam-webster.com/dictionary/ ethic#:~:text=%3A%20rules%20of%20behavior%20based%20on,that%20something%20is%20very%20 important

Neulicht, A. T., McQuade, L. J., & Chapman, C. A. (2010). *The CRCC desk reference on professional ethics: A Guide for rehabilitation counselors.* Elliot & Fitzpatrick.

Remley, T. P., & Herlihy, B. (2007). *Ethical, legal, and professional issues in counseling* (2nd ed.). Pearson Merrill Prentice Hall.

Remley, T. P., & Herlihy, B. (2016). *Ethical, legal, and professional issues in counseling* (5th ed.). Pearson Prentice-Hall.

Shuman, D. W., & Weiner, M. F. (1987). *The psychotherapist–patient privilege: A critical examination.* Charles C. Thomas.

Tarvydas, V. M. (1998). Ethical decision-making processes. In R. R. Cottone & V. M. Tarvydas (Eds.), *Ethical and professional issues in counseling* (pp. 144–154). Prentice Hall.

Tarvydas, V., & Cottone, R. R. (2000). The code of ethics for professional rehabilitation counselors: What we have and what we need. *Rehabilitation Counseling Bulletin, 43*(4), 188–196.

Van Hoose, W. H. & Paradise, L. V. (1979). *Ethics in counseling and psychotherapy.* Carroll Press.

Weston, A. (2008). *A 21st-century ethical toolbox* (2nd ed.). Oxford University Press.

Wheeler, A. M., & Bertram, B. (2012). *The counselor and the law: A guide to legal and ethical practice* (6th ed.). American Counseling Association.

Wheeler, A. M., & Bertram, B. (2015). *The counselor and the law: A guide to legal and ethical practice* (7th ed.). American Counseling Association.

CHAPTER 8

Career and Disability
Employment Needs and Job Placement

Rebecca R. Sametz, PhD, CRC, LPC, ETS, CMCC
Danielle Dede Nimako, PhD, CRC

Learning Objectives

As a result of reading this chapter, the student will be able to:

- Summarize the treatment of people with disabilities.
- Discuss employment statistics of persons with disabilities.
- Define and identify demand-side employment and its benefits.
- Demonstrate an understanding of accommodations for people with disabilities.

INTRODUCTION

Historically, people with disabilities have encountered significant barriers to employment. These challenges have highlighted the need for career services for persons with disabilities. Disability is a reality for many people globally and has been identified by the World Health Organization (WHO, 2011) to be a challenge faced by all nations for two reasons: an aging global population and increasing rates of chronic disease. One of the most significant societal impacts due to disability is the impact on the economy; in particular, the lower participation rates in the labor force (OECD, 2010).

Perhaps no other single activity continuously demands as much physical, emotional, and cognitive processing similar to that of work (Landy & Trumbo, 1980). Farruggia (1986) states that work absorbs the majority of an individual's waking hours and bestows a vast assortment of tasks to which individuals must respond to in one way or another. Because work is a dominate portion of our lives, understanding factors within one's work that are dissatisfying and satisfying will lead to higher retention rates and higher levels of reported job satisfaction. This chapter describes the vocational journey taken by many people with disabilities. It also highlights the key issues that people with disabilities encounter in the workplace and provides guidelines for helping them in overcoming these challenges.

Early Treatment of People With Disabilities

For much of history, people with disabilities were viewed as being undesirable. The term *eugenics* was first coined in the late 1800s by Francis Galton, who analyzed different human characteristics, such as intelligence, and concluded that they were hereditary. In his view, therefore, desirable and nondesirable traits could be passed down through generations (Norrgard, 2008). The belief that people with hereditary diseases or illnesses could dilute American's bloodlines had a huge impact on public and governmental beliefs and attitudes toward individuals with disabilities (Fox & Marini, 2017). This fear, combined with the American eugenics movement of the early 20th century, prompted U.S. lawmakers to pass laws that specifically restricted certain people or groups from entering the United States, as well as some city ordinances that kept them out of public view (Fox & Marini, 2017).

Due to the high influx of immigrants to the United States during the 1830s, the issue of disability became more pressing (Treadway, 1925). Outward attitudes and treatment toward persons with disabilities, as well as certain other immigrant populations, were blatantly prejudiced and discriminatory (Fox & Marini, 2017). A number of antidisability laws were passed between 1882 and 1924, with some of the original laws in effect until the 1980s. The concept behind these laws was to prevent the immigration of people who were considered undesirable. Popular beliefs promoted the idea that preventing people considered undesirable from entering the United States was a means of protecting not only the people but also the welfare of the country (Ward, 1907). As one of the driving forces behind early federal immigration law, the Immigration Act of 1882 manifested the beginning of the exclusion of persons with disabilities in America (Baynton, 2005). For instance, railroads and public transit systems were essentially granted permission to deny access to transportation for impaired people; school laws upheld segregating persons with disabilities by not allowing them to attend school or requiring that they be taught in a segregated room; employers were also permitted to discriminate in hiring those with disabilities; and all public venues, including restaurants, theaters, and so on, could deny access and frequently did so (Fox & Marini, 2017).

However, positive and empowering legislation was also passed during the early 20th century. The 1920s brought about the Smith-Fess Act, which promoted vocational guidance, occupational adjustment, and placement services for people with disabilities. A few years after the Great Depression of the 1930s, individuals with disabilities demanded their voices be heard, which led to the development of the League of the Physically Handicapped (Longmore & Goldberg, 2000). The organization's focus was to tackle discrimination issues rather than their medical impairments. Franklin Roosevelt was a member of the League of the Physically Handicapped and strived for the rehabilitation of those with disabilities, despite hiding his own paralysis from polio at age 39. In Roosevelt's autobiography, he talked about being intuitively aware of the negative societal attitudes toward disabilities and that if the public knew of both the extent of his disability and chronic pain he would be perceived as a weak, ineffective leader (Fox & Marini, 2012). Because of this awareness, Roosevelt had agreements with the media to not photograph or film him while using his wheelchair or while ambulating with his leg braces.

In 1935, Roosevelt signed the Social Security Act (Gallagher, 1994) and the State–Federal Vocational Rehabilitation Program was established as a permanent program (Parker et al., 2005). Even with these efforts to provide services and reduce society's stigma toward persons with disabilities, the unemployment gap when comparing placement rates to those without disabilities continued to grow. The lowest unemployment rate for persons with disabilities was during World War II because many able-bodied

Americans were involved in the war, and manufacturing jobs for the war effort increased dramatically (Yenlin, 1991).

When the war was over, tens of thousands of able-bodied men and women in the armed services returned home looking for work, and thousands of workers with disabilities were subsequently replaced and suddenly unemployed. The year 1943 marked the passage of landmark legislation with the Barden-LaFollette Act. The Barden-Lafollette Act also broadened the definition of disability; one of the benefits of this expanded definition allowed persons with mental illness or psychiatric disabilities to be eligible for rehabilitation services.

The 1954 Vocational Rehabilitation Act increased the amount of state vocational services available to persons with mental disabilities. Specifically, the federal government increased the amount of funding to states. The legislation also began providing grants to universities to train individuals to work with people with disabilities.

However, perhaps the single most important legislation to date concerning the civil rights of persons with disabilities was the 1990 passage of the Americans with Disabilities Act (ADA) by President George H. W. Bush. The five parts of the ADA address employment; extended access to state and federal government services, including public or paratransit transportation access; public accommodations for physical access to all public venues; access to telecommunications; and miscellaneous topics.

Note that with the aging of the U.S. population, millions of baby boomers will be moving into their golden years. Their financial portfolios, or lack thereof, will likely dictate the quality of their lives. Although Americans are living longer and healthier lives due to advancements in medicine, technology, and so forth, those with disabilities and little income may face precarious times ahead.

Statistics: Disability and Employment

The percentage of people with disabilities in the United States rose from 11.9% in 2010 to 12.6% in 2013, 2014, and 2015. As the U.S. population ages, the percentage of people with disabilities continues to increase. In the United States in 2015, less than 1.0% of those under the age of 5 had a disability; for those aged 5 to 17 years, the rate was 5.4%; and for those aged 18 to 64 years, the rate was 10.5%. Of those with disabilities, more than half were of working age (51%), while 41.2% were 65 and older. Disability in children and youth accounted for 7.2% (5 to 17 years) and 0.4% (younger than years; Kraus, 2017).

According to the 2016 Disability Statistics Annual Report, in the United States, 34.9% of people with disabilities aged 18 to 64 years living in the community were employed (Kraus, 2017). The employment percentage was more than double for people without disabilities (76.0%). Thus, the employment gap between people with disabilities and people without disabilities was 41.4%. Kraus (2017) notes that this employment gap widened steadily from 38.8% in 2008 to 41.1% in 2014. However, although progress has been made in increasing employment opportunities for people with disabilities, the 17.2% employment rate of people with disabilities stands in distressing contrast to the 65% rate of those without disabilities (U.S. Department of Labor, 2017).

Despite decades of social and legislative efforts to better integrate people with disabilities into the workforce, the gap in employment rates for persons with disabilities continues to remain largely higher than those without disabilities. Improving hiring outcomes for people with disabilities can help reduce employment disparities. In addition, increasing employment correlates with broader social and community integration and can help reduce negative beliefs toward people with disabilities (Barnes & Mercer, 2005).

Employers' Perceptions of Disability

It is important to understand employers' views on hiring people with disabilities and how such views develop across employers of all sizes. Until relatively recently, employers had the misperception that workers with disabilities tended to be undereducated or unqualified, unproductive, and expensive to hire (U.S. Department of Labor, 2014b). Strikingly, 43% of employees with disabilities report experiencing discrimination within the workforce (United States Department of Labor, 2014a). Overall, the academic literature and industry publications indicate that these employer attitudes are a significant impediment to increasing positive employment outcomes for people with disabilities (Bendick & Nunes, 2012; Davaki et al., 2013; U.S. Department of Labor, 2014a).

Research has shown that employers share concerns about the ability of people with disabilities to perform necessary job functions (Gröschl, 2005). Similarly, Bruyère and colleagues (2006) cited lack of skills or knowledge as a major concern for employers in hiring people with disabilities. However, a survey of 500 food service employers highlighted that having previously hired people with disabilities drastically improves employers' attitudes toward such workers (Chi & Qu, 2003). Because employers' attitudes are often among the most difficult to change barriers to hiring people with disabilities (Bruyère et al., 2006), it is important to understand the extent of and basis for these beliefs.

Employer attitudes about the ability and acceptance of prospective employees with disabilities may also vary by employer size. Fraser and colleagues (2010) conducted a Seattle-based focus group of companies and found that smaller businesses were more likely to see people with disabilities as unqualified or unable to perform tasks, while larger employers were more likely to express concerns over the ability to convince staff to accept employees with disabilities. A general trend of large employers viewing changing cultural attitudes as more difficult was also found by Jasper and Waldhart (2012) and Houtenville and Kalargyrou (2012). In their survey of human resource professionals, Bruyère and colleagues (2006) also concluded that larger employers were more likely to believe that employer attitudes toward people with disabilities were more difficult to change. Interestingly, the authors' survey results revealed no statistically significant difference between small and large employers' perceived challenges of hiring people with disabilities. The conflicting arguments and evidence for whether employer attitudes differ by employer size toward hiring and accommodating people with disabilities creates an opportunity to more rigorously test whether such differences exist.

Demand-Side Placement Services

Typically, professionals working with individuals with disabilities have been known to operate on the supply side of the labor market (Luecking et al., 2006; Symanski & Parker, 2005). The traditional supply-side approach to employment outcomes (i.e., providing medical, psychological, educational, and vocational services to improve functioning, physical stamina, and job skills) without taking into account organizational behaviors, employer needs, and the changing labor economy is no longer adequate for achieving meaningful employment outcomes for people with disabilities (Chan et al., 2010). The goal has primarily been to inform and prepare job seekers to facilitate their connection to jobs. The supply-side approach relies on offering employers a supply of workers who present, in various ways, with skills that will meet the needs of the labor market (Luecking et al., 2006). Even though these are important functions, an exclusive supply-side approach neglects the importance of influencing workplace operations in order to create a demand for rehabilitation services (Luecking et al., 2006).

There have been few attempts to adopt demand-side approaches by providing services directly to employers to help them meet their labor needs and change the nature of the work environment to be more accessible for job candidates with disabilities (Gilbride & Stensrud, 1999; Luecking et al., 2006). It is important to know how employers view interactions with clinical rehabilitation counselors and job seekers who are approaching them to negotiate customized positions (Chan et al., 2010). As such, many job development and placement researchers have recommended that both the consumer and the employer be viewed as rehabilitation customers (Gilbride & Stensrud, 2010).

Evidence indicates that employers are receptive to meeting the needs of clinical rehabilitation counselors who create a demand for workers with disabilities. Customized employment is a strategy for assisting individuals who are unlikely to compete for jobs with standardized job descriptions due to intensive support and accommodation needs. Customized employment strategies are designed to result in employment where job tasks are carved from an existing job, restructured from one or more existing job positions, or created to match the skills and accommodation needs of the individual job seeker. The key is to negotiate with the employer so that customized arrangements meet specific operations needs of the employer (Luecking et al., 2006).

In spite of the growing literature on employer perspectives on hiring people with disabilities, little is known about employer attitudes, willingness, and ultimately expectations about changing the nature of their hiring and operational procedures when considering applicants who cannot compete for "off-the-shelf" jobs (Luecking et al., 2006); that is, those individuals who may not have the skills, training, stamina, or life circumstances that will allow them to present themselves as viable candidates for positions listed by prospective employers. Individuals in this category may include individuals with significant accommodation needs, candidates for supported employment, youth transitioning from special education without a diploma, and individuals living or working in segregated settings. In order for successful employment to occur, innovative programming and strategies need to occur in order to assist individuals with disabilities, in the context of the proposed study specifically youth with disabilities, in determining potential employment options (Luecking et al., 2006). An innovative solution and strategy that has been identified by transition coordinators as a service that assists youth with disabilities in the transition from school to work and adult life is work-based learning.

Accommodations

Passed in 1990, the Americans with Disabilities Act (ADA) is perhaps the most widely cited disability policy. The ADA places the financial burden for accommodations, as well as the burden to prove if a requested accommodation is too costly to society (i.e., it is "unreasonable") or is too costly (i.e., an "undue hardship"), on the employer, leading some employers to have negative feelings toward the law (Sherwyn, 2005). Markel and Barclay (2009) explain that a requested accommodation is unreasonable if it disrupts workflow or is prohibitively expensive, while other accommodations such as providing assistive computer technology or a different break schedule are typically considered reasonable for employers.

Accommodations can include generalizable approaches such as job mentoring, internships or co-ops, and other training programs (U.S. Department of Labor, 2017). Such practices and supported employment programs are often managed through an intermediary state vocational rehabilitation agency or a public–private or private employment network that works to match prospective employees with employers (Unger, 1999).

SUMMARY

This chapter discussed the vocational journey taken by many people with disabilities by highlighting the challenges and barriers to employment that they may have and continue to encounter. It started with a discussion on the early treatment of people with disabilities. Antidisability immigration laws and policies that specifically restricted certain people or groups from entering the United States were examined before transitioning into the current statistics on disability and employment. The chapter highlighted key issues that people with disabilities encounter in the workplace and provided guidelines for helping people with disabilities in overcoming these challenges. It also described the importance of demand-side placement by stressing the need for professionals working with individuals with disabilities to adopt demand-side approaches with a goal of making work environments more accessible for job candidates with disabilities. The chapter concluded with suggesting general approaches in providing job accommodation.

Discussion Questions

1. Do you think that clinical rehabilitation counselors should increase their participation in demand-side placement services? Explain.
2. What major concerns do employers have regarding hiring people with disabilities?
3. As a clinical rehabilitation counselor, what measures can you adopt to improve the hiring outcome for your consumers?
4. What will you consider as reasonable accommodation or unreasonable accommodation, and why?
5. Over time, how have new laws and policy changes improved or diminished the lives of people with disabilities?

Case Study: Joe

Joe is a 53-year-old male diagnosed with diabetes who has just been discharged from the hospital with a new diagnosis of anxiety and major depression. He smokes one pack of cigarettes per day, does not exercise, and is about 50 pounds overweight. He does not drink alcohol or use street drugs. He reports trouble sleeping. Joe is married and has a college-age son who lives at home. Joe was originally hospitalized after experiencing the symptoms of a panic attack at work. His symptoms are now under control with medication. If he continues his medication, his prognosis is good. He had been employed as a 911 operator but lost his position due to the extended nature of the hospital stay. He states that he is feeling "stressed out" and is afraid that he will have another panic attack at work.

(Continued)

Case Study: Joe (*Continued*)

1. Do you believe that Joe could return to being a 911 operator? Why or why not.
2. What other types of employment could Joe explore based on his work history?
3. As a clinical rehabilitation counselor, what types of services do you feel are important to include in Joe's plan for him to be successful?

REFERENCES

Barnes, C., & Mercer, G. (2005). Disability, work, and welfare: Challenging the social exclusion of disabled people. *Work, Employment & Society, 19*(3), 527–545.

Baynton, D. (2005). Defectives in the land: Disability and American Immigration policy, 1882–1924. *Journal of American Ethnic History, 24*(30), 31–40.

Bendick, M., & Nunes, A. (2012). Developing the research basis for controlling bias in hiring. *Journal of Social Issues, 68*, 238–262.

Bruyère, S. M., Erickson, W. A., & VanLooy, S. A. (2006). The impact of business size on employer ADA response. *Rehabilitation Counseling Bulletin, 49*(2), 194–206.

Chan, F., Strauser, D., Gervey, R., & Lee, E. (2010). Introduction to demand-side factors related to people with disabilities. *Journal of Occupational Rehabilitation, 20*, 407–411.

Chi, C. G., & Qu, H. (2003). Integrating persons with disabilities into the work force: A study on employment of people with disabilities in foodservice industry. *International Journal of Hospitality and Tourism, 4*(4), 59–83.

Davaki, K., Marzo, C., Narminio, E., & Arvanitidou, M. (2013). *Discrimination generated by the intersection of gender and disability.* European Parliament: Policy Department C–Citizens Rights and Constitutional Affairs. http://www.europarl.europa.eu/RegData/etudes/STUD/2013/493006/IPOL-FEMM_ET(2013)493006_EN.pdf

Equal Employment Opportunity Commission. (2002). *Enforcement guidance: Reasonable accommodation and undue hardship under the Americans with Disabilities Act.* https://www.eeoc.gov/policy/docs/accommodation.html

Farruggia, G. (1986). Job satisfaction among private and public sector rehabilitation practitioners. *Journal of Rehabilitation Administration, 10*(1), 4–9.

Fox, D. D., & Marini, I. (2012). History of treatment toward persons with disabilities in America. In C. Stebnicki & I. Marini (Eds.), *The psychological and social impact of illness and disability* (6th ed.; pp. 3–12). Springer.

Fox, D. D., & Marini, I. (2017). History of treatment towards persons with disabilities in America. In C. Stebnicki & I. Marini (Eds.), *The psychological and social impact of illness and disability* (7th ed.). Springer.

Fraser, R. T., Johnson, K., Hebert, J., Ajzen, I., Copeland, J., Brown, P., & Chan, F. (2010). Understanding employers' hiring intentions in relation to qualified workers with disabilities: Preliminary findings. *Journal of Occupational Rehabilitation, 20*(4), 420–426.

Gallagher, H. G. (1994). *FDR's splendid deception.* Vandamere.

Gilbride, D., & Stensrud, R. (1999). Demand-side job development and system change. *Rehabilitation Counseling Bulletin, 42*, 219–229.

Gilbride, D., & Stensrud, R. (2010). Demand-side job development and system change. *Rehabilitation Counseling Bulletin*, 219–229.

Gröschl, S. (2005). Persons with disabilities: A source of nontraditional labor for Canada's hotel industry. *Cornell Hotel and Restaurant Administration Quarterly, 46*(2), 258–274.

Houtenville, A., & Kalargyrou, V. (2012). People with disabilities: Employers' perspectives on recruitment practices, strategies, and challenges in leisure and hospitality. *Cornell Hospitality Quarterly, 53*(1), 40–52.

Jasper, C. R., & Waldhart, P. (2012). Retailer perceptions on hiring prospective employees with disabilities. *Journal of Retailing and Consumer Services, 19*(1), 116–123.

Kraus, L. (2017). *2016 Disability statistics annual report.* Rehabilitation and Training Center on Disability Statistics and Demographics. University of New Hampshire. https://disabilitycompendium.org/sites/default/files/user-uploads/2016_AnnualReport.pdf

Landy, F., & Trumbo, D. (1980). *Psychology of work behavior.* Dorsey Press.

Livneh, H. (1982). On the origins of negative attitudes toward people with disabilities. *Rehabilitation Literature, 43*, 338–347.

Longmore, P. K., & Goldberger, D. (2000). The League of the Physically Handicapped and the Great Depression: A case study in the new disability history. *Journal of American History, 87*(3), 888–921.

Luecking, R. G., Cuozzo, L., & Buchanan, L. (2006). Demand-side workforce needs and the potential for job customization. *Journal of Applied Rehabilitation Counseling, 37*(4), 5–13.

Markel, K. S., & Barclay, L. A. (2009). Addressing the underemployment of persons with disabilities: Recommendations for expanding organizational social responsibility. *Employee Responsibilities and Rights Journal, 21*(4), 305–318.

Norrgard, K. (2008). Human testing, the eugenics movement, and IRBs. *Nature Education, 1*(1), 170.

OECD. (2010). *Sickness, disability and work: Breaking the barriers.* OECD Publishing.

Parker, R., Szymanski, E., & Patterson, B. (2005). *Rehabilitation counseling: Basics and beyond* (4th ed.). PRO-ED.

Sherwyn, D., Eigen, Z., & Gilman, G. (2006). Retaliation: The fastest-growing discrimination claim. *Cornell Hotel and Restaurant Administration Quarterly, 47*(4), 350–358.

Szymanski, E., & Parker, R. (2005). *Work and disability: Issues and strategies in career development and job placement.* PRO-ED.

Treadway, W. (1925). Our immigration policy and the nation's mental health. *The Scientific Monthly, 21*(4), 347–354.

Unger, D. D. (1999). Workplace supports: A view from employers who have hired supported employees. *Focus on Autism and Other Developmental Disabilities, 14*(3), 167–179.

U.S. Department of Labor. (2014a). Employer engagement strategy: Workforce inclusion. [White paper.]. Author. https://www.dol.gov/odep/pdf/20140604Busin essCaseEngagementWhitePaper.pdf

U.S. Department of Labor. (2014b). Persons with a disability: Labor force characteristics–2013. [News release.]. http://www.bls.gov/news.release/disabl.nr0.htm

U.S. Department of Labor. (2017). *Youth labor force participation rate and unemployment.* https://www.dol.gov/odep/stats/index.html.

Ward, R. (1907). The new immigration act. *The North American Review, 185*(619), 587–593.

World Health Organization. (2011). *World report on disability.* http://www.who.int/disabilities/world_report/2011/report/en/

Yenlin, E. H. (1991). The recent history and immediate future of employment among persons with disabilities. In J. West (Ed.), *The Americans with Disabilities Act: From policy to practice* (pp. 129–149). Millbank Memorial Fund.

CHAPTER 9

Vocational Rehabilitation Systems

Judith L. Drew, PhD, CRC

Learning Objectives

As a result of reading this chapter, the student will be able to:

- Explain the important role legislation has played in the development and history of the state–federal vocational rehabilitation (VR) system.
- Describe the similarities and differences between the state–federal VR system and private-sector rehabilitation.
- Define the role and function of clinical rehabilitation counselors in VR systems.
- Understand the complexity and importance of the work rehabilitation counselors do to improve the lives of people with disabilities and the variety of settings in which they might work.

INTRODUCTION

Today's vocational rehabilitation (VR) systems were not created in a vacuum. They are the culmination of many years of federal legislation and the impact of the disability rights movement that created a level playing field for people with disabilities to have equal access to employment, education, and housing in order to maintain their independence. This chapter focuses on two primary VR systems that serve very different consumer populations and are settings that offer many opportunities for employment and professional growth for clinical rehabilitation counselors.

With the acceleration of industrialization in the United States in the early 20th century, the need for vocational rehabilitation was born. People working in the new industrial jobs of that era were getting injured at high rates, prompting the passage of the Federal Employees Worker's Compensation Act in 1916 that allowed injured workers to receive compensation and medical treatment due to work-related injuries (Weed & Field, 2001). The Smith-Fess Act of 1920 is the legislation that bolstered the rehabilitation counseling profession and the state–federal rehabilitation counseling programs.

Over the next 70 years, legislation followed that provided funding for vocational rehabilitation services to soldiers and other individuals with disabilities by widening the net from serving veterans with war-related injuries to civilians with a range of significant disabilities. The Social Security Act of 1935 created the initial vocational rehabilitation (VR) program as part of the Social Security system. The VR program has grown in terms of the number of people of all disabilities and ages supported through this legislation and the funding provided through government appropriations.

The passage of these laws and the subsequent funding demonstrated the intent of the federal government to assist individuals with disabilities to have equal access to employment and education and the opportunity to live independently (Weed & Field, 1989). At the same time, the disability rights movement was growing in its attempt to influence legislation. It experienced incremental successes through the passage of the Rehabilitation Act of 1973 and its protections against discrimination for individuals with disabilities in employment and their access to goods and services and transportation.

The current VR program is authorized under the Rehabilitation Act of 1973. It provides states with funds based on a formula that considers numerous factors, including performance outcomes. The federal government's share of funding is 78.7%. States are required to match this funding with a 21.3% contribution to total VR program expenditures (federal plus nonfederal). The Department of Education oversees the funding and distributes it as grants to the state agencies that administer the state–federal VR program. In fiscal year 2017, federal funding for the VR program was over $3 billion, according to the Government Accounting Office (GAO, 2018).

Due to the increased advocacy of individuals with disabilities, their families, nonprofit rehabilitation agencies, and congressional support created through prior laws, the Americans with Disabilities Act (1990) was passed. This law was relevant to state and private VR systems because it prohibits discrimination against people with disabilities and provides a three-pronged definition of disability. Two titles of the act are relevant to the work of clinical rehabilitation counselors in public and private rehabilitation systems related to employment and community integration. The act opened doors to employment and greater community independence for people living with disabilities. Title I of the ADA prohibits discrimination in employment practices; Title III mandates the removal of architectural and communication barriers.

The federal government further expanded its commitment to full employment opportunities for people with disabilities through the passage of the Workforce Investment Act (WIA) of 1998 and its replacement, the Workforce and Innovation Opportunities Act (WIOA) of 2014. Titles I and IV of the WIOA relate to the public VR system, specifically. Title I authorized programs to provide job search, education, and training activities for individuals seeking to gain or improve their employment prospects and established the One-Stop Career system. Title I programs are administered by the U.S. Department of Labor (DOL), primarily through its Employment and Training Administration and work closely with the public VR system to serve their consumers.

Title IV of the WIOA amended the Rehabilitation Act of 1973 by funding VR services for individuals with disabilities that primarily are related to employment and independent living. It required that the public VR system collaborate with the workforce system and DOL through increased cooperative activities.

From these legislative initiatives, an industry of public VR and nonprofit agencies arose that offer services, including vocational rehabilitation assessment and evaluation, competitive employment, and supported employment, that still exists today. The VR system of today is substantially different than the systems created in the 20th century. There is an increased emphasis on reducing the number of individuals with disabilities receiving federal subsidies and helping them become independent and productive members of society regardless of having a congenital or acquired disability (Weed & Field, 2001). Additionally, the WIOA authorized state VR agencies to provide services to employers, such as outreach and technical assistance; emphasized the goal of placing VR consumers in mainstream employment, where they have competitive wages and are integrated with employees without disabilities; and required the Department of Education (DOE) and the DOL to develop one or more performance measures assessing how well VR and certain other workforce programs serve employers.

The Types of Vocational Rehabilitation Systems

The VR systems that exist today are generally recognized as three distinct sectors in rehabilitation counseling: (1) public (state–federal), (2) private nonprofit, and (3) private for profit (Roessler et al., 2018). The focus of this chapter is on the state–federal and the private for-profit VR systems. Because private nonprofits operate on a model that closely aligns with the state–federal systems, which is a primary source of their income, they follow a similar model of counseling to the state agencies. Goodwin (1992) predicted the rise of private for-profit rehabilitation settings when he noted that specializations were developing within the field of rehabilitation counseling. These specializations were offering increased opportunities for employment for master's graduates and currently represent a large number of employers of rehabilitation counselors as state agencies are experiencing retirements and counselors leaving for private-sector opportunities (Rubin et al., 2018).

Public Rehabilitation

The state–federal VR program interlaces funding between the state and federally funded programs as required by federal law, as previously described. The VR system assists individuals with disabilities to choose, prepare for, obtain, and maintain employment.

According to the Bureau of Labor Statistics (BLS), in 2018 the average employment rate for people with disabilities who are able to work was 19.3%, compared to 66.3% for those without disabilities. Consequently, employment is considered the most desirable outcome of services provided through the public VR program. Across the nation, individuals with disabilities who apply for VR services are expected to be interested in becoming employed and are advised that employment is the focus of VR services during their initial meeting with their counselor.

In 2020, the federal VR program will be celebrating its 100th anniversary. The program has undergone numerous changes to meet the employment needs and challenges faced by individuals with disabilities and the demands of public policy. However, the purpose of the program has remained constant since its inception. Rubin and Roessler (2008) wrote that "the end goals of the vocational rehabilitation process for people with disabilities are placement in competitive employment, personal satisfaction with the placement, and satisfactory performance on the job" (p. 289).

Robinson (2014) opined that the role of the VR counselor is as a guide to help consumers reach their full potential. Based on the fundamental principle of the right to choose that is codified in the Rehabilitation Act of 1973, VR consumers have the right to participate in services of their choosing and to discontinue those services at any point during the process from the initial intake to termination.

In his seminal text *Total Rehabilitation*, Wright (1980) emphasized that VR's goal is to assist individuals with disabilities to achieve their highest level of functioning in their "personal, social, and vocational roles." His work laid a clear road map for the VR process and the measurement of successful outcomes. Rubin and Roessler (2008) described the VR process as comprising four phases: evaluation, planning, treatment, and termination. Although they describe the phases as being sequential, today's VR counselors recognize that these phases can be revisited many times as consumers try out jobs in a variety of work settings to determine the best fit for their abilities, interests, and the unique nature of their disability.

The VR program has been transformed because of changes in work environments and public policies and an increasingly diverse consumer population that reflects a wide variety of disabilities and cultures. Also, new and more effective interventions, such as assistive technology, help individuals with disabilities achieve quality employment outcomes of their choosing. As efforts increase to provide competitive integrated employment options for consumers, the move to improve the variety and quality of supported employment services and the development and implementation of customized employment service systems continues.

Consumer Statuses & VR Status Codes

With the passage of WIOA (2014), the former system of VR case statuses has been replaced with a different approach to tracking and reporting consumers' progress. This approach captures the increased complexity of the services the VR system is providing in conjunction with meeting consumers' choices in a flexible, timely, and cost-effective manner.

Within the context of evaluation, planning, treatment, and termination, are multiple layers of services that can be provided. VR counselors monitor and track the timely movement of their consumers through eligibility for services to assessment, employment, and post-employment services to ensure that consumers are progressing toward their employment goals.

Although the Federal Register identifies more than 100 status codes for case movement, these codes fall under nine general categories: Application, Eligibility, Determination of Order of Selection, Development of the Individual Plan for Employment, Job Services, Employment, Case Closure, Post-Employment Services, and Pre-ETS. Within each of these categories, the Rehabilitation Services Administration (RSA) has identified specific data under WIOA that must be used to track consumers' progress through the system (U.S. Department of Education, 2019).

Application, Eligibility Determination, and Order of Selection

Referrals for services can come from individual consumers, parents, physicians, school systems, and attorneys. After the initial application for services has been submitted, eligibility determination occurs. Consumers must meet the federal definition of disability to be eligible for VR services. They must have (1) a physical, intellectual, or emotional impairment that is a substantial barrier to employment; (2) require vocational rehabilitation services to prepare for, secure, retain, or regain employment; and (3) be able to benefit from VR services in terms of an employment outcome. If consumers are receiving Social Security Disability Insurance (SSDI) or Supplemental Security Income (SSI), they are deemed eligible for VR services by their state VR program. If consumers are not found eligible initially, the VR counselor gathers data from a variety of sources, such as the school system and treating physicians, to confirm a disability and determine if consumers meet the criteria for category I, II, or III services and assigns them a category for order of selection based on U.S. Department of Education Policy Directive RSA-PD-19-03.

The order of selection (OOS) is used by VR agencies to prioritize providing services to people with the most significant disabilities. The three categories for OOS are category I, which includes individuals who have the most significant disabilities. Their disability must seriously limit their functioning in more than one of the following six areas: mobility, communication, self-care, self-direction, interpersonal skills, work tolerance, or work skills. To qualify for this category, consumers must also need multiple VR services over an extended period of time in order to become employed and must have one or more physical or mental disabilities as described in RSA-PD-19-03.

Category II includes those consumers who have significant disabilities, which means their disability limits them in at least one of the areas listed above but may not need extensive VR services over a long period of time. Category III consumers are individuals who have disabilities, but they are not as significant as the other categories and do not require extensive VR services to achieve employment.

Individualized Plan for Employment (IPE)

Consumers and their VR counselor work together to develop an employment plan called the Individualized Plan for Employment (IPE). The IPE considers the individual's unique strengths, resources, priorities, concerns, skills, abilities, preferences, capabilities, interests, and values, as well as barriers to employment. It identifies the employment goal that the individual has chosen, the length of time expected to reach the goal, the services that the individual chooses as necessary to reach their goal, and how the services will be provided.

In some states, services may be provided directly by the VR counselor, while in other states services may be available through other public sources such as the One-Stop Career Centers. Also, other services may be purchased from nonprofit or for-profit private agencies with funds provided by the state VR agency. Consumers have the option to develop the IPE with the assistance of the VR counselor or another individual or to complete the plan themselves.

The VR counselor is always available to assist in this process, and a VR counselor who works for the public VR program must approve the IPE before any services are provided or funded through the VR agency. The partnership between consumers with a disability and their VR counselor is a key to success in this process. As consumers move through the various services to achieve their goal of employment, the VR counselor provides career counseling, assistance with adjustment to an acquired disability, disability case management, and coordination of evaluations and employment services (RSA-PD-19-03).

The IPE describes the rehabilitation goal, what rehabilitation services are needed, and the providers required to achieve the goal. Also, the IPE requires the beginning and ending date of the services and a description of the services; the secondary goals needed to achieve employment and the service providers required to achieve the goals; objective information gathered from the assessment to substantiate the employment goal; clarification of the responsibilities of all parties involved in the IPE; the consumer's opinion regarding the objectives and services; a date for a periodic review if it is an annual plan; and the signature of all parties involved in the development of the plan (RSA-PD-19-03).

Services in an IPE that VR counselors or other agencies might provide include the following: Pre-Employment Training and Services (Pre-ETS) for transition-age youth; diagnostic evaluations, including vocational assessment, diagnostic testing, and psychological or neuropsychological testing; counseling and guidance to help plan vocational goals and services; transition services from school to career; college or vocational training; job training and job supports; job development and placement services; rehabilitation technology services; assistive technology services; vehicle modifications; housing modifications; or post-employment services.

Evaluation and Assessment

The goals of the assessment phase are to help consumers understand their strengths and areas of need related to their vocational functioning and to learn more about career opportunities in the labor market and VR services and supports that can help improve their functioning (Rubin & Roessler, 2001). To help consumers achieve this goal, VR counselors need to have an understanding of the local labor market; job functions; accessible vocational training programs; and an understanding of potential accommodations, assistive technology, and other services that can help improve a consumer's performance on the job (Roessler et al., 2018; Rubin & Roessler, 2001).

The first step in the evaluation and assessment phase is the review of a consumer's medical and school records, followed by the initial interview, referring a consumer for medical or psychological evaluations (as needed), and a vocational evaluation to determine the consumer's level of academic achievement, interest, abilities and personality characteristics. Once this information is collected, VR counselors meet with their consumers to review the results of the assessments and to determine the next steps in the process. Rubin and Roessler (2008) note that in this process a consumer's functional capacity can be determined using the combination of the assessments and the initial interview with the consumer.

What is not often understood in this process is the specific competencies that are needed by the VR counselor. Farnsworth and colleagues (2015) researched these competencies and found that the vocational evaluation process requires that the VR counselor have the ability to conduct a comprehensive file review and diagnostic interview; perform psychometric testing; engage in behavioral observations during the initial interview; interpret the data; and provide career counseling services. According to Roessler and colleagues (2018), the information gathered from the evaluation process helps the counselor guide consumers toward appropriate career and employment options. Additionally, it helps clarify the options for employment services as part of the IPE. Robinson (2014) opined that "a well-researched, documented, and empirically supported vocational rehabilitation plan improves the probability of successfully obtaining competitive work" (p. 7).

At times, consumers are not able to progress to employment because they may need educational remediation, short-term training, on-the-job training, or retraining to gain employment and be competitive in the labor market. VR counselors, in collaboration with their consumers, explore these options to determine what their consumers' choice will be to enhance their employment prospects. Once consumers complete their training programs, the goal is to find and keep competitive employment.

Provision of Services and Employment Services

As noted previously, the IPE is tailored to meet the individual needs of consumers and to incorporate their choice through a process of informed decision making and career counseling. For transition-age youth between the ages of 14 and 21, there is Pre-ETS. These services give students who are still in high school opportunities for job exploration, job tryouts, and assessments at work sites that are funded by the VR office in their state. Additionally, once they leave high school and age out of the school system, they become eligible for adult services, including a full range of job placement and job development supports, such as provided through the federal On-the-Job Training (OJT) program.

The consumers' involvement in goal setting increases their self-knowledge, creates opportunities for choice in plan development, and increases their motivation to achieve their goals and take responsibility for their choices. For consumers with a work history, one service provided during the plan development is a transferrable skills analysis (TSA) to determine if a consumer has transferable skills to other employment (Rumrill & Koch, 2014; Wagner et al., 2016).

Factors to consider when conducting a TSA are the length of time consumers have been out of the work environment, whether their skills are outdated, whether they are marketable, and whether they have been impacted by the onset of a disability. Using a TSA is often one of the most effective and expedient ways of assisting someone to return to work because it is based on using the consumer's skills from prior employment (Rubin & Roessler, 2018).

Strauser (2013) and Gilbride and Stensrud (2003) noted that job placement support for consumers to achieve good employment outcomes requires two approaches. One is consumer centered, which they call job search, and the other is employer centered, which they term job development.

Within the VR system, there are numerous employment services and categories for types of employment. Placement in competitive employment in integrated settings, supported employment, self-employment, and small business ownership are options mandated by the WIOA and are recognized in the legislation as viable employment outcomes. The WIOA defines *competitive employment* as work that is performed on a full-time or part-time basis (including self-employment) and for which an individual is compensated at a rate that is not less than the labor rate specified in the federal Fair Labor Standards Act of 1938 or the rate required by state minimum wage law. The rate cannot be less than the usual rate paid by the employer for the same or similar work performed by other employees who are not individuals with disabilities and who have similar training, experience, and skills. Also, the worker must be eligible for the same level of benefits provided to other employees and needs to work at a location typically found in the community where the individual with the disability is interacting with non-disabled peers. This regulation was specifically included in the WIOA to eliminate the use of subminimum wage employment. The act mandated that sheltered workshops be eliminated by the end of 2016.

Roessler and Rubin (2018) encourage VR counselors to use a consumer-centered approach to support and prepare consumers for finding appropriate employment. Services such as interview preparation and how to complete a job application are associated with better employment outcomes.

Critical competencies for VR counselors who are actively engaged in job placement and development with consumers include a solid understanding of a variety of workplace modifications, such as job restructuring, modification of a work schedule or equipment, restructuring of the work area, use of new equipment or tools, or access to assistive technology for consumers with visual or hearing impairments, can make the difference in a consumer's successful employment outcome (Job Accommodation Network, 2020).

Within the context of the VR system, many consumers with significant disabilities benefit from working at supported employment sites. Like, competitive employment settings, supported employment is integrated into the workplace, but the work demands are less in terms of the number of hours per week the individual may work and often include modified job duties. Supported employment is employment in an integrated setting with ongoing support services for individuals with the most significant disabilities for whom integrated employment has not been successful and who require intensive supports on the job site (Rehabilitation Act Amendments, 1986).

Post-Employment Services

Post-employment services are applicable for competitive integrated employment as well as for supported employment. The goal of these services is to provide supports or interventions (as needed) to ensure a consumer's successful employment. Some consumers will require direct intervention and support with the employer, whereas others may need the long-term, follow-up services of a job coach.

Termination

In the VR system, termination can occur under several circumstances. Most frequently, it is when a case is closed or a consumer has successfully remained employed for a period of 90 days. Closure can also occur due to transfer of the case to another counselor or discontinuation of services at the request of the consumer or by the VR counselor for lack of progress.

Private For-Profit Rehabilitation

Simply put, private for-profit rehabilitation counselors provide rehabilitation services on a fee-for-service basis for public agencies, private nonprofit organizations, insurance carriers, attorneys, employers, and school systems (Rubin & Roessler, 2001). The rise of private-sector rehabilitation counseling was noted by Weed and Field (2001) and Rubin and Roessler (2001) who opined that the labor market for vocational experts was on the rise due to several factors: (1) increased demand due to nationwide legislation mandating vocational rehabilitation services in state workers' compensation; (2) the need of employers to manage their increasing disability costs by hiring vocational experts who could provide case management services to return injured workers to work; (3) the ability of private VR counselors to provide cost-effective and timely services; (4) the entry of rehabilitation counselors into the field; (5) the growth in the number of rehabilitation counselors who had business acumen and entrepreneurial abilities to establish their own practices and companies; and (6) the passage of federal legislation protecting the rights of people with disabilities such as the Rehabilitation Act of 1973, the ADA (1990), and the ADA Amendments (2008).

The question of who is a vocational expert and what a vocational expert does has been debated over the past 50 years. Barros-Bailey (2014) found that by the 1960s physicians and other professionals with credentials were identified in case law as testifying as vocational expert witnesses. The profession has matured since that time due to the establishment of the CRC (Certified Rehabilitation Counselor) credential along with the formation of ethical standards to address codes of conduct and behavioral expectations in private-sector rehabilitation. Also, the advent of the American Board of Vocational Experts (ABVE) led the way to establishing minimum educational standards for vocational experts who did not hold a master's degrees in rehabilitation counseling (McCroskey et al., 2007).

In order to define what vocational rehabilitation experts are and what they do, many role and function studies were commissioned by the Commission on Rehabilitation Counseling Certification (CRCC) to provide an understanding of the competencies needed by vocational experts given the diverse settings in which they may practice (Weed & Field, 2001). Barros-Bailey (2014) noted that since 2009 programs offering certificates in vocational expert work have developed across the country as part of graduate program studies in rehabilitation counseling. These programs are meeting a critical need for greater expertise in the skills and competencies required in private-sector work.

Over the past 20 years, demand has increased for vocational expert counseling, consultation, and testimony in over 16 practice areas, including age discrimination; complaints related to discrimination and the ADA, FMLA, and IDEA; expert work with the Jones Act, Longshore and Harbor Works Act, and Federal Employees Retirement Act; opportunities for vocational expert evaluation and testimony in employment law, marital dissolution, and rehabilitative alimony; case management in long-term disability; vocational expert consultation in pension funds, second injury funds, student loan defaults, and trust fund management; and service provision in employee assistance programs (EAPs; Barros-Bailey, 2014; Rubin & Roessler, 2001).

Overall, there are more similarities than differences between the two VR systems. However, in some areas there are important differences. For instance, the federal VR system is publicly funded, whereas private-sector rehabilitation is supported through fees for services or sometimes government contracts. Most federal VR counselors have a master's degree in rehabilitation counseling. In contrast, some professionals who work as vocational experts in private VR programs may have degrees in other disciplines, such as nursing or psychology, and may occasionally be physicians. The development of the ABVE organization and the creation of the CRC credential were instrumental in clarifying the minimum requirements needed to be considered a vocational expert (Barros-Bailey, 2014).

Weed and Field (2001) found that multiple research studies conducted in the 1970s and 1980s showed the similarities between the two systems in terms of interest in the employment of people with disabilities, having similar attitudes and goals, providing counseling and evaluation services, and developing and writing vocational plans. They opined that research showed both systems engage in similar activities but with a "different emphasis" (Weed & Field, 2001, p. 8).

In contrast, there is a clear difference between VR counselors in the federal system and private-sector VR counselors in terms of the consumers on their caseloads. Federal VR counselors work with a diversity of consumers representing all disabilities who often have severe disabilities (Weed & Field, 2001). In the 1960s and 1970s, private-sector VR counselors tended to provide vocational expert testimony for the Social Security Administration's (SSA) Office of Hearings and Appeals as federal contractors. Today, private-sector VR counselors continue to provide testimony for the SSA but also work with a wide range of individuals who have acquired disabilities through work-related injuries, medical malpractice and negligence, or catastrophic injuries requiring life care plans.

Another interesting difference are the systems themselves. The federal VR system is a bureaucracy that can be slower in responding to referrals and in the length of time it takes to become employed. Often, this is due to the severity of the disability of the consumers and the range of services needed to become employed. The private-sector system can provide services more fluidly, efficiently, and rapidly because most VR experts work for small companies that offer a full range of services or the experts are self-employed in private practice. The time from referral to initial contact and beginning to provide services is often significantly less than the federal VR system (Weed & Field, 2001).

The goal of VR within workers' compensation and other return-to-work programs differs from the federal VR system. The federal VR system's goal is to maximize the consumer's full potential through employment and independent living. The goal of VR in the private sector is to return an injured worker or person with an acquired disability to work in the most cost-effective, expeditious manner, along with returning the consumer to the preinjury wage level, when possible (Weed & Field, 2001). Additionally, private-sector VR places an emphasis on early intervention and provision of services while minimizing the functional limitations of the disability through therapeutic interventions such as occupational or physical therapy or assistive technology (Rubin & Roessler, 2001).

Another goal of the private sector is to reduce the disability-related costs to employers and to encourage workplace health and safety programs (Rubin & Roessler, 2001). In the 1980s implementing workplace health and safety and return-to-work programs developed into its own specialization known as the Certified Disability Management Specialist (CDMS). Private-sector VR counselors who hold this certification have specific training and competencies in implementing and managing return to work and wellness programs within businesses. They are considered the in-house experts in return to work within their companies (Weed & Field, 2001).

Matkin (1985) developed and Lynch and Lynch (1998) improved upon a proposed system that is now known as the vocational rehabilitation hierarchy that is used by employers, insurance companies, courts, and private-sector VR counselors as a model plan for assisting consumers to return to work. The seven-step hierarchy outlines the following process to return consumers to work: (1) return to work at the same job (at the time of injury) with the same employer; (2) return to work at the same job with the same employer with modified duties to accommodate the worker's functional limitations; (3) return to work at a different job with the same employer; (4) return to work at the same job with a new employer (with or without modifications); (5) return to work at the same job with a new employer (with or without on-the-job training) with the same or different employer; (6) return to work after a training or educational program (in this system, shorter training programs are desirable to help consumers reestablish their connection with employment sooner); and (7) self-employment. With self-employment there needs to be evidence that the consumer has the skills necessary to be successful. However, this option is rarely used given the cost of developing a business plan, the skills needed by consumers to be successful, and the high failure rate.

The hierarchy takes into consideration the residual functional capacity of the consumer and the consumer's level of vocational experience. Much like the work of federal VR counselors, knowledge of medical issues, impact of disability on the ability to work, and competencies in TSA and labor market knowledge are critical to success (Rubin & Roessler, 2001; Weed & Field, 2001).

Although the goal of private VR is to return an individual to work, workers' compensation laws vary from state to state. VR counselors who might consider this aspect of counseling are encouraged to explore the workers' compensation laws of their state to determine if VR services are mandated and how they are funded. Each state's information can be found on the National Federation of Independent Business's website.

There is a significant difference in caseloads between the two VR systems. Caseloads for public VR are well over 100 consumers at varying levels of services leading to employment. For private-sector VR counselors, a typical case load ranges from 25 to 40 consumers, depending on the complexity of the cases and the pace at which the consumers are working to return to work.

An area where there are strong similarities is in how the evaluation phase progresses and the range of services provided. In both systems evaluating the vocational potential of a consumer follows a similar path. This path includes assessment and testing to measure educational achievement, interests, and aptitudes and use of a TSA to determine transferable skills and consumer access to the labor market (Weed & Field, 2001). The TSA process is based on the Vocational Diagnosis and Assessment of Residual Employability (VDARE) using the U.S. Department of Labor's *Dictionary of Occupational Titles*.

Once the VR counselor has identified job options and associated wages for the job, a private-sector VR counselor may be called upon to testify about the placeability and employability of the consumer. In the world of private-sector VR, *placeability* is defined as the ability of persons with a disability to find a job in their local area that meets their abilities and capabilities given their disability (Weed & Field, 2001). In forensic VR, labor market access is related to a loss of earning potential as a result of analyzing pre- and post-injury wages. Assessing pre- and post-injury earnings may be done by federal VR counselors, but their use of this information as VR counselors typically relates to helping consumers understand what the pay and opportunities may be for jobs they are considering. It does not include court testimony.

The two systems also differ in their approaches to job placement and job development. The federal VR counselor often is less engaged in job placement and labor market surveys, whereas private-sector VR counselors are very engaged in determining the availability of work for their consumers and conducting labor market surveys to determine if there are jobs available in their consumers' local area that match their consumers' job choices (Weed & Field, 2001).

An additional difference between the two VR systems is that federal VR counselors are able to arrange for the consumer to receive basic medical and other diagnostic exams, whereas private-sector VR counselors must ensure that consumers attend medical exams and then provide follow-up coordination of services if requested by the referring party.

Unlike federal VR counselors, VR counselors in private-sector work face multiple barriers to returning consumers to work following an injury. According to Robinson (2014), major hurdles in having successful closures for employment in private-sector VR are the disincentives inherent in the compensation systems that are used to provide financial support to injured workers and other individuals with disabilities. Workers' compensation payments, SSDI, SSI, veterans' benefits, and long-term disability payments "discourage full participation in VR and result in poorer rehabilitation outcomes" (Drew et al., 2001, para. 1). Duta and colleagues (2008) reported that VR consumers who received cash and/or medical benefits had lower rates of employment than consumers who had no such financial supports.

Work Incentive Benefit Experts

A variety of work incentives are built into the federal and private-sector VR systems. Both systems offer opportunities for on-the-job training. Whereas the federal sector can provide this service directly, the private sector must go through the U.S. Department of Labor's One-Stop Career Centers. On-the-Job Training (OJT) is a federal program funded by WIOA (2014) that encourages employers to hire and train skilled workers and get reimbursed for their efforts. The Work Opportunity Tax Credit (WOTC) is another benefit available. It provides a federal tax credit to employers for hiring individuals from certain target groups (e.g., disabilities) who have consistently faced significant barriers to employment. The WOTC is currently authorized through December 31, 2020.

Benefits counseling is an innovative service first established in 1999 by the Ticket to Work legislation. It is a free service provided by the federal VR system to assist people with disabilities to go to work. Each state has its own benefits counselors who work along with the federal VR counselors to answer consumers' questions regarding the impact on their federal and state benefits. It can be another practice area for private-sector VR counselors to incorporate into their skills or another resource that can be used to encourage consumers to return to work after injury. Benefits counselors assist consumers in deciding whether to work, how to keep their necessary benefits while they work, and how to avoid work-benefits conflicts.

Rehabilitation Case Management

Rehabilitation counselors have diverse job roles and need a variety of skills to help people with disabilities improve their quality of life and find and keep employment. Case management is seen by some as the management of the entire caseload, whereas others view it as the management of individual cases (Rumrill & Koch, 2014). Case management competencies are needed in both VR systems but with different emphases. According to Roessler and Rubin (2018), case management tasks include conducting intake interviews, service coordination, maintaining case records, and providing reports of progress to referral sources.

In their description of caseload management, Chan and colleagues (1998) opined that in case management VR counselors have two contradictory goals: trying to increase access to services while at the same time limiting costs. Although this statement is primarily focused on public VR services, it can be true of private-sector VR case management services as well, especially in the pressured environment of vocational expert services and case coordination. Often, VR counselors in both systems report that they did not feel well prepared to fulfill this role (Chan, 2003).

Effective caseload management involves understanding the intake interview and planning process; providing counseling and planning services; and arranging, coordinating, and purchasing services, as needed (Roessler & Rubin, 2018). Providing placement services, monitoring the consumer's progress, and supervision of assistants who sometimes help with bill payments are additional demands on the federal and private-sector VR counselor's time. Dealing with the demands of managing large caseloads in the federal VR system can lead to counselor burnout (Frankel & Gelman, 2004). Consequently, federal VR counselors must learn how to effectively manage and allocate their time and resources to complete their caseload tasks (Roessler & Rubin, 2018).

Greenwood and Roessler (2018) discuss the benefits of effective time management through daily planning and the use of technology to track activities and to monitor completion of important daily tasks. Tools suggested range from low-tech to-do lists and a calendar to the use of scheduling software and delegating administrative tasks to case technicians for processing daily paperwork. The authors suggest reducing procrastination by setting reminders on the computer and breaking down the daily work into smaller, more manageable components.

Successful caseload management requires federal and private-sector VR counselors to establish an effective and consistent process for managing time, interviewing, counseling, and planning and coordinating services. The counselor engaging in regular, weekly evaluations of their consumers' progress to determine if their consumers' goals have been achieved is an important part of the process (Greenwood & Roessler, 2018).

SUMMARY

Federal and private-sector VR systems share many similarities but differ in their approaches to case management and the practice settings. There are opportunities in private-sector VR to develop skills in forensic expert testimony and vocational assessments, disability case management, and return-to-work programs, along with certification as a benefits counselor or disability case manager in private industry. Federal VR counselors work with more severely disabled consumers to help them achieve their potential and eventually go to work, whereas the goal of private-sector VR is to return consumers to work in the most expeditious, cost-effective manner. Private-sector VR counselors have smaller caseloads, whereas federal VR counselors can have over 100 consumers on their caseload at any time. Although there are differences, the goal of both sectors is to provide quality, effective services for people with disabilities that result in consumers finding and keeping gainful employment.

Case Study: Charlie

Charlie is a 42-year-old man who has major depression and obsessive-compulsive disorder (OCD) that have been well controlled through medication and behavioral interventions for many years. He has a 15-year history as a psychiatric RN in a hospital that specializes in treating individuals with significant mental illness that require short-term in-patient hospitalization. He has been a good employee throughout his 15 years with the hospital, always arriving to work early and taking great care in completing his nursing notes at the end of each shift. He prides himself on the accuracy of his work and especially in keeping track of and documenting the medications he has given patients. During a period when the hospital was short staffed, Charlie agreed to cover extra shifts, including overnights.

With the added shifts and overnights, Charlie's OCD became less controlled. He started leaving the hospital at the end of his shift and then returning to the ward within a few minutes to double check the medications he had given to his patients. This behavior escalated from doing this only once or twice a week at the end of every shift to returning three to four times at the end of each shift to double-check his work. His supervising nurse manager noticed his behavior, counseled him about it, but he was still not able to control his obsessive need to check his work multiple times at the end of his shifts. He was eventually terminated.

Charlie sought the help of his state VR agency to determine if he could go back to work at the only job he had held for any length of time. His VR counselor determined he was eligible for services and began to develop Charlie's IPE with him. Answer the following questions as if you are Charlie's VR counselor.

1. As Charlie's VR counselor, would you conduct a TSA, or would you refer him for a vocational assessment to determine his employability options? Provide a rationale for your answer.
2. What medical information would you like to gather to better understand Charlie's treatment for depression and OCD, and why?
3. How would you factor in Charlie's medical information that you have gathered into the counseling process to help Charlie consider his re-employment options?
4. In your opinion, is Charlie's mental health stability a requirement for re-employment? If so, why? If not, why not?
5. Consider the VR process outlined in this chapter. What are the steps you would develop with Charlie in his IPE?

Discussion Questions

1. What are the similarities and differences between the public VR system and private-sector rehabilitation services?
2. What are the keys to providing effective caseload management?
3. What do you think might be the biggest challenge of managing large caseloads of more than 100 consumers?
4. Compare how evaluations are conducted in the private-sector VR system versus the federal VR system. Which might be more effective in helping individuals find employment, and why?

REFERENCES

Barros-Bailey, M. (2014). History of forensic vocational rehabilitation. In R. Robinson (Ed.), *Foundation of forensic vocational rehabilitation* (pp. 13–31). Springer.

Bureau of Labor Statistics. (2018). *Occupational outlook handbook.* https://www.bls.gov/ooh/

Chan, F., Leahy, M., Chan, C., Hilburger, J., & Jones, J. (1998). Training needs of rehabilitation counselors in the emerging mental health/managed care environments. *Rehabilitation Education, 12*(4), 333–345.

Chan, T. (2003). *Recruiting and retaining professional staff in state VR agencies: Some preliminary findings from the RSA evaluation study.* American Institute for Research.

Drew, D., Drebing, C., VanOrmer, A., Loardo, M., Krebs, C., Penk, W., & Rosenheck, C. (2001). Effects of disability compensation on participation in and outcomes of vocational rehabilitation. *Psychiatric Services, 52*, 1479–1484. https://doi.org/10.1176/appi.ps.52.11.1479

Dutta, A., Gervey, R., Chan, F., Chou, C., & Ditchman, N. (2008). Vocational rehabilitation services and employment outcomes for people with disabilities: A United States Study. *Journal of Occupational Rehabilitation, 18*, 326. https://doi.org/10.1007/s10926-008-9154-z

Farnsworth, K., Field, J., Field, T., Griffin, S., Jayne, K., & Van de Bittener, G. (2005). *The quick desk reference for forensic rehabilitation consultants.* Elliot & Fitzpatrick.

Frankel, A., & Gelman, S. (2004). *Case management* (2nd ed.). Lyceum Press.

Gilbride, D., & Stensrud, R. (2003). Job placement and employer consulting: Services and strategies. In E. Syzmanski and R. Parker (Eds.), *Work and disability* (2nd ed.; pp. 407–440). PRO-ED.

Government Accountability Office. (2018). Vocational rehabilitation. GAO-15-77.

Greenwood, R., & Roessler, R. (2018). Systematic caseload management. In R. Roessler, S. Rubin, & P. Rumrill (Eds.), *Case management and rehabilitation counseling* (5th ed.; pp. 241–254). PRO-ED.

Job Accommodation Network. (2020). *Homepage.* https://askjan.org

Lynch, R. K., & Lynch, R. T. (1998). Rehabilitation counseling in the private sector. In E. Syzmanski and R. Parker (Eds.), *Rehabilitation counseling: Basics and beyond* (3rd ed.; pp. 71–105). PRO-ED.

Matkin, R. E. (1997). Public and private rehabilitation counseling practices. In D. R. Maki & T. F. Riggar (Eds.), *Rehabilitation counseling: Profession and practice* (pp. 139–150). Springer.

McCroskey, B. J., Mayer, L., Lageman, H., Lowe, J., Grimley, C., Graham, G. M., Dunn, P., Dennis, K., & Streaters, S. (2007). The American Board of Vocational Experts National Certification Examination. *Journal of Forensic Vocational Analysis, 10*(1), 7–60.

National Federation of Independent Business. (2017, June 7). *Workers' compensation laws—state by state comparison.* https://www.nfib.com/content/legal-compliance/le/gal/workers-compensation-laws-state-by-state-comparison-57181/

Robinson, R. (2014). *Foundations of forensic vocational rehabilitation.* Springer.

Roessler, R., Rubin, S., & Rumrill, P. (2018). *Case management and rehabilitation counseling.* PRO-ED.

Rubin, S., & Roessler, R. (2008). *Foundations of the Vocational Rehabilitation Process* (6th ed). Pro-ed.

Rubin, S., Roessler, R., & Rumrill, P. (2018). *Foundations of the vocational rehabilitation process* (7th ed.). PRO-ED.

Rumrill, P., & Koch, L. (2014). Vocational rehabilitation counseling. In P. Hartung, M. Savickas, & B. Walsh (Eds.), *Handbook of career intervention* (pp. 139–155). American Psychological Association.

Strauser, D. (2013). *Career development, employment, and disability in rehabilitation.* Springer.

U.S. Department of Education. (n.d.). *Vocational rehabilitation state grants.* https://www2.ed.gov/programs/rsabvrs/index.html

U.S. Department of Education. (2019). Rehabilitation Services Administration, Policy Directive, RSA PD-19-03.

Wagner, S., Wessel, J., & Harder, H. (2016). Workers perspectives on vocational rehabilitation services. *Rehabilitation Counseling Bulletin, 55*, 46–61. https://doi.org/10.1177/0034355211418250

Weed, R., & Field, T. (1989). *The rehabilitation consultant's handbook* (1st ed.). Elliott & Fitzpatrick.

Weed, R., & Field, T. (2001). *The rehabilitation consultant's handbook* (3rd ed.). Elliott & Fitzpatrick.

Wright, G. N. (1980). *Total rehabilitation.* Little, Brown & Company.

CHAPTER 10

Assessment

Mona Robinson, PhD, LPCC-S, LSW, CRC
Denise Lewis, PhD, LPC, NCC

Learning Objectives

As a result of reading this chapter, the student will be able to:

- Explain the various categories of assessment tools and their appropriate use.
- Discuss how race, ethnicity, disability, age, gender, language, and other cultural factors should be considered when using assessments.
- Identify who can administer the various types of assessments.
- Articulate how to administer, interpret, and report the results of assessments in a culturally and ethically responsible manner.

INTRODUCTION

We begin this chapter by providing students with a working knowledge of psychological tests and other assessments (terms that are often used interchangeably). Psychological tests consist of numerous published and unpublished research instruments. Insurance companies as well as educational and occupational settings often require an initial assessment with some form of standardized test being conducted that is based on scientific data (Wright, 2014).

Two major types of tests and assessments are discussed in this chapter. The first type is psychological assessments that allow practitioners to evaluate consumer's traits, characteristics, preferences, personality, and cognitive skills and abilities. The second type is educational achievement tests that measure what content a student has already learned or mastered and is concerned with teaching and learning outcomes (Whiston, 2016; Wright, 2014).

Of particular interest in this chapter are the four distinct areas of assessment: (1) intelligence tests that measure an individual's level of intelligence and cognitive ability and can assist in evaluating intellectual disabilities or intellectual acuity; (2) aptitude tests that are used to determine an individual's skill or ability, assessing how they perform in an area in which they have no prior training or knowledge; (3) achievement tests that assess previous knowledge and are restricted to a specific subject or area of knowledge and are usually applied when a grade or level of study has been completed; and (4) interest tests that can assist one in identifying careers that address their level of interest and can provide guidance with occupational focus. In addition, several subcategories will be discussed, including behavioral, personality, and substance abuse screening tools. Counselors should understand that psychological testing and clinical evaluations require a greater depth of knowledge regarding the use of test data in the diagnostic process (Groth-Marnat, 2009; Whiston, 2016). Clinical interviews and other data sources, such as medical records, social history, educational records, employment data, and other alternative methods, should be considered along with the standardized test information.

Race, ethnicity, disability, age, gender, language, and other cultural factors that were not commonly considered when assessments were normed can result in lower test scores. Hence, test scores should not be used as the sole indicator when making decisions that can ultimately have lifelong consequences for consumers. Finally, counselors should exercise culturally relevant and ethical decision making when administering psychological assessment instruments while being mindful of potential forms of bias that may be present in interpretation (American Counseling Association [ACA], 2014; Commission on Rehabilitation Counselor Certification [CRCC], 2017; Remley & Herlihy, 2016; Whiston, 2016; Wright, 2014).

Test Administrator Qualifications

Before tests are administered it is important to have a good understanding of the qualifications that practitioners should possess. The ethical codes of both the Commission on Rehabilitation Counselor Certification (CRCC) and the American Counseling Association (ACA) elucidate the importance of meeting the training requirements associated with the appropriate areas of assessment being administered (ACA, 2014; CRCC, 2017). Historically, there are three levels of training that students should be familiar with: Level A, Level B, and Level C. More recently, Pearson Assessment, a large test publishing company, added a Level M qualification to account for medical providers in the field of psychiatry and neurology to administer clinical assessments consistent with their areas of expertise (Wright, 2014).

Level A requires practitioners to have an ethical use for administering the assessment. No specialized education in testing and assessment is necessary. Examples of such users include research assistants, vocational rehabilitation counselors, and admissions counselors who may work in schools, hospitals, and counseling centers (Wright, 2014). Examples of Level A tests include aptitude tests such as the ACT/SAT, GRE, and self-directed job search inventories.

Level B requires a master's degree in counseling, education, or psychology. Assessors should have advanced training in measurement statistics, reliability, and validity. Practitioners should be knowledgeable of the reliability and validity of the chosen instrument. Members of professional organizations can qualify to administer some of the tests if they are well qualified and trained in test administration and interpretation (Whiston, 2016; Wright, 2014). Examples of Level B tests include interest assessments, attention-deficit disorder scales, occupational preferences such as career inventories, preschool developmental assessments, achievement tests such as the Peabody Individual Achievement Test, and personality assessments such as the Myers-Briggs.

Level C requires practitioners to be highly educated; typically holding a doctoral degree in counseling, clinical rehabilitation counseling, rehabilitation psychology, clinical psychology, developmental psychology, and educational or school psychology. Practitioners should also hold advanced licensure from a state agency and be a member of professional organizations such as the ACA, American Psychological Association (APA), or the CRCC. Adherence to professional codes of ethics relative to education and training of those using C-level tests is imperative (Whiston, 2016; Wright, 2014). Examples of Level C tests include personality tests, such as the Millon Adolescent Personality Inventory (MAPI) and the Minnesota Multiphasic Personality Inventory (MMPI), and intelligence tests, such as the Stanford-Binet Intelligence Test.

The Assessment Process

During the assessment phase, rehabilitation counselors assist their consumers in understanding their strengths as well as areas that may require improvement as it relates to their vocational functioning. Rehabilitation counselors also help their consumers access information about careers, the labor market, and vocational rehabilitation resources that can aid in improving their overall functioning and quality of life (Rubin & Roessler, 2001). In order to assist consumers, rehabilitation counselors must be knowledgeable of the local and national economy, job requirements, reasonable accommodations, assistive technology, and other services that can increase their consumers likelihood of success in employment and training (Roessler et al., 2018; Rubin & Roessler, 2001).

During the initial intake, clinical rehabilitation counselors review all relevant medical and school records followed by the initial interview. Conducting a mental health status examination is also appropriate at this juncture. A decision is then made to determine whether the consumer should be referred for further medical or psychological evaluations. A vocational evaluation may be deemed necessary to determine the consumer's level of academic achievement, interest, abilities, and personality characteristics. Generally, the counselor will meet with the consumer again once all diagnostic information has been reviewed and a report is written. The information contained in the formal assessment report is used to plan the next steps in the process (Rubin & Roessler, 2008).

Farnsworth and colleagues (2015) reported that counselors should demonstrate competencies during the vocational evaluation process, such as having the ability to conduct a comprehensive file review and diagnostic interview; perform psychometric testing; engage in behavioral observations during the initial interview; interpret the data; and provide career counseling services. Roessler and colleagues (2018) further posited that the information gathered from the evaluation process helps the counselor guide consumers toward appropriate career and employment options.

Key Statistical Terms

The following terms are often used with regard to testing and assessment:

- *Reliability* is the consistency, dependability, and stability regarding an outcome score from an assessment. This means that if the test was repeated several times, the same score would be achieved as a result.

Variance in test scores can be attributed to factors such as the environment and the test taker's health and motivation. Reliability can also be attributed to the actual test and/or items on the tests (Balkin & Juhnke, 2018; Wright, 2014).

- *Validity* is whether the test is valid; that is, whether the test measures what it claims to measure.
- *Criterion validity* is a measure of fidelity and documents whether a particular measure is valid, employing correlations to determine the degree of agreement between the test score and another known criterion (Wright, 2014).
- *Concurrent validity* is a form of criterion validity. It is a measure that can be established by referencing scores from another measure or standard that is expressed as a correlation. If there is a high degree of correlation, then the measure has a degree of fidelity with the accepted measures of the domain (Wright, 2014).
- *Predictive validity* is a form of concurrent validity that determines if there is a direct observational assessment of the dimension; for example, whether there is a correlation between GRE scores and performance during the first year in a graduate program. In other words, the correlation between the criterion of graduate school success and the predictor, the GRE (Wright, 2014).
- *Construct validity* is an important type of validity. "Many authors of psychological assessment use an array of other related measures to document a new instrument's validity. This process of using multiple measures is central to establishing construct validity, an important conceptualization of validity needed in the development of new psychological assessments" (Wright, 2014, p. 346).
- *Discriminate validity* is a reflection of whether "elements of the new construct's measurements have low correlation with other constructs" (Wright, 2014, p. 347).
- *Convergent validity* reflects whether the correlations between new constructs actually correlate (Wright, 2014).
- *Content validity* is a measure of content being assessed with multiple test items. Content validity is particularly used in assessments such as achievement tests, admissions test and licensing examinations" (Wright, 2014, p.). Attention should be given to ensuring that the measurement is aligned with the course content and that the assessment of the student's learning should go beyond skills learned from textbook knowledge and include practicum and laboratory experiences (Wright, 2014).

Common Types of Assessments

The following are some of the types of assessments clinical rehabilitation counselors will encounter in their practice:

- *Achievement assessments* measure what content a student has already learned or mastered. Achievement tests assess previous knowledge and are restricted to a specific subject or area of knowledge and are usually applied when a grade or level of study has finished. They are generally used to assess subjects such as math, reading, and spelling (Balkin & Juhnke, 2018; Whiston, 2016).
- *Aptitude assessments* measure a student's potential or ability to learn. Aptitude is a prediction or forecast of future performance. An aptitude test is used to determine an individual's skill or ability, assessing how they perform in an area in which they have no prior training or knowledge. The concept behind these tests is that each test question has only one correct answer, and everyone can correctly solve all the test questions. This ability is considered independent of learning, past experience, and education (Balkin & Juhnke, 2018; Whiston, 2016).

- *Interest assessments* identify an individual's career interests and addresses their level of significance. This can be used to provide guidance with occupational focus. While many components of interest have been proposed, three major components have been identified most often: personality, motivation or drive, and self-concept. The two most widely cited determinants of interest are nurture, which emphasizes socialization and learning, and nature, which emphasizes genetics and the heritability of interests (Hansen, 2004).
- *Behavioral assessments* identify environmental factors that induce and maintain problem behaviors. This is generally conducted for students with disabilities engaging in challenging behaviors in the school setting. For example, the Functional Behavioral Assessment (FBA) requires the test taker to think beyond customary reactions to behavioral problems in schools and challenges them to develop a problem-solving format geared to addressing the cause of the challenging behavior (Albert, 2020).
- *Intelligence assessments* measure a person's level of intelligence and cognitive ability. These tests typically measure a broad range of cognitive functions involving verbal and nonverbal abilities (Haier, 2017) through a battery of tests that focus on four domains of intelligence: verbal comprehension, perceptual reasoning, working memory, and processing speed. Since their inception in the early 1900s, these assessments have become one of the primary tools for identifying children with mental retardation and learning disabilities (Benson, 2003).
- *Personality assessments* describe an individual's personality, including what they are like and how they are likely to think. They examine the characteristics that define the nature and disposition of an individual. Evaluating the nature of a person and their disposition to conduct themselves in certain ways can be used to examine differences in response style. This can help practitioners reach relevant conclusions and make useful recommendations in a wide range of clinical applications (Weiner & Green, 2017).
- *Substance abuse assessments* can be used to identify adolescents and adults likely to have a substance abuse disorder. Substance use is any consumption of alcohol or drugs. Substance use may not be a problem or lead to abuse or dependency in some people. Substance abuse is when someone continues to use drugs or alcohol even when it causes problems, such as trouble with work, family, or their health (Hart & Ksir, 2018).

Assessments by Setting and Type

Assessment and Clinical Interview Considerations

Assessment is a process for defining the nature of a problem, determining a diagnosis, and developing specific treatment recommendations for addressing the problem or diagnosis. Regardless of the type of assessment or screening tool being utilized, in order to achieve the best results, assessments and screening tools should be used as a part of the diagnostic process that includes conducting a clinical interview, mental status examination, and biopsychosocial interview, when appropriate.

Care should be exercised to ensure that the assessments under consideration for use are reliable and valid. Most publishers include these measurement data with the general information about the assessments so that clinicians can make the most appropriate choices when selecting instruments. Using tests with the appropriate validity and reliability is essential to the assessment process. Even when an assessment is valid and reliable, the use of other methods of assessment are necessary due to inherent test bias. For example, if a school is using assessment scores to assist a child in getting needed resources that cannot be accessed otherwise, the assessment would be appropriate, but the use of the assessment might also be viewed as harmful if it identifies a high number of minority students (including those with disabilities and language barriers) as needing extra support and thereby overwhelming the system. Thus, having information about the pros and cons of the assessment is necessary to ensure that the best decisions are made on behalf of the consumer. This includes information about unintended side effects and any ramifications of using the assessment or test (Wright, 2014).

Test Bias and Cultural and Ethical Considerations

Test bias often occurs because the tests were not normed on the populations that are being assessed. Test developers continue to try to make improvements as tests are upgraded by including samples from underrepresented populations. While progress continues in this area, most assessments and tests in use do not have minority group representation. This signifies the need for clinicians to use alternate methods of assessment to account for cultural differences. Clinicians should adhere to their respective codes of ethics to ensure they are following best practices.

Interpreting Assessments and Reporting Results

Most assessments can be conducted using paper and pencil or by computer. Specific details are included in the technical manual that accompany these tests to ensure that the assessments are being used appropriately. Manuals also provide information regarding the validity and reliability of the instrument.

Administration, interpretation, and reporting of results should be done in an ethical manner. Clinicians should adhere to four principles of ethical practice with regard to interpretation and reporting of results. The first principle is related to communicating with the test taker. Test takers should be informed about how long the test results will be kept on file. The second principle is confidentiality; test takers should be informed about who has access to their information. The third principle is related to interpretation of the test scores. Consumers should be informed about their test scores in an understandable manner free of psychological jargon. The fourth and final principle is also related to interpretation. Clinicians should never use a single score in isolation but rather use the scores in conjunction with other data sources (Joint Commission on Testing Practices, 2005).

Educational Assessment: WRAT5 Achievement Tests

The Wide Range Achievement Test, Fifth Edition (WRAT5) was published in 2017 and is an accurate and easy-to-administer way to assess reading, spelling, and math skills and identify possible learning disabilities. The WRAT5 is appropriate for individuals ages 5 to 85+. The test can be administered in approximately 15 to 25 minutes for those aged 5 to 7 years and 35 to 45 minutes for those ages 8 and up. The WRAT5 has been upgraded with data reflecting current populations based on recent census. The updates include improved identification of learning disabilities; digital administration, scoring, and reporting; and subtest improvements. The WRAT5 provides derived scores and interpretive information for four subtests: word reading, sentence comprehension, spelling, and math computation. Cronbach's alpha values for the subtests and composite range from the upper 0.08 to 0.09. Results of validity and reliability studies are reported in the manual. The test can be administered by persons with Level B qualifications. For more on the WRAT5, see https://www.pearsonassessments.com/WRAT5.

Vocational Assessment: ASVAB Aptitude Test

The Armed Services Vocational Aptitude Battery (ASVAB) is a multiple-choice test that helps users identify which Army jobs (Military Occupational Specialties) they would be best suited for. The ASVAB is administered by the United States Military Entrance Processing Command and is used to determine qualification for enlistment in the United States Armed Forces. ASVAB scores are used to determine if someone is qualified to enlist in the military and to assign them to an appropriate job in the military. While most ASVAB testing is conducted at a Military Entrance Processing Station (MEPS), the test can be taken at an ASVAB satellite location, known as a Military Entrance Test (MET) site if there is no MEPS in the applicant's area. The ASVAB is administered by computer at all MEPS and by paper and pencil at most MET sites. Regardless of whether the test is taken by computer or paper and pencil, the scores should be very similar.

The ASVAB tests are designed to measure aptitudes in four domains: verbal, math, science and technical, and spatial. ASVAB, the Armed Forces Qualifying Test (AFQT), covers the following areas: general science, arithmetic reasoning, word knowledge, paragraph comprehension, mathematics knowledge, electronics information, auto information, shop information, mechanical comprehension, and assembling objects.

The computerized ASVAB, called the CAT-ASVAB, is an adaptive test, which means that the test adapts to the examinee's ability level. The computer software selects items that are suitable based on responses to earlier items in the test. Because the CAT-ASVAB is targeted toward ability level, it is possible to administer a shorter test than is used in the paper-and-pencil administration. The average applicant takes about 1.5 hours to complete the CAT-ASVAB. The paper-and-pencil ASVAB, called the P&P-ASVAB, is a traditional test, which means that everyone takes the same set of questions at the same pace. In all, it takes about 3 hours to complete the P&P-ASVAB.

AFQT scores are reported as percentiles between 1 and 99. An AFQT percentile score indicates the percentage of examinees in a reference group who scored at or below that particular score. For current AFQT scores, the reference group is a sample of 18 to 23 year olds who took the ASVAB as part of a national norming study conducted in 1997. Thus, an AFQT score of 62 indicates that someone scored as well as or better than 62% of the nationally representative sample of 18 to 23 year olds. The test can be administered by persons with Level A qualifications. For more information on ASVAB testing, see www.Official-ASVAB.com.

Interest Test: Strong Interest Inventory

The Strong Interest Inventory was developed based on the work of John Holland, who believed that people desire to work in environments where they are best able to use their skills and abilities. Workplace selection is based on seeking environments that best match their personality and where they can be around others who are most like them. This enables them to be more successful and satisfied in their career choice.

The first Strong Interest Inventory was developed in 1927 and was based on studying the occupational interests of men and women. After several revisions, the most recent occurring in 2004, it is considered to be the most well-investigated and universal interest inventory. While the test received an overhaul in 2004, the Occupational Scales received a more recent revision in 2012, allowing for a more accurate representation of the general population's interests.

The Strong Interest Inventory is an assessment that helps match people's interests with potential educational, career, and leisure activities, using their preferences in a variety of areas to aid them in discovering what they would most enjoy doing with their work. Each career option and college major category has a set of interest themes associated with them. This inventory is designed to help people identify their work personality by exploring their interests in six domains: realistic, artistic, investigative, social, enterprising, and conventional (commonly referred to as RIASEC). It then breaks the RIASEC into 30 specific areas of interest that can be directly related to fields of study, careers, and leisure activities. Additionally, it describes an individual's personal style preferences in five work areas: work style, learning environment, team orientation, leadership style, and risk taking. Upon completion of the test, it ranks the individual's top 5 to 10 most compatible occupations from a list of 260 specific jobs. This information can be used by test interpreters and individuals to provide a picture of where a person's interests lie and which jobs or school majors would be most gratifying. The test can be administered by persons with Level B qualifications. For more on the Strong Interest Inventory, see https://careerassessmentsite.com/tests/strong-tests/about-the-strong-interest-inventory/.

Behavioral Tests: Functional Behavioral Assessment

A Functional Behavioral Assessment is required by federal law under the Individuals with Disabilities Education Improvement Act (2004). A Functional Behavioral Assessment uses measures to examine a student's behavior in order to understand what is behind any behavioral challenges that impact the student's functioning in the educational setting.

The Functional Behavior Assessment uses three measures to identify environmental factors that may be maintaining challenging behavior: indirect assessments, descriptive analysis, and functional analysis. Indirect assessments gather information from any source that is not a direct interview with the individual. This can include information gathered from interviews, checklists, and rating scales. Descriptive analysis includes the direct observation of the student in their natural environment. The descriptive analysis is the most objective of the three measures because it involves direct observation and exploration of the student's behaviors. Functional analysis involves creating an environment where various behavioral hypotheses can be evaluated.

Once the test is administered, the results are evaluated by a behavioral support team, which can include teachers, parents, psychologists, and counselors. This team works together to create a behavioral intervention plan (BIP) that describes the environmental changes that will need to take place to encourage necessary modifications to reduce the student's undesirable behaviors. The effective demonstration of a behavioral support plan should be validated in the level of instruction, curriculum, and other positive aspects of the school routine for students. The Functional Behavioral Assessment is used with students between the ages of 3 and 21 years. The test can be administered by persons with Level B qualifications.

Psychological Assessments: Intelligence & Achievement Tests

WAIS-IV

David Wechsler developed the Wechsler-Bellevue Intelligence Scale, a battery of verbal and nonverbal subtests to measure intelligence, in 1939 (Lichtenberger & Kaufman, 2012). After a number of revisions, the Wechsler Adult Intelligence Scale, Fourth Edition (WAIS-IV) was published in 2008. The WAIS-IV is considered the most advanced measure of adult cognitive ability in use today.

The structure of the WAIS-IV is more reflective of current cognitive ability theory and divides the scores into four specific domains: verbal, perceptual, working memory, and processing speed. The core battery of tests consists of 10 subtests that yield the Full Scale Intelligence Quotient (FSIQ) and four index scores. Five supplemental subtests are available that may be substituted for the core subtests or administered by the administrator to gain additional information.

The WAIS-IV is appropriate for individuals between the ages of 16 and 90 and can be administered online or as a paper-and-pencil test. This test can be administered with Level C qualifications. To learn more about WAIS-IV, see https://www.pearsonassessments.com/content/dam/school/global/clinical/us/assets/wais-iv/wais-iv-brochure.pdf.

Myers-Briggs Type Indicator

The Myers-Briggs Type Indicator (MBTI) is the most popular personality assessment tool and is considered the foundation for individual development. It is used to evaluate a person's psychological penchants to help them to identify their strengths and preferences, interests, and happiness. The MBTI was based on the work of Carl Jung, who identified psychological types theories that described how people are innately different both in terms of how they perceive and take in information and how they make decisions (Jafrani et al., 2017).

The MBTI was developed in the 1940s by Isabel Briggs Myers based on original research. The essence of the theory behind the MBTI is that much of the seemingly random variation in people's behavior is actually quite orderly and consistent due to basic differences in the ways individuals prefer to use their perception and judgment.

The MBTI is a paper-and-pencil self-report that is composed of 94 forced-choice items that yield scores on eight factors as well as four dimensions: Introversion–Extraversion, Sensation–Intuition, Thinking–Feeling, and Judging–Perceiving. Respondents are classified into one of 16 personality types based on the largest score obtained for each bipolar scale. The four-letter MBTI-type formula is a shorthand for how a person's four mental dimensions interact and which ones they prefer to use first. This is called type dynamics, and it is an important part of understanding the MBTI results. The test can be administered by persons with Level B qualifications. For more on the MTBI, see https://www.myersbriggs.org.

Substance Abuse Screening Tools

Adult Substance Abuse Subtle Screening Inventory, Fourth Edition (SASSI-4) was published in 2016 and is a screening tool used to determine whether a person needs a substance abuse assessment. *Substance abuse* refers to the harmful or hazardous use of psychoactive substances, including alcohol and illicit drugs. Substance use is any consumption of alcohol or drugs. *Substance use* may not be a problem or lead to abuse or dependency in some people. However, substance abuse is when someone continues to use drugs or alcohol even when it causes problems, such as trouble with work, family, or their health. Therefore, screenings such as the SASSI-4 and other screening tools are useful in determining if further services are necessary.

The SASSI-4 identifies the probability of a person having a substance use disorder and includes a prescription drug scale that identifies individuals likely to be abusing prescription medications. It also provides a measure of profile validity and clinical insight into the person's level of defensiveness and willingness to acknowledge experienced consequences of substance use disorder. SASSI-4 identifies individuals who have a high probability of being diagnosed with any type of substance use disorder, including alcohol. It is not a measure of the use of controlled substances. The test is appropriate for adults aged 18 years and older. An adolescent form is available for use with 12 to 18 year olds (SASSI-A2).

The SASSI-4 can be administered in either an individual or group setting and is usually conducted using paper and pencil. The test requires a fourth- to fifth-grade reading level and takes 15 minutes to administer and score. The SASSI-4 has an accuracy rating of 92% based on empirical studies. The test–retest stability coefficients for the SASSI-4 scale scores range from .78 to .99. The test can be administered by persons with Level B qualifications. For more on the SASSI-4, see https://sassi.com/sassi-4/.

SUMMARY

The importance of clinical rehabilitation counselors possessing the knowledge and skills to select, administer, and interpret pertinent assessments cannot be overstated. This chapter provided information on a variety of assessments that counselors should be knowledgeable of when working with their consumers, whether they are in a role where they actually conduct the assessment or refer their consumers to external evaluators. The results of assessments are used to guide future planning to increase the consumer's likelihood of success.

Test bias has long been documented regarding the use of standardized tests. This is due in large part to the fact that most commonly used assessments were normed on the White dominant male culture, without consideration for those from diverse backgrounds. As a result, persons who come from marginalized and underrepresented populations often tend to fare worse on standardized assessments (Balkin & Juhnke, 2018; Groth-Marnat, 2009). Thus, attention should be given to utilizing alternative methods of assessment when gathering information during the diagnostic process. Counselors should be familiar with instruments related to the assessment of personality, psychological conditions, career interests, and academic achievement.

People with varying mental and physical conditions often benefit from evaluations to help determine the most appropriate treatment plan or rehabilitation plan. Hence, counselors must be sensitive to cultural factors and conduct clinical interviews, psychosocial histories, and gather other materials to use in conjunction with assessment tools during the diagnostic process. Counselors should be cognizant of the fact that some people may not score well on standardized tests and that the scores are not always indicative of their actual capabilities. Therefore, it is imperative that counselors are knowledgeable of the process for selecting, administering, and interpreting assessments in an ethical and culturally relevant manner (ACA, 2014; CRCC, 2017; Remley & Herlihy, 2016; Wright, 2014).

Case Study: David

David is a 39-year-old White male who sustained an industrial injury while working as a custodian. His duties consisted of cleaning manufacturing plants, where he was responsible for lifting up to 50 pounds daily. David received his injuries when he was lifting a heavy object, during which time he felt his back "pull." David's diagnoses include protruding disc L5–S1, lumbosacral sprain, generalized anxiety disorder, depressive disorder, failed back syndrome/post-laminectomy syndrome lumbar, protruding disc L4–L5, and L5 radiculopathy lumbar. David sought treatment for anxiety and depression and is currently seeing a licensed professional counselor twice a month for counseling. Additionally, David is being prescribed medication for treatment of his depression by his physician of record for his physical conditions. David's school records indicate that he attended high school and was in special education classes from the 6th through 12th grade. He graduated with a Diploma of Completion. David's grades indicate that he performed well below average for his grade level throughout junior high and high school. David's past work history consists of working as an industrial cleaner (custodian) for 20 years. He is currently receiving workers' compensation benefits but was recently told his benefits will be ending. David is afraid he will lose his home if he doesn't have an income. He cannot return to his previous job and states, "I'm not college material." David has begun drinking on a daily basis and reported that his wife is threatening to leave him.

1. Identify three assessments that could be utilized in the case of David. Explain how and why you would utilize these assessments in David's case.

Discussion Questions

1. Discuss potential forms of bias that may be present when interpreting psychological evaluations. How should these issues be addressed?
2. Identify at least two types of assessments and discuss what they are used for.
3. Describe what other diagnostic information should be utilized when administering assessments. Why is this important?
4. Describe how a behavioral assessment can be used to facilitate positive behavioral changes in the school setting.
5. Discuss the three levels of test administrator qualifications and identify one test that can be administered by each.

REFERENCES

Albert, M. (2020). Functional behavioral assessment: Putting the function into functional behavioral assessments. *Ed.D. Dissertations, 420*, 1.

American Counseling Association. (2014). *ACA code of ethics.* https://www.counseling.org/Resources/aca-code-of-ethics.pdf

Balkin, R. S., & Juhnke, G. A. (2018). *Assessment in counseling: Practice and application.* Oxford University Press.

Benson, E. (2003). Intelligent intelligence testing. *Monitor on Psychology, 34*(2), 48.

Commission on Rehabilitation Counselor Certification (CRCC). (2017). *Code of professional ethics for rehabilitation counselors.* https://www.crccertification.com/code-of-ethics-3

Farnsworth, K., Field, J., Field, T., Griffin, S., Jayne, K., & Van de Bittener, G. (2005). *The quick desk reference for forensic rehabilitation consultants.* Elliott & Fitzpatrick.

Groth-Marnat, G. (2009). *Handbook of psychological assessment* (5th ed.). John Wiley & Sons.

Haier, R. J. (2017). Efficiency and the ability to integrate information. *The Neuroscience of Intelligence, 62*(19), Article 4.

Hansen, J. C. (2004). Assessment of interests. In S. D. Brown & R. W. Lent (Eds.), *Career development and counseling: Putting theory and research to work* (pp. 281–304). John Wiley & Sons.

Hart, C., & Ksir, C. (2018). *Drugs, society and human behavior* (17th ed.). McGraw-Hill Education.

Jafrani, S., Zehra, N., Zehra, M., Ali, S. M. A., Mohsin, S. A. A., & Azhar, R. (2017). Assessment of personality type and medical specialty choice among medical students from Karachi: Using Myers-Briggs type indicator (MBTI) tool. *Journal of Pakistan Medical Association, 67*(4), 520.

Joint Commission on Testing Practices. (2005). Code of fair testing practices in education. *Educational and Measurements: Issues and Practice, 24*(1), 23–27.

Lichtenberger, E. O., & Kaufman, A. S. (2012). *Essentials of WAIS-IV assessment* (2nd ed.). John Wiley & Sons.

Remley, T. P., & Herlihy, B. (2016). *Ethical, legal, and professional issues in counseling* (5th ed.). Pearson Prentice-Hall.

Roessler, R., Rubin, S., & Rumrill, P. (2018). *Case management and rehabilitation counseling.* PRO-ED.

Rubin, S., & Roessler, R. (2008). *Foundations of the Vocational Rehabilitation Process (6th ed).* PRO-ED.

Rubin, S., Roessler, R., & Rumrill, P. (2018). *Foundations of the vocational rehabilitation process* (7th ed.). PRO-ED.

Weiner, I. B., & Greene, R. L. (2017). *Handbook of personality assessment.* John Wiley & Sons.

Whiston, S. C. (2016). *Principles and applications of assessment in counseling* (5th ed.). Cengage Learning.

Wright, R. J. (2014). *Research methods for counseling: An introduction.* SAGE.

CHAPTER 11

Case Management

De'Amber L. Johnson, MS, LPC
Phillip D. Lewis, PhD, CRC, LADC-C
Perry Sanders, EdD, CRC

Learning Objectives

As a result of reading this chapter, the student will be able to:

- Define key terms used in case management.
- Identify the components of case management.
- Explain the function and process of case management.
- Describe the roles of the case manager.
- Understand the different sectors of case management.

INTRODUCTION

Historically, case management can be traced back to the 1920s. During that time, case management was practiced in psychiatry and social work that focused on long-term, chronic illnesses that were managed in outpatient, community-based settings. At the end of World War II, nurses often were employed as case managers to help return wounded veterans to work. These veterans often received multiple interventions as part of their rehabilitation. Today, case managers are used in many sectors, such as hospitals, nursing homes, mental health care, and vocational rehabilitation. They serve as liaisons between their consumers and the community by empowering and instilling hope in those who are seeking help in achieving their treatment goals. This chapter explores case management in depth by highlighting the major roles, functions, and processes of case management by reviewing the profession in an interdisciplinary model that can be used in many practice settings.

Defining Case Management

The Commission for Case Manager Certification (CCMC, 2018) defines *case management* as a collaborative process of assessment, planning, facilitation, care coordination, evaluation, and advocacy for services to meet individual and/or family comprehensive health needs through communication and available resources to promote cost-effective outcomes. Case managers work with the consumer to understand any existing problems and barriers in order to facilitate the consumer's use of personal and environmental resources for career, personal, social, and community adjustment following disabilities. Case management is a profession used in many sectors and serves as a tool to enhance the quality of life. The Commission on Rehabilitation Counselor Certification's (CRCC) scope of practice details the prerequisites for case management for rehabilitation counselors. According to the CRCC (2020), rehabilitation counseling is a systematic process that assists persons with physical, mental, developmental, cognitive, and emotional disabilities to achieve their personal, career, and independent living goals in the most integrated setting possible through the application of the counseling process. The counseling process involves communication, goal setting, and beneficial growth or change through self-advocacy, psychological, vocational, social, and behavioral interventions. The specific techniques and modalities utilized within this rehabilitation counseling process may include, but are not limited to:

- Assessment and appraisal
- Diagnosis and treatment planning
- Career (vocational) counseling
- Individual and group counseling treatment interventions focused on facilitating adjustments to the medical and psychosocial impact of disability
- Case management, referral, and service coordination
- Program evaluation and research
- Interventions to remove environmental, employment, and attitudinal barriers
- Consultation services among multiple parties and regulatory systems
- Job analysis, job development, and placement services, including assistance with employment and job accommodations
- Provision of consultation about and access to rehabilitation technology

As you begin your journey into the wonderful world of case management, it is important that you become familiar with the key terms provided in Table 11.1.

TABLE 11.1 Key Terms in Case Management

Term Consumer	Definition
Consumer	Also known as the patient or consumer. This is the individual who will receive the treatment.
Stakeholder	The person identified by each individual consumer to be directly involved in treatment.
Caregiver	The person who will be responsible for caring for the consumer.

(continued)

Term Consumer	Definition
Case manager	Professional responsible for overall care of the consumer to ensure personal, social, employment, and educational goals.
Case management process	The process of case management that involves the following phases: • Screening • Assessing • Planning • Implementing • Following-Up • Transitioning • Evaluating
Practice setting	Referred to as practice site, care setting, or work setting. This is the location in which the case management services are being provided.
Level of care	The level of treatment provided, ranging from primary to tertiary.
Benefits	The type of health and human services covered by a health insurance plan.
Services	Interventions, medical treatments, diagnostics, and other activities implemented to manage consumers' conditions, including health and human services issues and needs.

Roles of a Case Manager

When thinking of the profession of case management, *compassion* is the term often used to describe these professionals. People from diverse ethnic and demographic backgrounds with a range of physical and/or cognitive disabilities seek help from case managers. Case managers help ease difficult transitions for consumers so that they can make strides in their treatment. Case managers often are found in hospitals, physician offices or clinics, acute rehabilitation facilities, payer-based settings (insurance companies), palliative care settings, or home care. Hospice case managers combine the role of caregiver with case management and vocational rehabilitation. No matter the setting, case managers will have the same role, which includes five core tasks: (1) assessment, (2) planning, (3) implementation, (4) monitoring, and (5) reviewing. The primary function of case managers is to advocate for consumers/support systems and to serve as a liaison between the consumer and the community. Case managers understand the importance of achieving quality outcomes for their consumers and commit to the appropriate use of resources and empowerment of consumers in a manner that is supportive and objective (CMCC, 2018). These professionals are expected to follow all standards, guidelines, and ethical codes.

Case Management Models

Case management is a complex career whereby professionals coordinate a unique individualized treatment plan tailored to fit the needs of the consumer. Building a strong foundation and approach will contribute to a consumer's success in their treatment. Case management professionals can utilize four distinct models in their practice, which are outlined in Table 11.2.

TABLE 11.2 Case Management Models

Model	Description	Example
Brokerage model	The case manager provides little direct service to the consumer. Instead, they serve as a link between a consumer and community resources. The focus is on assessing needs, planning a service strategy, and connecting consumers.	Sue, a professional rock climber, fell 8 feet from a mountain. She broke her leg and arm and bruised her ribs. She healed but she had some cognitive dysfunction from hitting her head. Sue was assigned a case manager for rehabilitation where she was linked to a neuropsychologist to help with cognitive function. The main goal of this case management model was to link the consumer to the service needed for care.
Strengths-based clinical case management model	The case manager focuses on empowering consumers and their families. Case management and clinical services focus on creating consumer opportunities for growth, education, and skill development.	John is a lover of the arts! He loves painting and drawing, but after sustaining a traumatic brain injury, he feared he would lose these skills. The case manager used different exercises to help John become more enthusiastic about writing. The process was successful because the case manager identified his strengths and utilized them in the treatment process.
Clinical case management model	The clinical care provider serves as the case manager. Often, the case manager is a counselor or therapist. This model recognizes that many consumers face barriers to services that reach beyond simple questions of access.	Heather is an 18-year-old female senior in high school who had many hopes of going off to college. Heather was in a horrible car crash, which left her paralyzed on the right side of her body. The case manager coordinated her rehabilitation plan, including physical therapy and occupational therapy. The case manager was able to track Heather's progress through to a healthy recovery.
Intensive case management model	The case manager delivers high-quality services in a short amount of time. The consumer receives much more of the case manager's attention than if they were not in an intensive program. The relationship between the consumer and care coordinator is stronger in this model compared to the others.	Jane is a 14-year-old track runner who tore a ligament in her left leg. The case manager used intensive case management to refer Jane to a physiotherapist and then supported her by attending the appointments and checkups.

Phases of Case Management

Case managers within the rehabilitation counseling profession typically navigate through the five phases of the case management process with careful consideration of the consumer's cultural background, interests, motivation, needs, wishes, and values. The phases of case management are (1) referral, (2) intake and screening, (3) assessment, (4) care planning and service coordination, and (5) follow-up and reassessment.

Referral

Typically, a referral is from a secondary source in order for a consumer to seek and receive treatment. However, an individual who is seeking services also can contact their local agency themselves to obtain information regarding services. During this process, a person with a disability seeks consultation, review, and further action directing them to an intake and screening. Referrals should be documented in the consumer's case file prior to the screening and intake readiness phase.

Intake and Screening

During the intake and screening phase, the consumer will be asked a host of questions to gain insight into their mental and physical situation in order to assist in providing the best care possible. The objective of the intake and screening phase is to determine if a consumer would benefit from vocational rehabilitation counseling services. According to the CMCC (2018), the intake assessment phase serves to identify key concerns to address with the potential consumer.

Key tasks and information about the consumer/support system to gather during screening may include:

- Help the consumer evaluate and understand the service plan options available.
- Work with the consumer to agree on the personalized goals and priorities.
- Work with the consumer to determine what is the best process to meet consumer needs.
- Institute action to achieve their goals and meet their interests/expectations.
- Work with the consumer to get a clear understanding of his/her home environment.
- Work with the consumer to identify prior services they may have received in other settings.
- Work with the consumer to get a clear understanding of the consumer's physical, emotional, and cognitive functioning.
- Work with the consumer to get a clear understanding of the consumer's psychosocial network and support system.
- Work with the consumer to get a clear understanding of the consumer's self-care ability.

Assessment Phase

During the assessment phase, the case manager gathers pertinent information that will be important in identifying the consumer's needs. Assessment, although done initially, is an ongoing process and a way to observe changes over time. Assessment is rendered in an objective manner and is utilized as another means of gathering data about consumers (Denzin, 1973).

Care Planning and Service Coordination

The care plan is considered the road map that outlines the goals, objectives, and intended actions of the service provider and the consumer as they work together to carry out the consumer's service plan. Although case management is a specialty practice, case managers must be aware and knowledgeable of the multidisciplinary case management process.

Healthcare professionals have adopted the SMART goals and objectives for universality of treatment and development of the rehabilitation care plan. SMART goals are statements of the important results that the case manager is working to accomplish. SMART goals are used to address all of the case manager's major job responsibilities (Doran, 1981). Goals are intended to focus attention and resources on what is most important so that one can be successful in achieving priorities on the job. The SMART criteria are shown in Table 11.3.

TABLE 11.3 SMART Criteria

S	Specific	What will be accomplished? What actions will you take?
M	Measurable	What data will measure the goal? How much? How well?
A	Achievable	Is the goal doable? Do you have the necessary skills and resources?
R	Relevant	How does the goal align with the broader goals? Why is the result important?
T	Time-bound	What is the time frame for accomplishing the goal?

Common types of goals are to:

- Increase something
- Make something
- Improve something
- Reduce something
- Save something
- Develop someone

When writing SMART goals, it is important to ask yourself and other stakeholders a lot of questions. The answers will help fine-tune the strategy, ensuring that the goals are realistic and attainable. The SMART questions can be used as a guide. Achieving goals will allow the consumer to see their improvements. Timelines may be adjusted, as needed, but always document the changes as they occur. Throughout the case manager–consumer relationship, the case manager assists in coordinating services, maintaining compliance, and supporting the consumer to reach the outlined goals.

Service coordination follows the outline of the care plan and highlights what services will be initiated and how they will be organized in order to ensure timely, efficient, equitable, and consumer-centered services. Service coordination involves the identification of how the services will help in meeting the overall goal of service delivery to the consumer. One of the major components of being a case manager is to recognize what services exist within the community. Case management and other care plan coordinators are encouraged to familiarize themselves with community assets. Building rapport and having knowledge about what services are available is beneficial when assisting the consumer in reaching their goal of optimal and holistic wellness.

Follow-Up and Reassessment

The final case management phase is follow-up and reassessment. The treatment regimen and the consumer's advancement toward their goals are the focus of the follow-up phase. Reassessment occurs if the consumer has not made progress toward the outlined goals. If consumer function has not improved, case managers should begin to look at the effectiveness of the intervention through an evaluation of services and the development of a new care plan.

Interdisciplinary Case Management

Interdisciplinary case management occurs when the consumer's problems do not fall within one discipline. Individuals who seek rehabilitation counseling often will receive assistance from a team of professionals who will assist in their treatment by working toward the same goals. Rehabilitation counselors serve many populations, including those with cognitive and physical disabilities. It is their duty to assess and identify appropriate referrals in the community to best serve their consumers and families. In most cases the interdisciplinary team will include physicians, nurses, physical therapists, social workers, therapists, dieticians, and pharmacists. It is appropriate to note that this team will vary depending on the needs of the consumer. Communication is vital because there will be multiple individuals working with the consumer on their treatment plan. Once the interdisciplinary team has been identified to serve the consumer, the team will meet to coordinate and provide insight on what treatment would look like for the individual. Effective interdisciplinary meetings allow the care team, including the case manager, to be proactive in their planning, communication, and interventions with patients and families. Kirby (2011) acknowledged the overall goal of interdisciplinary meetings is to improve the team's ability to consistently deliver high-quality care.

Disability Case Management

Rehabilitation case management has been around for many years, serving individuals in the healthcare industry. Rehabilitation counselors are often confronted with unique challenges that require them to immerse themselves in the problem-solving activity of attempting to help their consumers overcome obstacles to independence and barriers to employment. But what is a disability? According to the *Oxford Dictionary* (2020), *disability* can be defined as a physical or mental condition that limits a person's movements, senses, or activities. Thus, the primary goals for disability case management are facilitating communication between stakeholders, advocating on behalf of consumers with disabilities, assessing and reviewing consumers' needs, and identifying appropriate interventions that promote a greater level of functioning for consumers. As mentioned earlier, case managers must use compassion when working with people with disabilities. In recent years, the education and training of counselors working with persons with a disability has become quite rigorous. Rehabilitation case managers are equipped with knowledge and resources that allow them to serve consumers through job coaching and other means of vocational assistance.

Private Rehabilitation

Private rehabilitation case management has grown significantly from its establishment in the early 1970s when it was referred to as insurance rehabilitation (International Association of Rehabilitation Professionals [IARP], 2020). Today's private rehabilitation profession has emerged to a place of prominence as a service to the community as it deals with vocational and disability issues in a broad range of civil litigation actions, federal and state workers' compensation programs, disabled veteran programs, and federal and state disability programs such as social security (IARP, 2020). Private rehabilitation professional works in a broad range of settings, helping to ease daily obstacles for those with disabilities.

Case Study: Kan

Develop a case plan for Mr. Kan Doolittle using one model and incorporating an interdisciplinary team.

Mr. Kan Doolittle is a 40-year-old Native American man that resides in a Metropolitan City. He was an average student in high school but earned a BS degree in communication from a local university. Prior to attending college, he entered the military from high school, where he served 4 years in the U.S. Army as a computer operator. He is married to his partner, and they are raising two adopted children that are now teenagers. His partner is employed with an income of $2,100 per month, and Mr. Doolittle receives $1,800 SSDI and Medicare. They have a supplemental health insurance policy through the wife's employment. Kan is an Insulin Dependent Diabetic, with corrected vision 20/200 OU from diabetic retinopathy. He worked 10 years as a computer operator with the Ajax Company. However, he was forced to quit work due to sudden vision loss. He has learned blindness skills through services from the local Rehabilitation Teacher for the Blind.

He uses low vision aids and braille for reading and writing skills. He has learned skills to perform daily independent living tasks without personal assistance through the local Rehabilitation Teacher. The Rehabilitation Teacher has referred him to you for services, which will enable him to gain education and/or training in hope of leading him to successful gainful employment.

Case Study: Cortney

Develop a case plan for Cortney using one model and incorporating an interdisciplinary team.

Cortney Barnes is a 30-year-old female residing in Oklahoma. She is a wife and mother to two children. She is a physical education teacher and has been teaching for more than 5 years. One day, while on a family vacation, her family was involved in a car accident. She was driving and was not wearing her seat belt. The collision left her entire family hospitalized. Everyone had a full recovery except for Cortney, who sustained a traumatic brain injury (TBI) and torn ligaments in both arms. Cortney wants to return to work but is unsure how her TBI and torn ligaments will affect her performance as a physical education teacher.

SUMMARY

Rehabilitation counselors play a major role in implementing, coordinating, and assessing consumer needs to ensure quality of life for people with disabilities. Case managers are competent individuals who are well-versed in the knowledge of service provisions needed for consumers with various physical and mental disabilities. Rehabilitation case managers educate their consumers so that they can make informed decisions. Rehabilitation case managers provide support by advocating and allowing the consumer to have autonomy in their treatment.

Discussion Questions

1. Define case management.
2. Identify the roles and functions of a case manager.
3. Discuss the purpose of an interdisciplinary approach to treatment.
4. Case managers use different models to approach treatment. What model do you like most? Explain.
5. What is the SMART model? How can it be best utilized?

REFERENCES

Chan, F., Chronister, J., Catalana, D., Chase, A., & Eun-Jeong, L. (2004). Foundations of rehabilitation counseling. *Directions of Rehabilitation Counseling, 15*, 1–11.

Commission for Case Manager Certification. (2018). *Case management philosophy and guiding principles.* Case Management Body of Knowledge. https://cmbodyofknowledge.com/content/case-management-philosophy-and-guiding-principles

Commission on Rehabilitation Counselor Certification. (2020). *Homepage.* https://www.crccertification.com

Denzin, N. K. (1973). *The research act: A theoretical introduction to sociological methods.* Transaction Publishers.

Disability. (2020). *Oxford Dictionary.* https:/www.oxforddictionary.com

Doran, G. T. (1981). There's a S.M.A.R.T. way to write management's goals and objectives. *Management Review, 70*(11), 35–36.

International Association of Rehabilitation Professionals. (2020). *Homepage.* https://www.rehabpro.org

Kirby, A. (2011, July 1). Case management Insider: Interdisciplinary meetings play critical role in inpatient setting. *Hospital Case Management.* https://www.reliasmedia.com/articles/130907-case-management-insider-interdisciplinary-meetings-play-critical-role-in-inpatient-setting

Lewis, P., Johnson, D., & York, B. (2019). Case Management. In. M. M. Joseph (Ed.), *Practicum and internship manual: A resource for rehabilitation and human services professionals.* Aspen Professional Services.

CHAPTER 12

Independent Living

Kent Crenshaw, MS, CRC
Mary-Anne M. Joseph, PhD, LPC, CRC

Learning Objectives

As a result of reading this chapter, the student will be able to:

- Define independent living.
- Outline the history of the independent living movement.
- Identify legislation related to independent living.
- Understand and apply concepts related to information and referral, advocacy, peer support, independent living skills training, and transition.

INTRODUCTION

Historically, people with disabilities (PWD) have been treated from the perspective of the medical model of disability, which posits that disabilities are impairments to be cured through medical intervention (Brisenden, 2007; Rogers, 1982). For hundreds of years, this resulted in PWD being treated as having diseases to be cured. Many lived lives in which they were undervalued and unacknowledged. This devaluation resulted in infringement on the human and civil rights of PWD. In contrast, the independent living (IL) model of disability views disability as a construct of society. Supporters of this model state that the problem is not the individual with the disability but rather the environment. The IL model posits that physical, programmatic, and attitudinal barriers are established and maintained in society (Barnes, 2014). From the perspective of the IL model, PWD seek and deserve the same human and civil rights as persons without disabilities. Through peer support, advocacy, skills training, and information and referral, independent living centers across the country now provide services to hundreds of thousands of people with disabilities each year (Haymen, 2019).

Before moving forward, it is essential to establish a clear description of independent living. A key distinction that must be made is that between independent living and assisted living. Although many people use the terms interchangeably, they are different concepts and practices. *Assisted living* is an option for PWD who may not be able to live alone but do not require intensive medical care. When one refers to an assisted living facility, they are often referring to a residential facility where PWD can go to live and have constant support and possible supervision. In contrast, *independent living* preserves and promotes the freedom of PWD by helping them to live and function as independently as possible (National Council on Independent Living [NCIL], 2020). In this chapter, independent living refers to services provided through a center for independent living (CIL), which is a consumer-controlled, community-based, cross-disability, nonresidential private nonprofit agency that is designed and operated within a local community by individuals with disabilities and provides an array of independent living services. CILs have been established throughout the United States to carry out the IL philosophy.

More than 700 CILs have been established throughout the United States that practice the cross-disability philosophy, which is the belief that all PWD share a common thread that brings them together. CILs are private nonprofit organizations that are operated by PWD. It is required that at least 51% of the CIL staff be PWD. Additionally, the board of directors for the CIL must have a minimum of 51% PWD (Northeast Independent Living Program [NILP], 2020). ILCs are not a place to live, rather they are agencies that provide information, support, and advocacy to support PWD to live in the communities of their choice. These CILs are the cornerstone of individual and systems advocacy for disability issues throughout the United States (NCIL, 2020).

The IL movement evolved from the community rights model, which espouses the belief that if an individual needs support to live in the community, then those supports should be provided. The IL philosophy emphasizes consumer control; the idea that people with disabilities are the best experts on their own needs; that they have a crucial and valuable perspective to contribute; and that they deserve equal opportunity to decide how to live, work, and take part in their communities (NCIL, 2020; Rogers, 1982). The IL movement was founded on the belief that PWD have a common history and a shared struggle. It posits that PWD are a part of a community and a culture that will advance the lives of people with disabilities.

A key component of the IL philosophy is the belief that PWD have the right to control and direct their own lives (Budde & Bachelder, 1986; DeJong, 1979; The League, 2020). It emphasizes the notion that PWD should not be limited by adverse measures that are not placed upon persons without disabilities. For PWD to minimize their physical and/or psychological dependence upon others, they need to be able to govern their own lives. This entails the ability to make independent and effective life choices based on culturally and personally appropriate options. Those who support the IL philosophy also believe in the right to risk taking and the right to fail as part of the learning process. Through peer support people learn from each other how to problem solve and live more independently (NILP, 2020).

Such life choices include the right of PWD to select where, with whom, and how to live. These choices also include their determination of how they utilize their time (The League, 2020). Moreover, PWD have the right to actively participate in all aspects of community life to the extent they deem appropriate and necessary. The philosophy of IL supports the rights of PWD to engage in risk taking as they move toward personal, educational, vocational, and social success (DeJong, 1979; The League, 2020), while understanding that one must take responsibility for their actions as they make life choices. As do all people, PWD have the right to fail and earn the potential benefits associated with failure. Both failure and success lead to an increase of knowledge and information; these experiences greatly enhance a person's potential for increased development of self-determination and independence.

Dr. Adolf Ratzka said it best:

> Independent Living does not mean that we want to do everything by ourselves, do not need anybody or like to live in isolation. Independent Living means that we demand the same choices and control in our every-day lives that our non-disabled brothers and sisters, neighbors and friends take for granted. We want to grow up in our families, go to the neighborhood school, use the same bus as our neighbors, work in jobs that are in line with our education and interests, and raise families of our own. We are profoundly ordinary people sharing the same need to feel included, recognized and loved. (cited by Independent Living Institute [ILI], 1997)

History of Independent Living

Although not recognized as such in its early stages, the IL movement began as early as the 1850s in the United States (DeJong, 1979). During this time, persons who were deaf began working to develop local groups to advocate for their interests. Over time, these small organizations grew into national associations such as the National Association for the Deaf, which was established in 1880 (Pennsylvania State Independent Living Council [PA SILC], 2020). During the 1930s, members of society began to engage in protest demonstrations that denounced the discrimination of PWD in federal programs. During the 1940s, organizations such as the National Federation of the Blind, the American Federation of the Physically Handicapped, and Paralyzed Veterans of America were formed to promote the treatment of persons with varying types of disabilities.

The IL movement emerged during the 1960s from the disability rights movement, which was closely tied to the civil rights movement. The IL movement was focused on eliminating disgraceful treatment, stereotypes, and discrimination in the areas of housing, education, transportation, and employment (PA SILC, 2020).

Timeline of Significant Events in IL History

1960s	Ed Roberts is the first student with a significant disability (respiratory quadriplegia secondary to polio) to enroll in a university, the University of California, Berkeley. Roberts was housed in the Cowell Residence Program on the campus of UC Berkeley. By 1969, the Cowell Residence Program, supported by the California Department of Rehabilitation, housed 12 students with disabilities (Brown, 2001; Fleischer, 2001; Zukas, 1975).
1969	A "Strategies for Independent Living" class is developed at UC Berkeley by students with disabilities. The course was developed under the university's group study program. The course was used to develop a proposal for the establishment of a facility similar to the Cowell Resident Program that would be under the direct control of residents. The students wrote a proposal to secure funding for a Physically Disabled Students' Program (PDSP; Brown, 2001; Fleischer, 2001; Zukas, 1975).

(continued)

Timeline of Significant Events in IL History (*Continued*)

1970   The Physically Disabled Students Program is founded by Ed Roberts, John Hessler, Hale Zukas, and others at the UC Berkeley (Brown, 2001; Fleischer, 2001; Zukas, 1975).

1972   The first Center for Independent Living is founded by disability activists, led by Ed Roberts, in Berkeley, California. These centers were created to offer peer support and role modeling and are run and controlled by persons with disabilities. This center became the model for hundreds of independent learning programs across the United States (NCIL, 2020).

1974   Ed Roberts is appointed the director of the California Department of Rehabilitation. Wade Blank founded the Atlantis Community, a model for community-based, consumer-controlled, independent living (NCIL, 2020).

1977   The 504 sit-in is held at the San Francisco office of the U.S. Department of Health, Education and Welfare. The sit-in, led by Judith Heumann and organized by Kitty Cone, lasted for 28 days and included more than 150 people. As a result, on April 28, 1977, Joseph Califano signed both the Education of All Handicapped Children (now known, as the Individuals with Disability Education Act) and Section 504 (Disability Rights Education and Defense Fund [DREDF], 2020).

1977   Independent Living Research Utilization (ILRU) is established in Houston, Texas. The ILRU provides research, education, and consultation in the areas of independent living, home and community-based services, and the Americans with Disabilities Act (ILRU, 2020).

1977   The Disability Rights Education and Defense Fund (DREDF) is founded in Berkeley, California. The DREDF is dedicated to improving the lives of people with disabilities through legal advocacy, training, education, public policy, and legislative development. It has developed a variety of strategies for collecting, synthesizing, and disseminating information related to the field of independent living (DREDF, 2020).

1982   Max Starkloff, Charlie Carr, and Marca Bristo establish the National Council on Independent Living (NCIL). The NCIL is the longest-running national, cross-disability, grassroots organization run by and for people with disabilities. Its mission is to advance independent living and the rights of people with disabilities, and it envisions a world in which people with disabilities are valued equally and participate fully (NCIL, 2020).

(continued)

Timeline of Significant Events in IL History (*Continued*)

1983   The American Disabled for Accessible Public Transit (ADAPT) is established. The ADAPT fights for the rights of PWDs to live as equals, free and able to pursue liberty and justice and a life of quality. ADAPT grew out of the Atlantis Community, which fought to free its members from institutions and nursing homes so they might live in the community with the rest of humanity. Fighting at the local level, they realized their fight was universal for PWD and decided to share their experience. In 1990, ADAPT changed its name to American Disabled for Attendant Programs Today (ADAPT, 2020).

1983   The World Institute on Disability (WID) is founded by Ed Roberts, Judy Heumann, and Joan Leon in Oakland, California. It is one of the first global disability rights organizations founded and continually led by PWD. WID works to advance the rights and opportunities of over one billion people with disabilities worldwide, bringing research and policy into action and operationalizing inclusion. Their work centers on digital tools for optimizing community living and employment; accessibility solutions; and excellence in disability inclusive emergency preparedness, disaster risk reduction, and climate resilience (WID, 2020).

1986   The Rehabilitation Act of 1973 is amended to include Title VII, Part A, which funds services for independent living rehabilitation (oxymoron) to individuals determined "eligible" for such services.

1986   National Council on the Handicapped issues "Toward Independence," citing the need for federal civil rights legislation (eventually passed as the Americans with Disabilities Act of 1990).

1986   The Association of Programs for Rural Independent Living (APRIL) is founded by 12 directors of rural CILs meeting in Houston. APRIL is a national, grassroots, consumer-controlled, nonprofit membership organization consisting of centers for independent living, their satellites and branch offices, statewide independent living councils, other organizations, and individuals concerned with the independent living issues of people with disabilities living in rural America (APRIL, 2020).

1999   The U.S. Supreme Court rules in *Olmstead v. L.C. and E.W.* that the "integration mandate" of the Americans with Disabilities Act requires public agencies to provide services "in the most integrated setting appropriate to the needs of qualified individuals with disabilities." The ruling emphasized that unjustified segregation of persons with disabilities constitutes discrimination in violation of Title II of the Americans with Disabilities Act (U.S. Department of Justice, 2020).

(continued)

Timeline of Significant Events in IL History (*Continued*)

2004   The first Disability Pride parades are held in Chicago and around the country. Disability Pride parades seek to change the way people think about and define disability, to end the stigma of disability, and to promote the belief that disability is a natural and beautiful part of human diversity in which people living with disabilities can take pride. The first Chicago parade was funded with $10,000 in seed money that Sarah Triano received in 2003 as part of the Paul G. Hearne Leadership award from the American Association of People with Disabilities. The first Disability Pride parade was held on July 18, 2004, and parades are now held in Chicago every July (Ability Strong Parade, 2020).

2009   President Obama marks the 10th anniversary of the Supreme Court Olmstead decision by designating 2009 as "The Year of Community Living," dedicated to identifying ways to improve access to housing, community supports, and independent living arrangements for older people and PWD (U.S. Department of Justice, 2020).

2010   The Department of Justice revises regulations for Titles II and III of the ADA, known as the Standards for Accessible Design. Title II prohibits discrimination on the basis of disability in all services, programs, and activities provided to the public by state and local governments, except public transportation services. Title III prohibits discrimination on the basis of disability in the activities of places of public accommodations (i.e., businesses that are generally open to the public and that fall into one of 12 categories listed in the ADA, such as restaurants, movie theaters, schools, day care facilities, recreation facilities, etc.; U.S. Department of Justice, 2020).

2014   The Stephen Beck, Jr. Achieving a Better Life Experience Act (the ABLE Act) is passed. The ABLE Act amends Section 529 of the Internal Revenue Service Code of 1986 to create tax-free savings accounts for individuals with disabilities. The bill aims to ease financial strains faced by individuals with disabilities by making tax-free savings accounts available to cover qualified expenses, such as education, housing, and transportation. The bill supplements, but does not supplant, benefits provided through private insurances, the Medicaid program, the supplemental security income program, the beneficiary's employment, and other sources (Social Security Administration, 2020).

(continued)

Timeline of Significant Events in IL History (*Continued*)

2014   The Workforce Innovation and Opportunity Act (WIOA) is passed. The act transferred IL programs to the National Institute on Disability, Independent Living, and Rehabilitation Research (NIDILRR) and the assistive technology programs to the Administration on Community Living (ACL). This also led to the creation of the IL Administration. The transition of these three important programs reflects their strong alignment with ACL's current efforts and mission—to maximize the independence, well-being, and health of older adults and people with disabilities and the families and caregivers of both. Additionally, WIOA included statutory changes that affect IL programs, including the addition of new core services, shifts in the process of developing and adopting state plans, and changes in the functions of the SILC (ACL, 2016).

IL of Services

CILs provide five core services to persons with disabilities. These services include: (1) information and referral, (2) advocacy, (3) peer support, (4) independent living skills training, and (5) transition.

Information and Referral Services

Information and referral (I&R) services are provided to PWD, their family members, business professionals, and members of the community via in-person meetings or telecommunication. The intent of I&R services is to provide members of society with information about disability-related resources, rights, organizations, and programs (Christenson & Howard, 2017). This service is often essential for these constituents because they are often unaware of the available services and resource within the community.

The provision of I&R services often helps PWD to learn about services in the community that can aid them in their rehabilitative process or in the fulfillment of their activities of daily living. Oftentimes, CIL staff will refer PWD and/or their family members to state agencies, such as the local Department/Division of Rehabilitation Services, Social Security, and the Department of Housing, depending on their particular needs. The Department/Division of Rehabilitation Services provides assistance with employment and employment-related training. The Social Security Administration can provide assistance with benefits, and the Department of Housing can provide possible housing benefits and services.

Likewise, CIL staff may provide business professionals and members of the community information on services for persons with disabilities. The CIL staff may accomplish this through direct one-on-one information and referral sessions, community events, or conferences and through the use of other marketing tools and social media.

For instance, a person with a disability who is homeless would be referred to the local homeless society or coalition. The CIL staff may also provide the individual with information about affordable housing. In another instance, a person in the community may call in to ask about accessible transportation. This person may be referred to the local department of rehabilitation services, where they could possibly get financial assistance and an appropriate evaluation.

Advocacy

Advocacy is the act of speaking on behalf of another person when that person is unable to speak on their own behalf (Disability Rights and Resources [DRR], 2020; Woodside & McClam, 2013). Advocacy may also be needed for a person who attempts to speak out for themselves but the person finds that they are not being heard. CILs promote various types of advocacy, including individual advocacy and system advocacy.

System advocacy promotes change in the community, including promoting change that is needed to ensure that PWD have equal access to community resources and other opportunities that allow them to live independently. It is an effort to change policies, rules, or laws that determine how services are provided. Individual advocacy addresses issues of discrimination, abuse, and/or neglect on a one-on-one basis. This form of advocacy is the practice of helping PWD to gain the services they need by exercising their rights and engaging in self-advocacy. The most important form of advocacy is self-advocacy. Self-advocacy involves helping a person learn how to actively participate in the planning and development of their life goals (DRR, 2020).

It is best practice to teach consumers how to engage in self-advocacy so they can learn how to independently ask for what they need. This is of vital importance because the consumer knows their needs and desires better than anyone; this qualifies them to be their best advocate. Self-advocacy has the potential to empower consumers to change their own life situations; it also encourages consumers to move away from the notion of depending on others to solve their problems.

CIL staff should consider six key courses of action in preparing PWD to be effective self-advocates. First, CIL staff should work collaboratively with the consumer to help them develop a clear plan of action. Second, they should make themselves familiar with the environment in which the consumer is experiencing challenges so that the CIL staff are better equipped to engage the other parties involved in the advocacy issue. Third, CIL staff should develop a clear understanding of all those involved in the advocacy issue. This knowledge will ensure that the CIL staff communicate with the appropriate personnel who can effectively address the consumer's concerns. Fourth, CIL staff should engage in the use of appropriate techniques of persuasion and collaboration when advocating on the behalf of their consumers. The fifth key concept is related to direct systematic challenges if these persuasive and collaborative methods of advocacy prove to be ineffective. Finally, the CIL staff should ensure that they document all advocacy activities. Keeping accurate and effective records is essential to the effective and efficient provision of advocacy services to PWD. Such documentation also serves as a record for future reference in case of subpoena or other court-mandated reporting (Woodside & McClam, 2013).

Engagement in advocacy is in line with the IL model of disability. As noted earlier, this model views disability as a construct of society. The premise of this model is that problem at hand is not the individual but rather the environment. It posits that physical, programmatic, and attitudinal barriers are established and maintained in society (Barnes, 2014), therefore warranting the need for advocacy.

As an example of system advocacy, community groups promoting transportation and housing for people with disabilities may contact the CIL to ask questions about group advocacy. In the case of individual advocacy, an individual who needs assistance with their IEP meeting may reach out to the CIL for assistance. The CIL staff may meet with the consumer to discuss their IEP concerns. The staff may also attend the IEP meeting to play the role of advocate at the consumer's request.

Peer Support

Peer support is the active engagement in activities that allow a person with a disability to share their personal experiences with another person with a disability, with the goal of moving toward a greater level of independence and empowerment (DRR, 2020). Peers can engage in peer listening, peer education, peer mentoring, and peer training. When PWD are able to connect with other individuals with disabilities, they can develop a sense of comradery and validation. That person can essentially serve as a sounding board and a potential pool of reflection. Sharing of similar stories of struggles and perseverance can have a profound impact on a person with a disability who may be overwhelmed by the challenges of their disability.

Likewise, PWD can educate one another about the resources in the community that they have used to overcome their own struggles. Additionally, they can share techniques that they utilize to minimize the challenges of completing activities of daily living. The shared body of knowledge that develops out of peer education can often be more valuable than information that comes from a professional who may not have lived with a similar disability. Additionally, peer mentors can provide their counterparts with disabilities with a real-life success story that motivates them to continually work toward their personal, social, educational, and/or vocational goals. The inspiration of the success of another person with a disability has the potential to encourage another individual to persevere and overcome the hurdles of their everyday experiences.

Peer listening, educating, and mentoring culminate in the essence of peer training. These peer support services help to teach PWD how to overcome the barriers they encounter in society. Peers have the ability to teach one another new skills and techniques for accomplishing tasks and pushing past discrimination and limitations. Peer support services may occur on an individual, one-on-one basis, or they may occur in a group setting. This core service is deeply rooted in the cross-disability philosophy, which is the belief that all PWD share a common thread that brings them together.

Peer support services may be provided on an individual or group basis. For instance, the CIL may provide a call line where consumers can call in and talk to a person with a disability so they can share their experience and learn from a peer. Group peer support services may include group talks such as "chat and chew" where a group of people get together and share information about community services.

Independent Living Skills Training

Independent living skills training is intended to help consumers learn what they may require to live autonomously (Sheehan, 2012). This service preserves and promotes the freedom of PWD by helping them to continue to live and function in a self-sufficient manner to the greatest extent possible (NCIL, 2020). IL skills training may include training about community resources and self-advocacy.

When engaging in the provision of IL skills training, CIL staff collaboratively develop a clear plan of action with the consumer. CIL staff should take time to explore the consumer's area(s) of challenge or difficulty and help the consumer explore options for improvement and greater independence. Educating the consumer about their options for moving toward the accomplishment of their IL goal will aid the consumer in developing new means of taking control of their life and enhancing their level of independence.

CIL staff may provide IL skills training that may include things such as financial planning, literacy, sewing, or a couponing course. These services may also include CIL staff working with PWD in the areas of transport. The staff may help PWD learn how to utilize community transportation resources. Additionally, the CIL staff may help consumers with disabilities engage in recreational activities, such as bowling and exercise classes.

Transition

When providing transition services, CIL staff are working to facilitate the transition of individuals with significant disabilities from nursing homes and other institutions to home and community-based residences, with the requisite supports and services. During this process the CIL staff may provide system advocacy. Such advocacy may be geared toward helping the consumer move to the home or residence of their choosing. This system advocacy may also be intended to help a person with a significant disability remain in the community as opposed to being placed in an institution. Such services would include things such as nursing home transition and transition retention, providing services to consumers that help them maintain their independent living status.

Additionally, CIL staff also work with youth with significant disabilities who are eligible for individualized education programs under section 614(d) of the Individuals with Disabilities Education Act (20 U.S.C. 1414[d]) and who have completed their secondary education or otherwise left school in their transition to life following the school setting (Holt et al., 2017). CIL staff work with students with significant disabilities who are preparing to get out of high school who are seeking volunteer and internship opportunities. CIL staff may also help parents of students with severe disabilities gain information about day centers and other facilities that work with young adults with severe disabilities.

IL Legislation

Clinical rehabilitation counselors must be knowledgeable about the legal mandates associated with independent living. Since the 1960s, a wide range of legislation has been passed with regard to the provision of IL services. Table 12.1 summarizes some of the more important legislation affecting IL services.

TABLE 12.1 Important IL Legislation

Year	Legislation	Brief Description
1965	Civil Rights Act	Prohibits discrimination on the basis of race, religion, ethnicity, national origin, and creed (later, gender was added as a protected class).
1965	Architectural Barriers Act	Requires that buildings or facilities that were designed, built, or altered with federal dollars or leased by federal agencies after August 12, 1968, be accessible.
1970	Urban Mass Transit Act	Requires that all new mass transit vehicles be equipped with wheelchair lifts.
1973	Rehabilitation Act	Key language prohibits discrimination in federal programs and services and all other programs or services receiving federal funding.

(continued)

Year	Legislation	Brief Description
1975	Developmental Disabilities Bill of Rights Act	Establishes protection and advocacy (P&A).
1975	Education of All Handicapped Children Act	Requires free, appropriate public education in the least restrictive environment possible for children with disabilities. This law is now called the Individuals with Disabilities Education Act (IDEA).
1978	Title VII of the Rehabilitation Act Amendments	Provides for consumer-controlled centers for independent living and created the National Council of the Handicapped.
1980	Amendments to the Rehabilitation Act	Provides for the Consumer Assistance Program (CAP), an advocacy program for consumers of rehabilitation and IL services.
1984	Voting Accessibility for the Elderly and Handicapped Act	Promotes the fundamental right to vote by improving access for handicapped and elderly individuals to registration facilities and polling places for federal elections by requiring access to polling places used in federal elections and available registration and voting aids, such as printing instructions in large font.
1985	Mental Illness Bill of Rights Act	Requires protection and advocacy services (P&A) for people with mental illness.
1988	Civil Rights Restoration Act	Counteracts bad case law by clarifying Congress's original intention that under the Rehabilitation Act, discrimination in ANY program or service that is a part of an entity receiving federal funding—not just the part which actually and directly receives the funding—is illegal.
1988	Air Carrier Access Act	Prohibits discrimination on the basis of disability in air travel and provides for equal access to air transportation services.
1988	Fair Housing Amendments Act	Prohibits discrimination in housing against people with disabilities and families with children. Also provides for architectural accessibility of certain new housing units, renovation of existing units, and accessibility modifications at the renter's expense.
1990	Americans with Disabilities Act	Provides comprehensive civil rights protection for people with disabilities. The ADA prohibits discrimination against people with disabilities in the areas of employment, public service, public accommodations, telecommunications, and other miscellaneous areas.
1990	Individuals with Disabilities Education Act	Makes available a free appropriate public education to eligible children with disabilities throughout the nation and ensures special education and related services to those children.

(continued)

Year	Legislation	Brief Description
1992	Rehabilitation Act Amendments	Restructured Title VII to set standards for CIL to create independent statewide IL councils.
1998	Workforce Investment Act	Provides workforce investment activities, through statewide and local workforce investment systems, that increase the employment, retention, and earnings of participants and increase occupational skill attainment by participants and, as a result, improve the quality of the workforce, reduce welfare dependency, and enhance the productivity and competitiveness of the nation.
2008	American with Disabilities Act Amendments Act	Emphasizes that the definition of disability should be construed in favor of broad coverage of individuals to the maximum extent permitted by the terms of the ADA and generally shall not require extensive analysis.
2010	21st Century Communications and Video Accessibility Act	Updates telecommunications protections for people with disabilities. The CVAA followed a string of laws, passed in the 1980s and 1990s, that were designed to ensure that telephone and television services would be accessible to all Americans with disabilities. But these laws were not able to keep up with the fast-paced technological changes that our society has witnessed over the past decade. The law contains groundbreaking protections to enable people with disabilities to access broadband, digital, and mobile innovations.
2018	The ABLE Act	Eases financial strains faced by individuals with disabilities by making tax-free savings accounts available to cover qualified expenses such as education, housing, and transportation.

SUMMARY

This chapter explored the concept of independent living, highlighting its philosophy of preserving and promoting the freedom of PWD by helping them to continue to live and function as independently as possible. The history of this great field speaks to the very essence of the need for continued improvement and support in this arena of rehabilitation and counseling. While many pieces of legislation have contributed to the field of independent living, many more may be needed as we enhance our perception of the true meaning and purpose of IL.

When providing individuals with core services, IL professionals must ensure that they are educating their consumers throughout the process to empower them so they might move closer and closer to living an autonomous life. Additionally, it is essential that these professionals educate themselves about the community and its resources that have the potential to benefit the lives of PWD. The passion and dedication that is required to serve in the area of IL must not be taken lightly. When training, teaching, supporting, educating, and advocating on the behalf of PWD, one must always be sure to place themselves in the shoes of the consumer and ask themselves, "Is this what I would want for myself?"

Case Study: Alex

Alex came into the local center for independent living on a cold rainy day. When greeted by the intern at the front door, Alex stated that he just wanted to get in from the cold as he sat in a chair near the door. Alex appeared disheveled and somewhat unclean. The intern allowed Alex to remain seated, and she sought a staff member to express her concerns about Alex's appearance and reason for entering the center. The staff member made her way to the front of the office and asked Alex if they could speak in a private environment. While speaking to Alex, the staff member learned that Alex was recently a resident at the local mental health hospital that had closed a few months ago. After being released, Alex did not have anywhere to live, so he has been living on the street. With this information in mind, the staff member began to seek out local resources that could be beneficial to Alex.

1. What information would you provide to Alex?
2. To what community agencies would you refer Alex?

Case Study: Debra

Debra, a member of the local transportation coalition group (a community organization) contacted the director of the local center for independent living to ask for assistance with an upcoming advocacy opportunity. Debra, on behalf of the group, expressed that many of the group's members are people with disabilities who utilize the local paratransit services provided through the local public bus system and that they have been experiencing a significant amount of challenges accessing these services. She shared that members of the transportation coalition have been denied rides and had experienced scheduling challenges and mistreatment by drivers. They also stated that when they expressed their discontent with the services, their concerns were often dismissed by the staff and the acting director. They also expressed that the staff and the director often appeared insensitive to disability and disability-related issues. They recently learned that the director had resigned his position. In light of this change, the members of the transportation coalition wanted to work with the mayor to see if they could advocate for someone who may be more suitable for the position and who may be able to have a positive impact on the receipt of services.

1. Develop an advocacy plan with key discussion points and recommendations for the group's meeting with the mayor.

Case Study: Cameron

The director of the local center for independent living received a call from a parent of a child, Cameron, who recently acquired a disability after a car accident. The child was diagnosed with a spinal cord injury that resulted in paralysis of his lower extremities that necessitated him using a manual wheelchair. He also has a mild traumatic brain injury. The parent expressed that the school has scheduled a meeting to develop the Cameron's IEP and that she would like someone to attend the meeting with her to assist her in obtaining the best services for her child.

1. What services could the CIL staff request for inclusion on the Cameron's IEP?

Discussion Questions

1. What is the independent living model of disability? Discuss the importance of this model.
2. What is the difference between independent living and assisted living?
3. Identify and describe six areas that are the focus of the independent living movement.
4. List and describe the core services of independent living. Provide an example of each.
5. What are the key provisions and amendments of the Rehabilitation Act that specifically address independent living?

REFERENCES

Ability Strong Parade. (2020). *History: Disability pride parade across America.* https://www.abilitystrong-parade.org/history.html

Administration for Community Living. (2016). *Key provisions of the independent living final rule.* https://acl.gov/sites/default/files/about-acl/2016-11/Key%20Provisions%20of%20the%20Independent%20Living%20Final%20Rule%20-%20External%20version%20final1.pdf

American Disabled for Attendant Program Today. (2020). *Our journey.* https://adapt.org/our-journey/

Association of Programs for Rural Independent Living (APRIL). (2020). *About Us.* Retrieved from: https://www.april-rural.org/index.php/about-us

Association of Programs for Independent Living (2020). *A little bit of history.* https://www.april-rural.org/index.php/about-us/about-us-page

Barnes, C. (2014). Independent living, politics and policy in the United Kingdom: A social model account. *Centre for Disability Studies at the University of Leeds, 1*(4).

Brisenden, S. (2007). Independent living and the medical model of disability. *Disability, Handicap & Society, 1*(2), 173–178. https://doi.org/10.1080/02674648666780171

Brown, S. (2001). *Freedom of movement: IL history and philosophy.* http://www.ilru.org/ilnet/files/bookshelf/freedom/freedom14.html

Budde, J., & Bachelder, J. (1986). Independent living: The concept, model, and methodology. *Journal of the Association for Persons with Severe Handicaps, 11*(4), 240–245.

Christenson, D., & Howard, R. (2017). *Get to the core of it: Best practices in the CIL core services—information and referral.* ILRU and the IL-NET.

DeJong, G. (1979). Independent living: From social movement to analytic paradigm. *Archives of Physical Medicine and Rehabilitation, 60,* 435–446.

Disability Rights Education and Defense Fund. (2020). *Short history of the 504 sit-in.* https://dredf.org/504-sit-in-20th-anniversary/short-history-of-the-504-sit-in/

Disability Rights and Resources. (2020). *Advocacy.* https://drradvocates.org/resources/links-of-interest/advocacy/

Fleischer, D. (2001). *The Disability rights movement.* Temple University Press.

Haymen, B. (2019). *People with disabilities are entitled to civil rights, options, and control over choices in their own lives.* Access Living.

Holt, J., Jones, D., Petty, R., Roth, H., & Christensen, H. (2017). *ABCs of nursing home transition: An orientation manual for new transition facilitators.* ILRU and IL-NET.

Independent Living Institute. (1997). *Homepage.* http://www.independentliving.org

Independent Living Research Utilization. (2020). *Core area of expertise.* https://www.ilru.org

National Council on Independent Living. (2020). *About independent living.* https://ncil.org/about/aboutil/

Northeast Independent Living Program. (2020). *The history of the independent living movement.* https://www.nilp.org/history-of-independent-living-movement/

The League. (2020). *The independent living movement (IL).* https://www.the-league.org/about/the-independent-living-movement/

Pennsylvania State Independent Living Council. (2020). *History of independent living.* https://pasilc.org/independent-living/history-independent-living/

Rogers, J. C. (1982). The spirit of independence: The evolution of a philosophy. *American Journal of Occupational Therapy, 36*(11), 709–715.

Sheehan, T. (2012). *Get to the core of it: IL skills training.* ILRU and IL-NET.

Social Security Administration. (2020). *Spotlight on achieving a better life experience (ABLE) accounts.* https://www.ssa.gov/ssi/spotlights/spot-able.html

Sweet, M. (2012). *Get to the core of it: IL individual advocacy.* ILRU and IL-NET.

U.S. Department of Education, Office for Civil Rights, Free Appropriate Public Education for Students with Disabilities: Requirements Under Section 504 of the Rehabilitation Act of 1973, Washington, D.C., 2010.

U.S. Department of Justice, Civil Rights Division (2020). *Olmstead: Community integration for everyone.* https://www.ada.gov/olmstead/olmstead_about.htm#:~:text=The%20Decision,the%20Americans%20with%20Disabilities%20Act

Woodside, M., & McClam, T. (2013). *Generalist case management: A method of human service delivery* (4th ed.). Brooks/Cole Cengage Learning.

World Institute on Disability. (2020). *Vision, mission and values.* https://wid.org/about/vision/

Zukas, H. (1975). CIL history: Report of the state of the art conference. Center for Independent Living, Berkeley, CA.

CHAPTER 13

Assistive Technology

Robert Stevens, PhD, LPC, CRC
Mona Robinson, PhD, LPCC-S, LSW, CRC
Bill Bauer, PhD, ALPS, LPC, CRC

Learning Objectives

As a result of reading this chapter, the student will be able to:

- Outline the principles of assistive technology.
- Describe how assistive technology benefits people with disabilities.
- Understand the laws that pertain to assistive technology.
- Know how to access assistive technology for those living in rural settings.
- Know the various assistive technology resources that are available.

INTRODUCTION

Assistive technology (AT) provides a means for many people with disabilities to live a more independent life. Rehabilitation counselors often are actively engaged in the provision of assistive technology resources and devices to a wide range of consumers (Gamble et al., 2006). As such, a working knowledge of the principles of assistive technology and the various resources available for consumers can aid these counselors in effectively serving their consumer population. Rehabilitation counselors should be knowledgeable of the laws pertaining to assistive technology and be well-versed in the principles of assistive technology. They should also be aware of assistive technology resources that are available in rural settings and know the various resources related to funding the acquisition of assistive technology devices for consumers in need of such supports.

Defining Assistive Technology

Professionals in the field of rehabilitation counseling need to be aware of two main definitions of assistive technology (AT). The Technology Related Assistance to Individuals with Disabilities Act of 1988 (Tech Act) defines an *assistive technology device* as "any item, piece of equipment, or product system, whether acquired commercially off the shelf, modified, or customized, that is used to increase, maintain, or improve functional capabilities of individuals with disabilities." It defines an *assistive technology service* as "any service that directly assists an individual with a disability in selection, acquisition or use of an assistive technology device."

The IDEA defines an *assistive technology device* as "any item, piece of equipment, or product system, whether acquired commercially off the shelf, modified, or customized, that is used to increase, maintain, or improve functional capabilities of a child with a disability. Exception.—The term does not include a medical device that is surgically implanted, or the replacement of such device." The IDEA is very important to consider when providing support and services to transition age youth and children with disabilities. The legislation also provides for evaluation needs, selection design and fit of assistive technology devices, coordination of related services, and technical training for rehabilitation professionals.

Assistive Technology Services

In practice, assistive technology services can mean many different things. One broad definition of *assistive technology services* comes from Bouck (2017), based off the Tech Act:

> Assistive technology services is when a rehabilitation professional assists a consumer directly in matching/finding appropriate assistive technology device(s) to assist the consumer to increase their quality of life. This involves some of the following actions being taken: evaluations being sought in the person with the disabilities environment, obtaining the assistive technology device (borrow, purchase, lease, etc.), coordinating expects to train both the person with the disability and also their caregiver (if applicable) on how to use said assistive technology device, providing technical assistance or a phone number for the user(s) to request assistance as necessary, and training for other people (teachers, aids, family members, rehabilitation professionals) to know how to use the device as well to assist the person with the disability as needed. (pp. 3–4)

Rehabilitation professionals providing assistive technology services must keep in mind to maintain a person-centered, rather than a device-centered, approach (Cook & Polgar, 2015). They must listen to their consumers' needs in order to provide the services needed to increase their quality of life. Losing focus of the consumers' needs and only focusing on the assistive technology, which may be inconveniently expensive, can actually set the consumer up for failure. Sometimes it can be difficult to find a specific match for a consumer for a number of reasons, including the consumer's ability to physically manipulate the device, whether the device is stressful for the consumer to use, the device is too advanced for the consumer's cognitive abilities, the device isn't portable or easy to use, and so on. If a consumer does not like a device or understand how to use it, then the consumer will likely abandon the device altogether. This is why a proper evaluation by the rehabilitation professional and consultations by other members of the rehabilitation team (occupational therapist, physical therapist, speech language pathologist, etc.) are so vital when providing assistive technology services.

Principles of Assistive Technology

The principles of assistive technology have been widely defined and described. For the purposes of this text, this chapter focusses on six key principles: (1) consumer choice/person-centered technology; (2) use of the device increases the consumer's quality of life; (3) the selection of the assistive technology device is evidence based; (4) the device has universal properties; (5) the device is easy to use and maintain; and (6) proper training on the device has been completed or is ongoing.

The first two principles have already been presented in this chapter. If the consumer has no voice in the selection of the assistive technology device being selected and the rehabilitation professional is not looking at the consumer's needs, then it will not be a good match for the consumer. Proper assessment and evaluation are essential to ensure that the consumer's needs are being heard and worked on. The second principle follows closely, by reiterating that if the consumer's needs are not being met with the device then the rehabilitation professional has done a disservice to their consumer, and their quality of life has not been improved. Again, proper evaluation and assessment are critical.

Insurance agencies and other funding sources often require evidence as to why the assessment has led to a specific piece of assistive technology being recommended for purchase, lease, and so forth. Cook and Polgar (2015) stress the importance of being able to show successful outcomes from the implementation of an assistive technology device with other consumers who have a similar disability and a similar need to increase their quality of life. If such evidence is lacking, the consumer may be denied funding for the assistive technology purchase.

Another principle to keep in mind is universal properties of assistive technology. Funders may be less likely to pay for an expensive piece of assistive technology if it can only be used in one setting (e.g., school) but not used in other settings (e.g., community, home, etc.). Assistive technology that can be used in multiple settings by the consumer to increase their quality of life will have a better chance of being funded and be used more often by the consumer.

Lastly, it is essential that the consumer, as well as any family, caregivers, teachers, or therapists, are trained on how to use the assistive technology device. Note that not all consumers have the intellectual/cognitive abilities to be taught how to use the device with one training session. A plan must be developed to ensure initial training, follow-up training as needed, and technology assistance when/if the assistive technology has a problem. This is why it is key to know the consumer's needs and to perform a complete assessment so as to ensure that the assistive technology requested is not too advanced for the consumer to use successfully on a day-to-day basis.

Assistive Technology Legislation

Numerous pieces of federal legislation have been passed that provide for or address increased access to assistive technology to people with disabilities, including the Tech Act of 1988, the Americans with Disabilities Act of 1990, the Assistive Technology Act of 1998 (amended in 2004), the Rehabilitation Act of 1973 (amended in 1992, 1998), and the Individuals with Disabilities Education Act (IDEA) of 2004.

Section 508 of the 1998 amendments to the Rehabilitation Act of 1973 required federal agencies to make their electronic and information technology (EIT) accessible to people with disabilities. The law (29 U.S.C § 794 [d]) applies to all federal agencies when they develop, procure, maintain, or use electronic and information technology. Under section 508, agencies must give individuals with disabilities public access to information similar to what they would give to those without disabilities.

The U.S. Access Board is responsible for developing information and communication technology (ICT) accessibility standards to incorporate into regulations that govern federal procurement practices. In January 2018, the Access Board's final rule went into effect that essentially updated accessibility requirements covered by section 508 with regard to market trends and innovations in technology and refreshed guidelines for telecommunications equipment subject to section 255 of the Communications Act. The standards are globally recognized.

Title II amended the Rehabilitation Act of 1973 (RA, as amended by the Workforce Investment Act of 1988) to require increased coordination on disability, assistive technology, and universal design research among federal departments and agencies that are members of the Interagency Committee on Disability Research and other federal departments and agencies.

Title III includes provisions to make grants to states for the federal share of alternative financing programs to allow individuals with disabilities and their family members, guardians, advocates, and authorized representatives to purchase assistive technology devices and services. The programs must include alternative financing mechanisms, which may include: (1) a low-interest loan fund; (2) an interest buy-down program; (3) a revolving loan fund; (4) a loan guarantee or insurance program; (5) a program operated by a partnership among private entities for purchase, lease, or other acquisition of assistive technology devices or services; or (6) another approved mechanism that meets the requirements of this title.

The Tech Act of 1988 law supports states by providing them with federal funds to develop systems to access assistive technology and services as well as information and referral. All states have developed programs to assist their consumers with disabilities regarding assistive technology. States can work with centers for independent living, hospitals, education agencies and schools, rehabilitation agencies, and One-Stop offices that were developed as a part of the Workforce Investment Act of 1998.

The Americans with Disabilities Act (ADA) of 1990 provides civil rights protection and mandates accessibility and accommodations for people accessing public facilities, employment, state and local government agencies and services, transportation, and communication. With the passage of this act, all new facilities renovated or built using state or federal funding must be accessible. In addition, restaurants, grocery stores, retail stores, as well as privately owned transportation systems must comply with this act. The website www.ada.gov is an outstanding resource for information and guidelines for the ADA.

Although not included in the original hallmark special education ruling of Education for All Handicapped Children Act of 1975 (Public Law 94-142), the 1997 amendments to IDEA specifically require that assistive technology be considered for every student with a disability as part of the Individual Education Plan (IEP) process. Assistive technology may be considered either as special education and related services or as supplementary aids and services on a student's IEP; however, assistive technology must be addressed in the IEP as part of the child's curriculum, whether at school or as part of community-based employment. Note that although the IDEA continues to be the umbrella for defining assistive technology, an exception was added in 2004 that states:

> Assistive technology device means any item, piece of equipment, or product system, whether acquired commercially off the shelf, modified, or customized, that is used to increase, maintain, or improve the functional capabilities of a child with a disability. The term does not include a medical device that is surgically implanted, or the replacement of that device.

The National Assistive Technology Act Technical and Training Center is a resource hub for a variety of assistive technology information for consumers, families, and centers (see https://www.at3center.net/repository/atactinformation).

Types of Assistive Technology Devices

A variety of assistive technologies are available to meet the needs of people with different types of disabilities:

- *Mobility impairments:* Walkers, canes, wheelchairs, prosthetics, scooters, devices to allow community involvement, adjustable height and tilt tables.
- *Cognitive devices:* Computers; tablets; applications (apps); technology for reducing distractibility; devices to help with memory loss, to assist with organizational skills, and task completion.
- *Hearing impairments consumer:*
  - Assistive listening devices (ALDs) help amplify sounds, especially where there is a lot of background noise. ALDs can be used with a hearing aid or cochlear implant to help the wearer hear certain sounds better.
  - Augmentative and alternative communication (AAC) devices help people with communication disorders to express themselves. These devices can range from a simple picture board to a computer program that synthesizes speech from text.
  - Alerting devices connect to a doorbell, telephone, or alarm that emits a loud sound or blinking light to let someone with hearing loss know that an event is taking place.
  - Closed captioning, hearing devices, infrared systems, and personal amplifiers.
  - Voice activation systems; text to speech, speech to text, or speech recognition software; alternative keyboards; online programs in alternative formats; computer-embedded accessibility options.
  - The website of the National Institute on Deafness and Other Communication Disorders (NIDCD) is a valuable resource (www.nidcd.nih.gov).

- *Visual impairments consumer:*
  - Text enlargement, service dogs, canes, electronic mobility aids and apps, screen readers, refreshable Braille displays (raises and lowers different combinations of braille pins in braille cells).
  - Smartphones, cell phones, computers, and GPS devices.
  - For a comprehensive list of assistive technology for people who experience vision loss, see the American Federation of the Blind website at www.afb.org.

- *Fine motor impairments:*
  - Pencil grips, automatic page turners.
  - Low-tech devices such as adapted erasers, sticky notes, Velcro, page protectors.
  - Mid- to high-tech devices such as adapted keyboards, adapted calculators, word prediction software, computers, electronic tablets, portable word processors, adaptive utensils.

- *Daily living devices:* Devices that help with cooking, reaching, cleaning, toileting; location devices; medicine reminders; environmental aids to help with stabilization at home (rails, ramps).
- *Behavior/sensory issues:* Weighted blanket, weighted vest, noise-cancelling headphones, fidget toys/devices, calming music/lights, specialized cushions/chairs (bean bag chair).

The Assistive Technology Team

The assistive technology team is an important part of the process of obtaining the correct assistive device that an individual with a disability needs to increase their quality of life. The assistive technology team may be made up of different experts, depending on the type of assistive device being requested. The following is a list of potential people who would be part of this interdisciplinary team:

- Individual with the disability
- Family members/caregivers
- Medical doctor (primary care physician or specialty physician)
- Physiatrist
- Physical therapist
- Occupational therapist
- Speech language pathologist
- Audiologist
- Assistive technology specialist
- Special educator (K–12) or disability services representative (college/university setting)
- Rehabilitation counselor
- Rehabilitation engineer
- Social worker, mental health counselor, or case manager
- Prosthetist

A wide range of people may be part of the assistive technology team. Each member of this team may have to do their own assessment and report to be able to obtain funding to purchase the specific type of assistive technology for an individual. Each member of the team plays a valuable role in advocating for the person with a disability.

Assistive Technology in Rural Settings

Access to assistive technology services and information to people with disabilities in rural America can be somewhat problematic. Approximately 27% percent of Americans live in rural areas (Figure 13.1; United States Census Bureau, 2020). About 4.5 million of these people live on farms. Of those rural Americans, approximately 12.6 million have a disability.

The U.S. Census Bureau (2020) defines *rural* as communities with populations of 2,500 or less or areas where there are no towns at all. Using this definition, there are 61,685,330 rural residents. But this definition oversimplifies *rural*. Some communities of 2,500 are located a stone's throw from a major city. People in those rural communities may be less remote and isolated than other rural Americans because they have access to the services a city provides.

Opportunities for community integration and employment are limited for people with disabilities because of the lack of:

- Accessible public transportation
- Telecommunication services (e.g., cell phone services, internet access)
- Health care
- Rehabilitation services

FIGURE 13.1 **Rural America**

When thinking about providing assistive technology services to people in rural America, cultural factors should be considered, which may include the following:

- Unchanging family dynamics
- Religious upbringing that may not allow technology to enter the home
- Slow-paced lifestyle
- Fear of the bigger cities
- Work avoidance on weekends
- Nonsupport of school funding, high dropout rates
- Lack of knowledge of assistive technology rights and services available

Possible solutions to these issue may include:

- Increased school and community collaborations.
- Schools providing databases of unused and used assistive technology devices.

- Assistive technology vendor fairs at schools or community gathering places.
- Provision of assistive technology services and repair at the home of the consumer.
- Teleconferencing.
- Pooling and blending of funds from various agencies.
- Personal planning instead of service planning
- Train educators on rural cultural competence regarding assistive technology.

Case Study: Adam

Adam is a 30-year-old man with spina bifida who lives in rural Appalachia. He is a person with paraplegia as a result of his condition of spina bifida. Currently, he is a wheelchair user. He obtained his driver's license when he was 20 years of age by utilizing the services of a driving training program that was offered at a local university. He currently drives using hand controls on his steering wheel because he has no functional use of his legs. His physical ability has regressed from childhood from walking with leg braces and canes, to a manual wheelchair, to an assisted push wheelchair, to currently using a modified electric wheelchair.

Education

He attended public schools and had access to the general education curriculum as appropriate based on his IEP provided by the school district. His category of impairment was listed on his multifactored evaluation as Orthopedic/Other Health Impairment. He had an aide who helped him with his medical and catherization needs.

Upon graduation from high school, he utilized the services of the state Medicaid agency to pay for gasoline for his van to drive to medical appointments. He is of average intelligence, with particular interests in travel, mapping, video making, spending time with his siblings, and reading books. He graduated with an associate degree in computer applications from a local community college. When needed, he used the services of the disability coordinators office at the college.

Physical Skills

Adam currently is unable to walk and finds it difficult to perform some fine and gross motor skills to control his hands to do some basic tasks. He was catheterized in school up until the eighth grade, and then he learned to catheterize himself. In elementary and high school, he had an attendant with him throughout the day who assisted him with physical tasks within the school environment, as well as restroom tasks. He was in inclusive classrooms where he engaged with a typical curriculum with supports to learn, communicate, and complete all tasks within the classroom setting. He has had numerous surgeries since childhood related to a shunt. He has an occasional severe headache that alerts him to go to the ER for an assessment on the functioning of his shunt.

Communication Skills

Adam's verbal skills are excellent.

1. What are some considerations you can use to assist Adam?

Assistive Technology Resources/Funding

When it comes to high school and/or college students needing to obtain assistive technology, it is important to have all specific needs built into either their IEP or their disability service plan (college) to ensure that every effort is put in place to obtain the assistive technology that is needed so that the person with a disability can be successful in their educational goals. The transition from high school to college can be facilitated by the state's vocational rehabilitation services if services are requested. When funding is available, it is possible that certain types of assistive technology that are considered essential to the educational process can be purchased or lent to a student with a disability while they are enrolled in college. For example, many universities will assist people with disabilities to access assistive technology such as the Livescribe smartpen (https://us.livescribe.com/). The pen not only allows a student with a disability to take notes but also records the lecture so they can go back and listen to points they may have missed. This is a reasonable accommodation and a great resource for students with disabilities. However, it is up to the student to advocate for themselves to obtain assistive technology such as this from either their disability services office on campus or the local office of their state's vocational rehabilitation agency.

Medicare

Currently, no single private insurance plan or public program will pay for all types of assistive technology under any circumstances. However, Medicare Part B will cover up to 80% of the cost of assistive technology if the items being purchased meet the definition of durable medical equipment. This is defined as devices that are "primarily and customarily used to serve a medical purpose, and generally are not useful to a person in the absence of illness or injury." To find out if Medicare will cover the cost of a particular piece of assistive technology, call 1-800-MEDICARE (1-800-633-4227; TTY/TDD: 1-877-486-2048). Additional information is available on the Medicare website (www.medicare.gov).

Medicaid

Depending on the state, Medicaid will pay for some assistive technology. Keep in mind, though, that even when Medicaid does cover part of the cost, the benefits usually do not provide the full amount needed to buy expensive pieces of equipment, such as power wheelchairs. A list of toll-free numbers for the state Medicaid programs can be found at http://www.cms.hhs.gov/medicaid/allStateContacts.asp.

State Departments of Vocational Rehabilitation

The Rehabilitation Act defines *rehabilitation technology* as "the use of technology, engineering, or scientific principles to meet the needs of and address barriers faced by people with disabilities in areas which include, education, rehabilitation, employment, transportation, independent living, and recreation" (29 U.S.C. 705 [30]). According to this act, rehabilitation technology is divided into three categories: rehabilitation engineering, assistive technology devices, and assistive technology services. Rehabilitation technology also includes vehicular modifications, telecommunications, sensory, and other technological aids and devices and does not include the purchase and repair of a vehicle (9 CCR § 7024.7).

To find out where the state vocational rehabilitation services agencies are located nearest you, please note the following website: https://www.csavr.org/stateagencydirectory.

State Technology Act Grantees

The Assistive Technology Act provides resources that allow state AT programs to provide access for funding or partial funding of assistive devices, services, or referrals. People within the community can access these services by contacting the state technology act grantee. Information about these programs can be accessed via the AT3 Center website (https://www.at3center.net/stateprogram).

Assistive Technology Resources

National Organizations

AbleData

AbleData is a database that provides comprehensive information on assistive technology products, solutions, and resources to improve productivity and daily living tasks for people with disabilities. AbleData is supported by the National Institute on Disability, Independent Living, and Rehabilitation Research (NIDILRR) of the U.S. Department of Health and Human Services (https://abledata.acl.gov).

Disabilities, Opportunities, Internetworking, and Technology (DO-IT)

The DO-IT Center is dedicated to empowering people with disabilities through technology and education. It promotes awareness and accessibility—in both the classroom and the workplace—to maximize the potential of individuals with disabilities and make communities more vibrant, diverse, and inclusive (https://www.washington.edu/doit/).

Center on Technology and Disability (CTD)

Funded by the U.S. Department of Education's Office of Special Education Programs (OSEP), the Center on Technology and Disability (CTD) is designed to increase the capacity of families and providers to advocate for, acquire, and implement effective assistive and instructional technology (AT/IT) practices, devices, and services (https://www.ctdinstitute.org/).

Early Childhood Technical Assistance Center (ECTA Center)

The ECTA Center assists states in building effective, efficient service systems; increasing the implementation of evidence-based practices; and enhancing outcomes for young children and their families.

Center for Parent Information and Resources (CPIR)

CPIR serves as a central resource of information and products to the community of Parent Training Information (PTI) Centers and the Community Parent Resource Centers (CPRCs) so that they can focus their efforts on serving families of infants, toddlers, and young children with disabilities (https://ectacenter.org/).

Case Study: Jose

Jose is a 34-year-old Latin American male who recently was in a car accident on his way to work. Jose suffered many broken bones and a traumatic brain injury. Jose is married to his wife Jolissa, and they have three children. Jose was in a coma for 30 days and has spent the last 90 days in rehabilitation (physical, occupational, and speech pathology). Jose has to use a walker for short distances, but due to fatigue he relies on a manual wheelchair for most of his mobility. He has problems with memory (taking his medications, remembering appointments, etc.) as well. The rehabilitation team at the rehabilitation hospital has decided that Jose is getting close to being ready to go home. They have hired you as their rehabilitation consultant to go with Jose's wife to tour their home and look at any other barriers that Jose may encounter that assistive technology could assist with. As you tour the home, you see that the house needs a lot of work to make it accessible for Jose to be able to use. The home has stairs in both the front and back entryways, narrow doorways into the bathrooms and closets, and thick carpet in the living room and bedrooms, just to name a few things. You have your work cut out for you, but you know you are ready for this task.

1. What are some considerations you can use to assist Jose?

Case Study: Lijiang

Lijiang is a 19-year-old Asian American female who sustained a spinal cord injury (SCI) in a diving accident. After months of extensive physical and occupational therapy, Lijiang is finally able to move back home with her parents. Lijiang has come to you as a rehabilitation/assistive technology expert for assistance. Lijiang plans to return to college for the spring semester. She will be living on campus in a dorm, and she is unsure what assistive technology she will need to be a successful college student. Currently, the rehabilitation hospital has fitted Lijiang with a power wheelchair and a transfer bench. Lijiang will have a personal assistant who will come to assist her with bathing and other activities of daily living. Lijiang has a laptop computer, but currently, she has trouble using the keyboard and mouse that came standard with her computer.

1. What are some considerations you can use to assist Lijiang?

SUMMARY

According to Dicianno and colleagues (2015), approximately 50 million U.S. citizens (1 in 6 people) have a disability, whether acquired or congenital. Rehabilitation technology is concerned with improving the quality of life for people with a disability. Rehabilitation technology is a "total approach to rehabilitation," combining medicine, engineering, and related science, to improve the quality of life of individuals with a disability. Many technologies were not specifically designed for people with disabilities; however, they have been the beneficiaries of such advancements in technology. Similarly, improvements in technology that were designed for people with disabilities have benefitted people without disabilities. Development of technologies such as the internet, wireless communication, and accessible architecture continue to be beneficial to everyone. Universal design coupled with extensive legislation has dramatically increased accessibility for people with disabilities (Reinkensmeyer et al., 2017). While we have come a long way with regard to technology, many more improvements are needed in this area, and the field continues to grow as technology enhances.

Discussion Questions

1. Define and discuss your understanding of assistive technology services from the Tech Act of 1988 as outlined in this chapter.
2. Pick one of the principles of assistive technology and discuss your understanding of how this principle would assist you as the rehabilitation expert to assist an individual with a disability to obtain the needed assistive technology.
3. This chapter described three types of assistive technology: low, mid, and high tech. Provide three examples of each.
4. What impact did the Tech Act have on the community, workplace, and education?
5. Why is the composition of the interdisciplinary team important to the success of an individual with disabilities who might benefit from assistive technology?

REFERENCES

Bouck, E. C. (2017). *Assistive technology.* SAGE.

Cook, A. M., & Polger, J. M. (2007). *Cook and Hassey's assistive technology: Principles and practices* (3rd ed.). Mosby Elsevier.

Cook, A. M., & Polgar, J. M. (2015). *Assistive technologies: Principles and practices.* Elsevier.

Dicianno, B., Lieberman, J., Schmeler, M., Elisa, A., Souza, S., Cooper, R., Lange, M., Liu, H., & Jan, Y. (2015) Rehabilitation Engineering and Assistive Technology Society of North America's position on the application of tilt, recline, and elevating leg rests for wheelchairs literature update. *Assistive Technology, 27*(3), 193–198. https://doi.10.1080/10400435.2015.1066657

Gamble, M. J., Dowler, D. L., & Orslene, L. E. (2006). Assistive technology: Choosing the right tool for the right job. *Journal of Vocational Rehabilitation, 24*(2), 73–80.

Reinkensmeyer, D. J., Blackstone, S., Bodine, C., Brabyn, J., Brienza, D., Caves, K., DeRuyter, F., Durfee, E., Fatone, S., Fernie, G., Gard, S., Karg, P., Kuiken, T. A., Harris, G. F., Jones, M., Yue, L., Maisel, J., McCue, M., Meade, M. A., & Mitchell, H. (2017). How a diverse research ecosystem has generated new rehabilitation technologies: Review of NIDILRR's Rehabilitation Engineering Research Centers. *Journal of NeuroEngineering Rehabilitation, 14*(1), 109. https://doi.10.1186/s12984-017-0321-3

United States Census Bureau. (2020). *One in five Americans living in rural areas.* Retrieved from: https://www.census.gov/library/stories/2017/08/rural-america.html

CREDITS

Fig. 13.1: Source: https://www.arc.gov/images/appregion/AppalachianRegionCountiesMap.pdf.

Forensic Rehabilitation Services in the United States

Thomas D. Upton, PhD, CRC
Jennifer Sánchez, PhD, CRC, LMHC
Matthew Sprong, LCPC, CRC

Learning Objectives

As a result of reading this chapter, the student will be able to:

- Outline the development and evolution of forensic rehabilitation services.
- Compare and contrast the fundamental skills necessary for work within public versus private vocational rehabilitation settings.
- Describe employment opportunities that rehabilitation counselors can fulfill to meet evolving societal need in the private (forensic) sector.

INTRODUCTION

Public rehabilitation service delivery has existed for 100 years in the United States. Within this time, the field has matured and defined educational and clinical preparation, and professional opportunities abound. Rehabilitation counselors are in high demand, and their roles are constantly evolving. This chapter presents information on rehabilitation counselor preparation and explores the development and growing demand for rehabilitation counselors in the private sector.

The development of public vocational rehabilitation (VR) is intimately linked with several factors. Specifically, these include federal legislation, the goodwill of others, and the guiding premise that investment in rehabilitation services geared toward employment will yield exponential returns in the form of tax revenue and diminished reliance on governmental subsidies (Rubin et al., 2016). On June 2, 1920, President Woodrow Wilson signed the Smith-Fess Act, establishing legislation that extended VR services to all citizens with disabilities (Leahy & Syzmanski, 1995; Rubin et al., 2016; Wright, 1980). Furthermore, the roles of rehabilitation counselors mirrored federal legislation, and the majority of rehabilitation counselors were employed by the public VR system (Leahy & Syzmanski, 1995; Rubin et al., 2016; Upton, 2011; Wright, 1980).

In the beginning of the public VR system, interested professionals who had training in relevant social services, such as a special education, social work, and so on, were hired as rehabilitation counselors (Rubin et al., 2016; Wright, 1980). Over time, however, it became increasingly evident that merely having a desire to help persons with disabilities was not sufficient. Clearly, comprehensive training was needed, and the federal government recognized this need through the 1954 amendments to the Vocational Rehabilitation Act (Rubin et al., 2016; Wright, 1980). In short, the federal government made training grants available for universities to develop and provide specialized training for persons who were seeking to pursue careers as rehabilitation counselors. As funding became available, these programs were developed, and mechanisms for financial support of students ensued. Students with an interest in the social sciences may have been swayed toward rehabilitation counseling due to the availability of financial support for graduate school training. These grants continue to be available for programs that train rehabilitation counselors who are committed to working in the public VR system. These financial incentives shaped rehabilitation education and the curriculum.

For decades rehabilitation researchers have sought to understand what are the requisite roles and functions of rehabilitation counselors (e.g., Beardsley & Matkin, 1984; Chan et al., 2003; Frain et al., 2013; Leahy et al., 2009; Muthard & Salomone, 1969). Clearly, the shift in roles followed three trends. First, the exact nature of specified training and practice changed with regard to societal needs. In other words, persons with disabilities being served and services provided (e.g., training, supported employment) were evolving. Second, ongoing mandates to serve persons with more severe impairments were being fulfilled. The final trend required a higher frequency of positive employment outcomes, while serving persons with more severe impairment, and dwindling governmental funding resources. In an attempt to ensure standard levels of competence across university training programs, the Council on Rehabilitation Counseling Education (CORE) was established in 1972 and reviewed the educational and clinical training requirements of rehabilitation programs and subsequently accredited those programs determined to have met current standards (Stebnicki, 2009). This created considerable professional work and also strengthened the professional status of rehabilitation counselors.

Evolving Scope of Practice

While rehabilitation counselors seem to find themselves working within a number of employment settings (e.g., public VR agencies, community rehabilitation agencies, Veterans Administration programs, education programs, employee assistance programs, health care, forensic consulting), they all possess similar knowledge, abilities, and skills (Lewis & Upton, 2011). These settings provide unique services that target enhancing overall vocational opportunity and employment options for persons with varying disabilities. Although exact work tasks vary among employment settings, rehabilitation counselors have a unified knowledge base from which to serve persons with various disabilities. Therefore, all graduates of CORE-accredited programs should have the capacity and ability to: "Conduct and utilize labor market analyses and apply labor market information to the needs of individuals with a disability"; "Identify transferable skills by analyzing the consumer's work history and functional assets and limitations and utilize these skills to achieve successful job placement"; "Describe employer-based disability management concepts, programs, and practices"; "Describe the purpose of forensic rehabilitation, vocational expert practice, and the reasons for referral of individuals for services"; "Describe the purposes of life-care planning and utilize life-care planning services as appropriate"; "Demonstrate knowledge of disability insurance options and social security programs"; and

"Explain the functions of workers' compensation, disability benefits systems, and disability management systems" (CORE, 2014, pp. 8, 14–15).

Leahy and colleagues (2013) performed job task analyses of certified rehabilitation counselors (CRCs) to identify the job skills and knowledge domains required for rehabilitation counselors. They identified three major job functions: (1) job placement, vocational assessment, and career counseling; (2) counseling, psychosocial interventions, and case management; and (3) demand-side employment, workers' compensation, and forensic services. These job skills were gathered from a sample of CRCs across a variety of employment settings, with 25% from private, proprietary rehabilitation companies; 8% from private, nonprofit rehabilitation organizations; 37% from governmental rehabilitation agencies; 9% from postsecondary educational institutions; and 4% from mental health centers. They identified four major knowledge domains: (1) job placement, consultation, and assessment; (2) case management and community resources; (3) individual, group, and family counseling and evidence-based practice; and (4) medical, functional, and psychosocial aspects of disability. These areas of competence were obtained from a separate (comparable) sample of CRCs across work settings, including 25% from private, proprietary rehabilitation companies; 7% from private, nonprofit rehabilitation organizations; 41% from governmental rehabilitation agencies; 7% from postsecondary educational institutions; and 4% from mental health centers.

The data that indicated that most rehabilitation counselors find employment in the public VR sector was shocking because nearly all of the approximately 100 CORE-accredited programs at the time followed prescribed curricula and clinical training to maintain accreditation so that graduates could be qualified to take the CRC examination. The CRC is the oldest (since January 1974) rehabilitation credential (Leahy & Holt, 1993). Rehabilitation counselors must meet stringent eligibility requirements to earn the designation of CRC, which demonstrates that holders of this credential are "qualified rehabilitation professionals" and provides assurance to employers and consumers that services provided meet the national standards of quality and adhere to rigid standards of ethical practice (Commission on Rehabilitation Counselor Certification [CRCC], 2017).

Significant Changes in Accreditation

Following discussions that spanned more than 20 years, a landmark merger between the CORE and the Council for Accreditation of Counseling and Related Educational Programs (CACREP) was finally realized. On July 1, 2017, the CACREP took over review and accreditation of rehabilitation counseling programs, in addition to other specialty counseling (e.g., clinical mental health, school) programs. Students in all CACREP-accredited programs are expected to learn general curriculum areas in counseling, as well as specialized knowledge and skills in their clinical area of emphasis, such as rehabilitation counseling (CACREP, 2015).

This major shift prompted rehabilitation scholars (Leahy et al., 2019) to conduct an updated skill and competency study to inform future versions of the CRC exam. The knowledge domains/subdomains were grouped as: (1) rehabilitation and mental health counseling, including rehabilitation and mental health counseling theories and techniques, crisis and trauma counseling, and employment counseling; (2) employer engagement and job placement, including job placement and job development, occupational analysis, and demand-side employment; (3) case management, including health care and disability management, caseload management, and community resources; (4) medical and psychosocial aspects of chronic illness and disability; (5) research methodology and evidence-based practice; and (6) group and family counseling. These data were gathered from CRCs across a variety of rehabilitation practice settings, with 24% from private, proprietary rehabilitation companies; 6% from private, nonprofit rehabilitation organizations; 34% from governmental rehabilitation agencies; 15% from postsecondary educational institutions; 10% from medical/psychiatric facilities; and the remaining 10% from other sectors.

The public sector still employs a majority of CRCs, but nearly one-third of CRCs are working in the private sector. It is clear from these data that a shift toward employment in the private sector is underway. This is in stark contrast to the time when nearly all rehabilitation counselors sought employment in the public VR system. Moreover, graduating master's level rehabilitation counseling students seek employment in the private sector. Some of these individuals eventually become forensic rehabilitation experts after they acquire the necessary knowledge, skills, abilities, and appropriate credentials to provide such services.

Students in CACREP-accredited clinical rehabilitation counseling programs must demonstrate contextual knowledge and skills surrounding "professional issues that affect rehabilitation counselors, including independent provider status, expert witness status, forensic rehabilitation, and access to and practice privileges within managed care systems" (CACREP, 2015, p. 26). Yet, rehabilitation counselors in the private sector indicate that they learn forensic-related topics through on-the-job training, specifically related to vocational evaluation (76%), service approaches to addiction (69%), disability policy and law (66%), and public policy (57%; Miller & Paris, 2017). Forensic rehabilitation is "the application of professional knowledge and the use of scientific, technical, or other specialized knowledge for the resolution of legal or administrative issues, proceedings, or decisions" (CRCC, 2015, p. 38). Forensic rehabilitation experts specialize in the provision of services regarding "litigation, such as worker's compensation, personal injury, product liability, medical/professional malpractice, catastrophic injury, and others" (International Association of Rehabilitation Professionals [IARP], 2020).

A recent study by forensic rehabilitation educators (Beveridge et al., 2016) to identify current training needs of rehabilitation counselors in the private sector revealed the following (in order of significance): multicultural competence (67%), private VR (52%), labor market research skills (43%), ethics (42%), forensic case management (36%), expert witness testimony techniques (35%), veterans' issues (27%), evidence-based treatments (22%), dual diagnosis (17%), emerging occupations (16%), DSM-5 (15%), counseling techniques (12%), assessment tools and healthcare providers (11%), fluidity of the job market (7%), consumer empowerment (5%), changes in the healthcare system (5%), building relationships with employers (4%), and online access to counseling (3%). A different study noted specific topics essential to preparation for private VR practice, including business law, business management and human resources, disability management, nonprofit management, forensic statistics, and forensic rehabilitation (Miller & Paris, 2017). Interestingly, a follow-up study revealed no significant differences in training needs between private and public VR counselors (Beveridge et al., 2019).

Factors Impacting the Shift to the Private Sector

This shift to the private sector is occurring for a number of reasons. Scholars such as Cioe and Upton (2011), Rubin and colleagues (2016), and Wright (1980) have consistently emphasized similarities and differences in service delivery in public VR versus private VR (forensic rehabilitation). Similarities include familiarity with medical and psychosocial aspects of disabilities, use of counseling skills, knowledge and utilization of local community resources, familiarity with occupational information, and a common interest in helping persons with disabilities. Differences also exist. In public VR, caseloads are larger (many times more than 100 consumers per counselor), eligibility criteria are determined by federal mandate, and services are provided free of charge to the recipients who receive them. In contrast, private VR counselors provide services that are covered by insurance, serve a smaller number of consumers, and have greater responsibility for returning injured consumers to work than their public VR counterparts.

Significant differences in salary and income potential also exist. The CRCC (2008) surveyed 1,220 CRCs to obtain an annual income index and found the average annual salary reported was $57,716; however, when factoring in the primary work setting, those who worked in a state VR agency (36%) earned an average annual salary of $47,600, compared to private practice practitioners (12%) who earned an average annual salary of $72,400. The American Counseling Association (ACA, 2014), using a similar approach to gauge counselor compensation, found that the average annual salary for rehabilitation counselors was $53,561, and almost half (45%) were working for state or local government. Most recently, IARP members were surveyed and reported an average annual income of $125,927.62 (median = $95,000; $n = 5 > \$500,000$); notably, those who reported "billable hour rate by case" earned an average annual income of $140,794.97, whereas those who reported being paid hourly for total hours worked earned an average annual income of $132,022.22, and those who reported earning a set annual salary averaged $90,022.95 (Beveridge & DiNardo, 2017). Reflecting on the requisite tasks of VR counselors in the public versus private sector and the associated significant pay discrepancy may influence counselors to consider taking rehabilitation knowledge and skills developed for the public VR setting and shifting application of these acquired skills into the private sector.

Successful employment as a rehabilitation counselor in the private sector places certain demands on rehabilitation professionals. First, one learns specialized skill domains that researchers (Beveridge et al., 2016, 2019; Leahy et al., 2013, 2019; Miller & Paris, 2017) have identified. Second, rehabilitation counselors must understand and master existing employment-related resources such as the U.S. Department of Labor's (DOL) *Dictionary of Occupational Titles* (DOT; published 1938–1999) and its replacement, the *Occupational Information Network* (O*Net; free online database); the Bureau of Labor Statistic's (BLS) *Occupational Outlook Handbook* (OOH; free publication since 1948); the *Standard Occupational Classification* (SOC) system; the *Classification of Jobs* (COJ; hardcopy book); local labor markets and rehabilitation resources; and transferable skills analysis (Cary et al., 2018; Hollender et al., 2011). Third, it is imperative that rehabilitation counselors develop and use ethical guidelines and decision-making models to provide forensic rehabilitation services (Lewis & Upton, 2011; Robinson & Watson, 2019). These requisites for forensic rehabilitation service delivery are skills that all rehabilitation counselors should have developed through educational preparation and professional practice in the field of rehabilitation counseling. Upon reading this list, readers who are rehabilitation counselors may think these requirements reflect information they already mastered during rehabilitation counselor education and professional services.

Forensic Beginnings

Professional rehabilitation counselors are similar to other professionals in that they may choose to change one's work roles or employment focus. These changes may happen due to curiosity, career development desires, or out of necessity due to employment layoffs. Whatever the reason, seasoned and relatively new rehabilitation counselors may see that the skill sets they have mastered can be readily applied in a private (forensic) rehabilitation employment.

Social Security

Many professionals entering the private sector do so by seeking work within the Social Security Administration (SSA) and may become certified as a Vocational Expert (VE) who can be called to take part in the federal disability determination process (Sleister, 2000; Upton, 2003; Weikel, 1986). The SSA is a setting that follows a standard model that is the same across the United States and requires the rehabilitation counselor to objectively participate in this process.

In this context, rehabilitation counselors are VEs and must complete four core processes. Typically, an hour-long hearing takes place. An administrative law judge, the claimant (person with a disability), their representative, and the VE are present. The judge runs the hearing, and specific information is gathered from the VE. First, the claimant's work for the past 15 years, known as past relevant work, must be reviewed and classified using the DOT definitions of strength ratings (i.e., sedentary, light, medium, heavy, and very heavy exertion levels) and skill ratings (i.e., unskilled, semi-skilled, and skilled work). Second, the VE provides expert testimony with respect to whether the person with the disability (who is referred to as a "claimant" by the SSA) is able to return to past work with specific physical, cognitive, or mental limitations. Finally, hypothetical questions are asked regarding the employability in the region of a person with functional limitations identical to the claimant. During this step, the VE may be asked to complete a transferable skills analysis that can identify residual skills and regional employment the claimant can seek. After the VE testimony, the claimant's representative (usually an attorney) has the opportunity to ask questions of the VE. Although this may be perceived as a stressful event, the context is nonadversarial and is usually a civil process that can serve as a springboard to additional forensic work.

Rehabilitation professionals exploring forensic work may find it useful to try this type of work. The SSA work requires minimal preparation (simply reviewing the case beforehand) and relies on the VE's knowledge regarding the DOT, an understanding of general functional limitations resulting from disabilities, and a clear awareness of the local labor market. One may become quite accustomed to this process, and if the rehabilitation counselor updates the regional labor market data regularly, this may be an enjoyable forensic service.

Workers' Compensation

Other venues exist in which rehabilitation counselors can provide forensic rehabilitation services. For instance, every U.S. state and territory has a workers' compensation mechanism (U.S. Department of Labor, n.d.). Workers' compensation programs were developed following industrialization in the United States. With workers sustaining injuries while on the job, protections were needed for workers and their employers (Rasch, 1985). This work uses a rehabilitation counselor's knowledge, skills, and abilities to provide opinions regarding overall employability. Typically, a forensic specialist completes a vocational evaluation and corresponding report, a labor market survey, job placement assistance, and expert testimony. A vocational evaluation report is a comprehensive document that is created from professional medical records, interview data, and vocational testing (Upton & Dallas, 2011). This report, usually completed for every workers' compensation case, clearly articulates the rehabilitation counselor's opinions about employability and also has the materials that were used to form these opinions. Following the vocational evaluation, a regional labor market survey or job placement services may follow. These distinct services will identify regional employment options and will help the injured worker seek and obtain work in regional employment openings. Ultimately, services provided are completed with relevant expert testimony.

Testimony is necessary of all the work so that the documentation can become evidence and be considered by the arbitrator (i.e., workers' compensation judge). The arbitrator's goal of re-employment of the injured worker is a guiding principle that all parties work toward.

This type of forensic work has a few additional details to consider. First, the work is adversarial, meaning one is usually involved either on the side of the petitioner (injured worker) or the respondent (insurance company contracted by the employer). Because there are two sides to every story, the rehabilitation counselor become aligned with one of the sides, and their services are based on the knowledge gained about the injured worker. Generally, typical services include a vocational evaluation, job-seeking skills training, job placement assistance, and expert testimony. All services provided must include clear documentation. Documentation must be objective, clear, and written with the understanding that everyone involved in this court case (i.e., attorneys, injured workers, and other professionals) will be seeing and relying on this information (Upton & Dallas, 2011). This increases the importance of clear, objective, and unbiased information.

Assessment of Earning

Although the first two specializations discussed are where rehabilitation counselors generally practice forensic work, life care planning and family law litigation are two other possible avenues for rehabilitation counselors to pursue. Within life care planning, rehabilitation counselors conduct a comprehensive assessment of factors that are associated with the life care needs (e.g., future medical services, long-term disability case management) of the injured person. Specialized coursework and material regarding life care planning is available. Obtaining an additional credential (i.e., Certified Life Care Planner [CLCP]) will help the rehabilitation counselor who engages in this specialty. With family law litigation, rehabilitation counselors are generally utilized to complement a judge's decision on how to address alimony (Upton & Mbugua, 2011). Becoming a member of the American Rehabilitation Economics Association (AREA) may be beneficial in determining the proficiencies that are needed to be effective in this type of specialty.

Marital Dissolution

Evaluations for marital dissolution cases where a severely injured person requires a life care plan is another avenue for work (Rasch, 1985). A typical referral is when a long-term marriage fails and one spouse is a successful professional (e.g., physician, dentist) and the other spouse has acquired a disability (e.g., lupus, fibromyalgia) and, therefore, has diminished capacity to earn a living. In this type of case, oftentimes an evaluation is completed with the ultimate goal of quantifying the spouse with a disability's earning potential. The goal is to quantify the spouse's earning potential, and the judge will then make any decision about alimony or spousal support (Shahnasarian, 2015).

Life Care Planning

For those who are catastrophically injured, a life care plan may be needed. According to the International Conference on Life Care Planning and the International Academy of Life Care Planners (IARP, 2015):

> The life care plan is a dynamic document based upon published standards of practice, comprehensive assessment, data analysis, and research, which provides an organized, concise plan for current and future needs with associated costs for individuals who have experienced catastrophic injury or have chronic health care needs. (p. 5)

A life care planner will begin the evaluation by reviewing pertinent medical records, conducting a comprehensive interview of the individual with the catastrophic injury and relevant family members, and discussing issues with the treatment team (e.g., physiatrist, psychiatrist, occupational therapist) to develop a comprehensive plan that may include the following areas, depending on the disabilities: projected evaluations, projected therapeutic modalities, medication, diagnostic testing and educational assessments, supply needs, wheelchair needs, wheelchair accessories and maintenance, home care or facility-based care needs, projected routine future medical care, orthopedic equipment needs, projected surgical treatment or other aggressive medical care, orthotic or prosthetic requirements, transportation needs, home furnishing and accessories, architectural renovations, aids for independent function, and leisure or recreational equipment (Weed & Berens, 2018). Individuals from several different professions can become certified to create life care plans, including physiatrists (physical medicine and rehabilitation doctors), nurses, and rehabilitation counselors. Although there has historically been turf wars between the different professionals (arguments are made that physiatrists and nurses know more about medical aspects of disability and are therefore more qualified), there is much to be said about training in the psychosocial aspects of disability that is included in the graduate-level training curriculum of rehabilitation counselors.

Individuals interested in becoming life care planners need to obtain the CLCP credential (course work can be taken at Capital University Law School, Fig Services, Inc., and Institute of Rehabilitation Education and Training [IRET; formerly through University of Florida]). When developing life care plans, it is essential that a CLCP bear in mind that the life care plan is a dynamic document, based on a comprehensive assessment, and provides an organized, concise plan for current and future needs (McCollom, 2005). These plans are oftentimes used for persons with brain injury, spinal cord injury, severe burns, or other injuries that are likely to have lifelong residual functional impairments. To prepare this work product, extensive collaboration with medical, psychological, and rehabilitation service providers takes place. Each contributes expertise to quantifying functional limitations and complete group problem solving to eradicate problems and provide estimates for future costs. This document presents all relevant medical/psychological issues, outlines current needs, and estimates lifetime costs based on needs deriving from specific functional limitations.

Personal Injury

As indicated throughout this chapter, specialization in certain types of forensic work is common. For example, rehabilitation counselors will often seek forensic work by testifying for the SSA. Although the process of testifying may appear appealing, and rehabilitation counselors may possess the necessary skills needed to be an effective VE, it is beneficial to observe the administrative hearing process prior to engaging in VE testimony independently. By observing hearings, a VE can gain knowledge on the process of the hearing, as well as the wording of the hypothetical questions. This will help the VE when reviewing the file for the first time and preparing to provide testimony during a hearing. Similarly, forensic rehabilitation services may be sought secondary to medical malpractice (Lehman & Phelps, 2005), personal injury litigation, or divorce cases (Shahnasarian, 2014). In each context, review of professional documentation, interview data, testing data, and other resources are used to synthesize opinions that are based on evidence and professional practices to offer sound findings.

Within workers' compensation or personal injury cases, one goal is to help the injured person return to their previous occupation. However, there may be barriers that prevent an injured person from returning to the previous work. For example, their functional limitations that resulted from the injury may preclude their ability to perform past work (e.g., a construction worker who has T-3 spinal fusion and is unable to stand/walk more than 2 hours in an 8-hour workday). The forensic specialist may be hired to review and utilize the functional limitations set forth by medical professionals, perform vocational testing, and conduct a vocational interview to determine if there is any other work that the injured person can perform. After identifying work that can be performed by the injured person and concluding that there are jobs the injured person can perform in the local labor market, the forensic specialist may be hired to provide job placement services. These specific types of services may involve helping the injured person with interviewing skills, developing a résumé, completing an application, and so on. If job placement services are rendered, the forensic specialist will also provide the injured person with approximately 10 jobs per week that are within the injured person's residual functional capacity. Although the primary certification held by rehabilitation counselors in forensic work is the CRC, other certifications (e.g., American Board of Vocational Experts [ADVE], Certified Case Manager [CCM], Qualified Rehabilitation Professional [QRP]) can be obtained by meeting specific qualifications, competencies, and educational requirements. Moreover, forensic professionals generally join the IARP to attend forensic-specific conferences and workshops.

Substance Abuse

The last specialization that will be discussed is substance abuse or addiction counseling. To practice as a substance abuse counselor (SAC) in a forensic setting, it is essential to adhere to the state-specific requirements. For example, in Illinois, certification (e.g., Certified Alcohol and Other Drug Counselor) or state licensure (e.g., Licensed Clinical Professional Counselor) is needed to practice. The Division of Alcoholism and Substance Abuse (DASA) is the governing body that oversees all treatment of persons with substance-related issues in Illinois. Within a forensic framework, counselors with requisite training can conduct DUI (driving under the influence) evaluations, offer DUI education courses, and provide substance abuse counseling. The DUI evaluation is required by law and is used to determine whether the defendant has a substance abuse problem. The counselor also recommends treatment, such as DUI classes or early intervention, outpatient, or inpatient substance abuse treatment (Azhari, 2012). Recently, rehabilitation professionals have begun to stress the importance of considering not only the short-term benefits but also the long-term negative effects of prescription pain medications for workers' compensation consumers (McCarthy & Wagner, 2014) and of the need to include addiction (or risk thereof) and its specific (or potential) vocational impact on the evaluee's ability to safely engage in competitive work in forensic vocational evaluations (Stoneburner & Rockett, 2017).

Diagnosis and treatment of substance use disorders requires specific addiction-related knowledge and clinical skills. At minimum, SACs should be competent in the administration, scoring, and interpretation of intermediate screening instruments, such as the *Substance Abuse Subtle Screening Inventory* (SASSI; Miller, 1985), a brief self-report screening measure for substance use disorders. The SASSI also assesses for risk of legal problems and misuse of prescription medications and has specific versions for use with adults (SASSI-4), adolescents (SASSI-A2), vocational rehabilitation consumers (SAVR-S2), and persons who speak American Sign Language (SAS-ASL). Furthermore, with additional training, SACs can conduct diagnostic evaluations with comprehensive substance use assessment instruments, such as the *Addiction Severity Index* (ASI; McLellan et al., 1980)—a structured clinical interview used to assess for problems associated with substance use disorders. The ASI-6 (current version) is considered comprehensive, yet brief, and assesses for various problems, including employment/financial, family/social relationships, and recent illegal activity/ interactions with the criminal justice system; it should only be used by counselors with specified training (Sánchez et al., 2019).

Case Study: John

The following is a typical case that a private forensic rehabilitation counselor would receive from an attorney. After reviewing the case study, review the specialty areas in forensic rehabilitation and create a plan for how you would spend your time with this individual.

John Smith is a 44-year-old single male who has a significant other and a three-year-old son. His family moved to the border of Illinois and Indiana when he was 5 years old, and he has lived on the border since then. Mr. Smith has three siblings, two older brothers and one sister, who live in the same region. Following a work-related injury, Mr. Smith moved in with one of his brothers who works in construction. Mr. Smith has not worked since his injury and is in constant pain, but he wants to get his life back so he can be productive again. Mr. Smith completed 10 years of school and has a GED.

Mr. Smith worked as a construction laborer. Since his injury, he has had two failed back surgeries at L-5 and S-1. The surgeons say he is physically healed, but he still experiences daily pain. Mr. Smith's pain had been managed with narcotics (with breaks for physical therapy after surgeries 1 and 2), but recently, his prescription for oxycodone has been discontinued. He has used a TENS unit with limited success and more recently has used physical therapy to minimize his pain.

1. What are some considerations you can use to assist John?

SUMMARY

This chapter introduced readers to forensic rehabilitation services in the United States. It seems clear that it is an emerging sector of employment that is building upon the professional development of rehabilitation counseling in the United States. Although specific specializations within forensic rehabilitation were discussed, other avenues of employment may exist as well. As a way to close this manuscript, two insights from Upton (2011) are shared:

> Theme 1: Rehabilitation counselor roles continue to evolve and private vocational rehabilitation [forensic] service delivery is a viable career option that more rehabilitation counselors are pursuing.

> ...

> Theme 2: Rehabilitation counselors who specialize in private [forensic] vocational rehabilitation meet broad societal needs in [America's] contemporary culture. (p. 221)

Discussion Questions

1. In the 1920s, when public vocational rehabilitation was started, what two outcomes were expected?
2. How are students learning the required knowledge, abilities, and skills of clinical rehabilitation?
3. This chapter introduced an exposure to forensic rehabilitation that may lead one toward a new and innovative specialty that may require further exploration. How might this information be useful for rehabilitation counselors?
4. How might someone interested in becoming a vocational expert gather more information about these opportunities?
5. How does the evolving scope of practice fit with forensic rehabilitation services for rehabilitation counselors?

REFERENCES

American Counseling Association. (2014). *Counselor compensation study*. Author.

Azhari, S. (2012, January 22). *Explaining the Illinois DUI evaluation process*. Illinois DUI. https://www.illinoisdui.us/2012/01/22/explaining-the-illinois-dui-evaluation-process/

Beardsley, M. M., & Matkin, R. E. (1984). The Abbreviated Task Inventory: Implications for future role and function research. *Rehabilitation Counseling Bulletin, 27*(4), 232–245.

Beveridge, S., & DiNardo, J. (2017). 2016 IARP survey on salary and impressions of the CORE/CACREP merger. *The Rehabilitation Professional, 25*(2), 87–96.

Beveridge, S., Durant, S., & Penrod, J. (2019). Application of the KVI-R to assess and compare training needs for private and public state-federal rehabilitation counselors. *Rehabilitation Research, Policy, and Education, 33*(2), 126–143. https://doi.org/10.1891/2168-6653.33.2.126

Beveridge, S., Karpen, S., Chan, C., & Penrod, J. (2016). Application of the KVI-R to assess current training needs of private rehabilitation counselors. *Rehabilitation Counseling Bulletin, 59*(4), 213–223. https://doi.org/10.1177/0034355215590770

Cary, J. R., Gamez, J. N., & Choppa, N. J. (2018). Labor market survey/research: An approach centered on the individual and grounded in objective and reliable data. *The Rehabilitation Professional, 26*(1), 5–18.

Chan, F., Leahy, M. J., Saunders, J. L., Tarvydas, V. M., Ferrin, J. M., & Lee, G. (2003). Training needs of rehabilitation counselors for contemporary practices. *Rehabilitation Counseling Bulletin, 46*(2), 82–91. https://doi.org/10.1177/00343552030460020201

Cioe, N. J., & Upton, T. D. (2011). The historical context and importance of private vocational rehabilitation. In T. D. Upton (Ed.), *Private rehabilitation: Evolving opportunities* (pp. 20–42). Aspen Professional Services.

Commission on Rehabilitation Counselor Certification. (2008). *2008 salary report: An update on salaries in the rehabilitation counseling profession*. Author.

Commission on Rehabilitation Counselor Certification (CRCC). (2017). *Code of professional ethics for rehabilitation counselors*. Author.

Council for Accreditation of Counseling and Related Educational Programs. (2015). *2016 CACREP standards*. Author.

Council on Rehabilitation Education. (2014). *CORE standards for graduate rehabilitation counselor education programs and self-study document*. Author.

Frain, M., Bishop, M., Tansey, T., Sánchez, J., & Wijngaarde, F. (2013). Current knowledge and training needs of Certified Rehabilitation Counselors to work effectively with veterans with disabilities. *Rehabilitation Research, Policy, and Education, 27*(1), 2–17. https://doi.org/10.1891/2168-6653.27.1.2

Hollender, H., Upton, T. D., & Anuar, A. (2011). The utilization of existing resources. In T. D. Upton (Ed.), *Private rehabilitation: Evolving opportunities* (pp. 68–84). Aspen Professional Services.

International Association of Rehabilitation Professionals. (2015). *Standards of practice for life care planners* (3rd ed.). Author.

International Association of Rehabilitation Professionals. (2020). *Overview of forensic services in rehab.* https://connect.rehabpro.org/forensic/news/forfocus/forinrehab

Leahy, M. J., Chan, F., Iwanaga, K., Umucu, E., Sung, C., Bishop, M., & Strauser, D. (2019). Empirically derived test specifications for the Certified Rehabilitation Counselor Examination: Revisiting the essential competencies of rehabilitation counselors. *Rehabilitation Counseling Bulletin, 63*(1), 35–49. https://doi.org/10.1177/00343552188008

Leahy, M. J., Chan, F., Sung, C., & Kim, M. (2013). Empirically derived test specifications for the Certified Rehabilitation Counselor Examination. *Rehabilitation Counseling Bulletin, 56*(4), 199–214. https://doi.org/10.1177/0034355212469839

Leahy, M. J., & Holt, E. (1993). Certification in rehabilitation counseling: History and process. *Rehabilitation Counseling Bulletin, 37*(2), 71–80.

Leahy, M. J., Muezen, P., Saunders, J. L., & Strauser, D. (2009). Essential knowledge domains underlying effective rehabilitation counseling practice. *Rehabilitation Counseling Bulletin, 52*(2), 95–106. https://doi.org/10.1177/0034355208323646

Leahy, M. J., & Syzmanksi, E. M. (1995). Rehabilitation counseling: Evolution and current status. *Journal of Counseling & Development, 74*(2), 163–166. https://doi.org/10.1002/j.1556-6676.1995.tb01843.x

Lehman, J., & Phelps, S. (2005). *West's encyclopedia of American law* (2nd ed.). Thomson/Gale.

Lewis, T., & Upton, T. D. (2011). Preparation for private vocational practice. In T. D. Upton (Ed.), *Private rehabilitation: Evolving opportunities* (pp. 42–67). Aspen Professional Services.

McCarthy, J., & Wagner, J. (2014). Use and abuse of prescription pain medication in workers' compensation: Assessment, guidance, and implementation of consumer protocols. *The Rehabilitation Professional, 22*(2), 95–108.

McCollom, P. (2005). Field review: Revised standards and practice for life care planners. *Journal of Life Care Planning, 4*(2/3), 67–74.

McLellan, A. T., Luborsky, L., Woody, G. E., & O'Brien, C. P. (1980). An improved diagnostic evaluation instrument for substance abuse patients: The Addiction Severity Index. *Journal of Nervous and Mental Disease, 168*(1), 26–33. doi:10.1097/00005053-198001000-00006

Miller, G. A. (1985). *The Substance Abuse Subtle Screening Inventory (SASSI) manual*. The SASSI Institute.

Miller, K. R., & Paris, D. (2017). Educational preparation for private sector rehabilitation practitioners. *Rehabilitation Professional, 25*(4), 167–174.

Muthard, J. E., & Salomone, P. R. (1969). The roles and functions of the rehabilitation counselor. *Rehabilitation Counseling Bulletin, 13*(Suppl 1), 81–168.

Rasch, J. D. (1985). *Rehabilitation of workers' compensation and other insurance claimants: Case management, forensic, and business aspects.* Charles C. Thomas.

Robinson, R., & Watson, E. (2019). Private sector rehabilitation counseling ethics: Evolution of the 2017 CRCC code. *The Rehabilitation Professional, 27*(1), 23–33.

Rubin, S. E., Roessler, R. T., & Rumrill, P. T., Jr. (2016). *Foundations of the vocational rehabilitation process* (7th ed.). PRO-ED.

Sánchez, J., Muller, V., Barnes, E. F., & Childs, J. R. (2019). Assessment of psychopathology. In D. R. Strauser, T. N. Tansey, & F. Chan (Eds.), *Assessment in rehabilitation and mental health counseling* (pp. 99–131). Springer. https://doi.org/10.1891/9780826162434.0007

Shahnasarian, M. S. (2014). *Assessment of earning capacity* (4th ed.). Lawyers & Judges Publishing Company.

Shahnasarian, M. (2015). Consultation in litigation. In P. J. Hartung, M. L. Savickas, & W. B. Walsh (Eds.), *APA handbook of career intervention*, Vol. 2. Applications (pp. 521–534). American Psychological Association. https://doi.org/10.1037/14439-038

Sleister, S. L. (2000). Separating the wheat from the chaff: The role of the vocational expert in forensic vocational rehabilitation. *Journal of Vocational Rehabilitation, 14*(2), 119–129.

Stebnicki, M. A. (2009). A call for integral approaches in the professional identity of rehabilitation counseling. *Rehabilitation Counseling Bulletin, 52*(2), 133–137. https://doi.org/10.1177/0034355208324263

Stoneburner, R. C., & Rockett, S. L. (2017). Evidence-based vocational evaluation recommendations for the consideration and consequences of opioid/opiate usage in forensic vocational evaluations. *The Rehabilitation Professional, 25*(4), 141–154.

Upton, T. D. (2003). Vocational expertise in the disability determination process. *Journal of Rehabilitation Administration, 27*(1), 25–31.

Upton, T. D. (Ed.). (2011). *Private rehabilitation: Evolving opportunities.* Aspen Professional Services.

Upton, T. D., & Dallas, B. (2011). Workers' compensation. In T. D. Upton (Ed.), *Private rehabilitation: Evolving opportunities* (pp. 109–135). Aspen Professional Services.

Upton, T. D., & Mbugua, A. (2011). Frequent venues of service delivery. In T. D. Upton (Ed.), *Private rehabilitation: Evolving opportunities* (pp. 85–107). Aspen Professional Services.

U.S. Department of Labor. (n.d.). *Division of Federal Employees' Compensation (DFEC): State workers' compensation officials. Office of Workers' Compensation Programs.* https://www.dol.gov/owcp/dfec/regs/compliance/wc.htm

Weed, R. O., & Berens, D. E. (2018). *Life care planning and case management: Handbook* (4th ed.). Routledge.

Weikel, W. J. (1986). The expanding roles of the counselor as a vocational expert witness. *Journal of Counseling and Development, 64*(8), 523–524. https://doi.org/10.1002/j.1556-6676.1986.tb01188.x

Wright, G. N. (1980). *Total rehabilitation.* Little Brown and Company.

Index

Symbols

21st Century Communications and Video Accessibility Act, 2010, 164

A

abandonment, 82
ABLE Act of 2018, 164
AbleData, 178
abuse and exploitation of disabled
  abandonment, 82
  emotional or psychological, 81–82
  financial or material exploitation, 82
  impact of, 83
  intervention and treatment, 83–84
  neglect, 82
  physical, 81–82
  self-neglect, 82
  sexual, 81–82
access board, 23–24
achievement assessments, 134
acquired disabilities, 62–63
acute disabilities, 62
ADA Amendments Act (ADAAA) of 2008, 26–27, 164
Adult Substance Abuse Subtle Screening Inventory, Fourth Edition (SAS-SI-4), 139
advocacy, 160
African Journal of Disability, 33
Air Carrier Access Act of 1988, 163
alerting devices, 173
American Board of Vocational Experts (ABVE), 122
American Counseling Association (ACA), 92
  Code of Ethics. *See* Code of Ethics (ACA)
American National Standards Institute (ANSI), 21
American Rehabilitation Economics Association (AREA), 187
Americans with Disabilities Act of 1990 (ADA), 7, 25, 51, 109, 116, 163, 171–172
  employment, 25
  key definitions of, 26
  public accommodations, 26
  state and local governments, 25–26
  telecommunications, 26
aptitude assessments, 134
Architectural Barriers Acts (ABA) of 1968, 7, 21–22, 162
Aristotle, 4
Armed Services Vocational Aptitude Battery (ASVAB), 136–137
art therapy, 84
assisted living, 154
assistive listening devices (ALDs), 173

Assistive Technology Act
  of 1998, 25–26
  of 2004, 25
assistive technology (AT)
  definition, 169–170
  device, 170, 173
  in rural settings, 174–176
  legislation, 171–173
  principles, 171
  resources/funding, 177–178
  services, 170
assistive technology team, 174
attention deficit/hyperactivity disorder (ADHD), 71
augmentative and alternative communication (AAC) devices, 173
autonomy, 92

B

Barden-LaFollette Act of 1943, 6, 21
Bartlett v. New York State Board of Law Examiners, 1997, 18–19
behavioral assessments, 135
behavioral intervention plan (BIP), 138
beneficence, 93
bibliotherapy, 84
bipolar disorder, 72
blindness/low vision, 69
Braille, Louis, 5
Buddhism, 34

C

CACREP-accredited clinical rehabilitation counseling programs, 184
case management, 143
  assessment. *See* assessment
  assessment phase, 147
  care planning and service coordination, 147–148
  case managers, 145
  client records. *See* client records
  definition, 144
  disability, 149
  follow-up and reassessment, 148
  intake and screening phase, 147
  interdisciplinary, 149
  key terms used, 144–145
  models, 145–146
  phases, 146–148
  private rehabilitation, 149
  psychotropic medications, monitoring. *See* psychotropic medications
Center for Independent Living (CIL), 154
Center for Parent Information and Resources (CPIR), 178
Center on Technology and Disability (CTD), 178

Certified Disability Management Specialist (CDMS), 123
Certified Rehabilitation Counselor examination, 9
certified rehabilitation counselors (CRCs), 183
charity model of disability, 56
children with disabilities, perceptions of
  17th- and 18th-century America, 3
  in ancient Rome and Greece, 2
  Middle Ages, 2–3
child with disabilities, parenting, 64–65
China, 34
Christian fatalism, 33
chronic disabilities, 62
Civil Rights Act
  of 1871, 15
  of 1964, 15
  of 1965, 162
Civil Rights Restoration Act of 1988, 163
Clerc, Laurent, 4
clinical mental health, 1
Clinical Rehabilitation and Clinical Mental Health program, 9
clinical rehabilitation counseling, 7–8
  accreditation, 183–184
  as a specialized practice, 9
  CORE-accredited programs, 182–183
  private sector, 184–185
  recommendations for, 84–85
clinical rehabilitation counselors, 1, 8, 32, 38
  scope of practice, 182–184
coaching. *See* life coaching
Code of Ethics (ACA)
  and decision-making models. *See* decision-making models
cognitive behavioral counseling, 84
collectivist cultures, 34
Commission on Rehabilitation Counseling Certification (CRCC), 8, 92, 122
community engagement, 68
  benefits of, 67–68
  characteristics of, 67
  social interconnection and, 68
Community Mental Health Centers Act of 1963, 6
competitive employment, 121
concurrent validity, 134
confidentiality, 94
Confucianism, 34
congenital disabilities, 62–63
construct validity, 134
consumer–counselor relationships, 8
content validity, 134
convergent validity, 134
Council on Rehabilitation Education (CORE), 8–9
Counseling and Related Educational Pro-

About the Editors

Dr. Mary-Anne M. Joseph, PhD, LPC, CRC has over 10 years of experience in the field of rehabilitation. She has served as a practitioner and a professor in education and vocational rehabilitation. Currently, Dr. Joseph is a tenured Associate Professor in the Department of Rehabilitation Studies at Alabama State University.

Dr. Joseph is a Certified Rehabilitation Counselor, as well as a Licensed Professional Counselor. She holds a PhD in Counselor Education and Supervision from Ohio University and a Master of Science in Rehabilitation Counseling from Winston-Salem State University. Dr. Joseph is committed to research in teaching and learning in rehabilitation and human services and is the author of several publications, including: *The Ethics of Undergraduate Rehabilitation Education, Development and Implementation of a Quality Curriculum/Program, Ethical Considerations for Working with Transition Aged Youth and Students with Disabilities,* and *Transition Vocational Rehabilitation.*

Dr. Joseph received the Sylvia Walker Education Award in 2017. She was awarded the College of Health Science Faculty of the Year Award in 2014 from Alabama State University. Dr. Joseph regularly teaches both undergraduate and graduate courses in rehabilitation services and rehabilitation counseling. She often presents scholarly works at state, regional, and national conferences. Dr. Joseph is a professional member of the National Rehabilitation Association, the National Association on Multicultural Rehabilitation Concerns, the American Counseling Association, the American Rehabilitation Counseling Association, and the Association for Counselor Education and Supervision.

Dr. Mona Robinson, PhD, LPCC-S, LSW, CRC, is a Professor and Program Coordinator for the Counselor Education Program and the Human Services Program at Ohio University. She is the immediate past chair of the Department of Counseling and Higher Education at the university. She holds a MA in Rehabilitation Counseling and PhD in Rehabilitation Services from The Ohio State University.

Dr. Robinson has served as a counselor and administrator of vocational rehabilitation counseling and employment services to persons with severe mental illness and other barriers to employment. Her areas of expertise include psychiatric rehabilitation, disability advocacy, multicultural counseling, ethics, and dual diagnosis.

Dr. Robinson serves as the Institute Director for study abroad programs held in Italy and Botswana. Dr. Robinson is currently First VP for the National Council on Rehabilitation Education (NCRE). She has served as Past-President of the National Association of Multicultural Rehabilitation Concerns, the Ohio Rehabilitation Association, and the Ohio Rehabilitation Counseling Association (ORCA). She is a member of several professional organizations, including, but not limited to, the American Counseling Association, the American Rehabilitation Counseling Association, the Association for Multicultural Counseling and Development, and the National Rehabilitation Counseling Association. She is an editorial consultant for the *Journal of Applied Rehabilitation*, an editorial board member for the *International Journal of Applied Guidance and Counseling*, and a CACREP site team chair.

Dr. Robinson has won several state and national awards for distinguished teaching and outreach. She has traveled extensively internationally and taught classes in both South Korea and Yogyakarta,

Indonesia. She has been an invited speaker at various conferences in Honolulu, Hawaii; Thimphu, Bhutan; Gaborone, Botswana; and Reggello, Italy. She is a recipient of the 2017 Virgie Winston-Smith Lifetime Achievement Award and 2018 NAMRC Fellow Award. Dr. Robinson is the 2019–2020 invited interviewee for the Professional Counselor Lifetime Achievement in Counseling Series.

About the Contributors

Bill Bauer, PhD, ALPS, CRC, has an undergraduate degree from Ohio University in Special Education, focusing on several cognate areas and certifications/licensures, including emotional disturbance, intellectual disabilities (mild to severe), learning disabilities, autism, and physical/orthopedic and other health impairments. He earned a graduate degree in School Administration (focus on Supervision) from Ohio University. He also earned a master's degree in Rehabilitation Counseling and a PhD in Rehabilitation Services from The Ohio State University. His dissertation focused on high school transition-aged youth and leadership.

Dr. Bauer is a Certified Rehabilitation Counselor, as well as a Licensed Professional Counselor in West Virginia and Ohio. He is an Approved Licensed Professional Supervisor (ALPS) in West Virginia as well. He is a well-known advocate for disability rights and is a founding member of the Disability Rights of Ohio Board, Board Chair of the Ohio Rehabilitation Services Commission (now Opportunities for Ohioans with Disabilities), and past chair of the Ohio State Advisory Panel for Exceptional Children and the State Council for Exceptional Children–Teacher Education Division. He is also a certified instructor in Mental Health First Aid for adults, youth, and higher education. Bauer is from southeastern Ohio, born and raised in Marietta, Ohio. He has been a schoolteacher, principal, and interim superintendent. He recently retired from Marietta College as a Professor of Education after an extended career. He has authored journal articles about Appalachian culture and counselor competencies and is a chapter author of a book focusing on Disability Pride and the cycle it takes for one to become more accepting of their own disability. He speaks around the world on disability and culture issues.

Brian L. Bethel, PhD, LPCC-S, LCDC III, RPT-S, is a Professional Clinical Counselor-Supervisor (LPCC-S), a Licensed Chemical Dependency Counselor (LCDC III), and a Registered Play Therapist-Supervisor (RPT-S), with specialized training in counseling children, adolescents, and families. Dr. Bethel earned his PhD in Counselor Education and Supervision from Ohio University, where he also earned dual master's degrees in Clinical Counseling and Rehabilitation Counseling. He is currently on the faculty of Capella University in the Department of Educational Psychology. With more than 20 years of clinical practice, Dr. Bethel brings a diversity of strengths to his clinical practice. As the founder and director of Interplay Counseling and Consultation Services, LLC, Dr. Bethel operates a private counseling practice and provides educational services to community organizations. He has dedicated much of his professional career to working with individuals impacted by trauma and continues as a mental health clinician for a child advocacy center that serves children and families across southern and southeastern Ohio.

In addition to his counseling practices, Dr. Bethel serves as an independent trainer and consultant. He has provided consultation services to various schools, social service agencies, court systems, and foster care agencies. Dr. Bethel serves as an independent trainer and consultant with the Ohio Human Services Training System and the Ohio Child Welfare Program, where he was recognized for his training excellence as a recipient of both the Rising Star Award in 2007 and the Linda Pope Award in 2014. In 2018, Dr. Bethel was awarded an Award of Excellence in Research from the Association for Play Therapy for his research on the use of play therapy for children with disabilities. Dr. Bethel is a frequent presenter at professional conferences and is recognized as an innovative and exciting presenter on the local, state, national, and international levels.

Sekeria Volece Bossie, PhD, LPC-S, NCC, CAMS, ACAS, is a faculty member at Alabama State University in the Rehabilitation Studies Department. She received her Bachelor of Social Work, Master of Community Agency Counseling, and Educational Specialist Degree in Community Agency Counseling from Jacksonville State University in Jacksonville, Alabama. She received her PhD in Professional Counseling from Amridge University in Montgomery, Alabama. She is a Licensed Bachelor Social Worker, a Licensed Professional Counselor, and is a Licensed Professional Counselor Supervisor. She is also certified as a Nationally Certified Counselor, a Certified Anger Management Specialist, and an Advanced Certified Autism Specialist. She has extensive experience with both youth and adults with mental health diagnoses, behavioral disorders, autism spectrum disorder, intellectual limitations, and/or physical disabilities, as well as those individuals coping with stressors, substance abuse/addiction, and general changes and challenges of life. Dr. Bossie's research interests include, but are not limited to, areas related to autism, behavior management, families, quality of life, ADHD, foster care youth outcomes, at-risk youth, and disadvantaged/marginalized populations. She is an Assistant Professor at Alabama State University in the College of Health Science Rehabilitation Studies Department. She is also the owner of Behavior Education Consultation and Training Services, LLC (BECT Services). This agency provides in-home and in-office mental health counseling, behavioral intervention, and reunification services in various counties throughout Alabama. BECT Services also partners with the Alabama Department of Human Resources and private foster care agencies to provide mental health and behavioral health services to foster children and training and/or education services to foster parents. Additionally, BECT Services provides professional continuing education services specifically focusing on licensed social workers and licensed counselors.

Sharon Brown, PhD, CRC, is a tenured Associate Professor at Alabama Agricultural & Mechanical University in northern Alabama. She currently serves as Coordinator for the Rehabilitation Counseling Program and Director of Bulldog Learning Independence Fostering Education and Employment (LIFE). She earned a doctoral degree in Rehabilitation Education and Disability Adjustment at The Ohio State University in 1997, a master's degree in Rehabilitation Counseling from Kent State University in 1985, and a bachelor's degree in Rehabilitation Services from Wilberforce University in 1984.

She has more than 25 years of experience in higher education with a history of grant development, which began with a $494,000 Capacity Building grant to develop the first graduate degree program in Rehabilitation Counseling at Wilberforce University in 2004. She has accrued over $946,000 in nine successful grants over the past 15 years. Her most recent grant was funded with the Alabama Council on Developmental Disabilities in the amount of $225,000 to establish an inclusion program for young adults with intellectual disabilities on a college campus. This is the first of its kind at a historically Black college or university.

Louvisia Conley, MEd., EdS, is currently a doctoral student at the University of Memphis, earning her EdD in Instruction and Curriculum Leadership in Special Education. She earned her master's in Rehabilitation Counseling from Auburn University and Educational Specialist in School Counseling from the University of Memphis. She earned both of her undergraduate degrees in Management Information System and Professional Studies in Rehabilitation and Disability Services degrees from the University of Memphis. Ms. Conley currently works for the University of Memphis Institute on Disability (UMID) as Co-Faculty Instructor.

Kent Crenshaw, MS, CRC, is the Executive Director of the Independent Rights and Resources (IRR). During his time at the center, the number of consumers has grown from 12 to over 400. IRR serves any person with a disability who desires to live more independently. The IRR's mission is "to provide a set of core services geared toward promoting self-help, equal access, peer role modeling, personal growth and empowerment." Mr. Crenshaw has advocated for people with disabilities through the county, serving on several boards, including the National Council on Independent Living, the State of Alabama Independent Living Council, and the Alabama Medical Equipment Board and as a spokesman at several conventions and meetings addressing discrimination and barriers that exist in society for people with disabilities. Mr. Crenshaw is a graduate of Auburn University at Montgomery. He earned his Master of Education from Auburn University and is a Certified Rehabilitation Counselor. He is an instructor at Alabama State University, where he involves his students with community service as it relates to people with disabilities.

Franco Dispenza, PhD, LP, CRC, is an Associate Professor in the Department of Counseling and Psychological Services at Georgia State University in Atlanta, Georgia. He currently serves as the coordinator of the PhD program in Counselor Education and Practice. His research and scholarship focus on culturally diverse populations and psychosocial and vocational aspects of chronic illness, disability, sexuality, and trauma. He also has secondary interests in practitioner training and education.

Carmela Drake, PhD, LPC, is an Assistant Professor and Bachelors of Science in Rehabilitation Services with Concentration in Addiction Studies (BSRS) Coordinator at Alabama State University. She received her PhD in Human Services, with a concentration in Counseling Studies from Capella University. She obtained her MS in Counseling and Human Development from Troy State University. She possesses two certifications in the addictions field: Certified Adolescent Alcohol and Drug Professional (CAADP), as well as a Certified Compulsive Gambling Counselor, level III (ACGC-III) in the state of Alabama. Dr. Drake is also a Licensed Professional Counselor (LPC) in the state of Alabama. She has worked with individuals with substance use disorders and/or mental illness for over 20 years. Dr. Drake serves as the President on the Board of Directors for the Council on Substance Abuse in Montgomery, Alabama. Dr. Drake also serves as the Faculty Athletics Representative (FAR) at Alabama State University. She served as President-Elect for 2019–2020 with the Alabama Association for Marriage and Family Counseling (ALAMFC) and currently serves as president for ALAMFC for 2020–2021.

Judith L. Drew, PhD, CRC, obtained her PhD from The Ohio State University in Rehabilitation Services and Counselor Education. She has been teaching Rehabilitation and Mental Health Counseling courses in higher education institutions for over 20 years. Currently, she is an Assistant Professor at Salve Regina University where she is the Program Director for the MA degree programs in Rehabilitation Counseling, Clinical Rehabilitation, Mental Health Counseling, and two CAGS programs.

Dr. Drew has been a guest lecturer and speaker for regional, national, and international conferences on assessment and transition issues for youth. Dr. Drew's research and writing interests include evidence-based practice models for assessment and employment services for people with disabilities, career counseling with underserved populations, and the intersection between governmental disability employment policies and the real-world implementation and application of those policies. She has coauthored several articles on vocational rehabilitation issues. Additionally, she coauthored two book chapters on forensic vocational assessment that focused on principles of vocational assessment in forensic cases and forensic assessment in civil litigation.

Dr. Drew also is the president of VocWorks in Cumberland, Rhode Island. She has been in private practice for over 29 years. Her private practice focuses on counseling work, including adjustment to disability and career and rehabilitation counseling; school-to-work transition assessments; expert testimony and forensic assessments; and staff development and training both for-profit and nonprofit organizations in diversity, inclusion, workplace performance, supported employment for people with disabilities, and job accommodations.

Dr. Drew was appointed by the Governor of Rhode Island to serve as chair of the State Rehabilitation Council and has served in that capacity for over 5 years. She served as a Commissioner on the Governor's Commission on Disabilities for over 10 years.

Dothel W. Edwards, Jr., RhD, CRC, CLCP, has over 20 years of experience as a rehabilitation educator in higher education. Presently, he is a Full Professor in the Department of Rehabilitation Studies in the College of Health Sciences at Alabama State University (ASU). At ASU, he served in the capacities of chair of the Department of Rehabilitation Studies (September 2009–November 2013), Program Coordinator of the Master of Rehabilitation Counseling program (September 2009–November 2013), and interim Program Coordinator of the Bachelor of Science in Rehabilitation Service with a Concentration in Addiction Studies program (February 2013–November 2013). From July 2001 until May 2008, he served in the capacity of Assistant Professor and Program Coordinator of the accredited Rehabilitation Counseling & Case Management graduate program at Fort Valley State University in Fort Valley, Georgia. From July of 1999 until July 2001, he served as an Assistant Professor and Clinical Coordinator in the Department of Rehabilitation Services at the University of Maryland Eastern Shore. In addition to his full-time faculty responsibilities at ASU, he provides vocational expert witness testimony (as a contractor) for the Social Security Administration Office of Disabilities Adjudication & Review offices of Atlanta, Georgia, and Orlando, Florida; the Office Hearings Operations National Hearing Center offices of Baltimore, Maryland, and Falls Church, Virginia, and he served as a registered Rehabilitation Supplier under the Georgia State Board of Workers' Compensation. His research interests are workplace bullying in higher education, quality of life issues among persons with developmental disabilities, multicultural counseling, professional ethics in vocational rehabilitation, life care planning, and forensic rehabilitation. Dr. Edwards has copublished one book, coauthored several book chapters, authored and coauthored several manuscripts in peer-reviewed journals, and he has conducted many presentations and trainings relating to the above-mentioned topics.

Angela L. Hall, PhD, is an Assistant Professor of Rehabilitation Studies in the College of Health Sciences at Alabama State University. She received her PhD in Rehabilitation Counseling and Special Education in May of 2018 from Auburn University. She has an MEd in Community Mental Health Counseling and a BA in English and History, both from Auburn University at Montgomery. Before coming to Alabama State University, she worked for Auburn University as a research associate and instructor in the Department of Special Education, Rehabilitation, and Counseling. Dr. Hall's research interests include the identity development of marginalized groups, specifically, individuals with disabilities, as well as incarcerated women with disabilities. She considers herself an advocate and ally for any socially marginalized group, including individuals with disabilities, racial and ethnic minorities, and members of the LGBTQ community.

De'Amber L. Johnson, MS, LPC, is a native of Tulsa, Oklahoma, where she currently resides with her three beautiful daughters. She graduated from Langston University–Tulsa in 2007 with a BA in Psychology and went on to earn a Master of Science in Rehabilitation Counseling in 2017. Currently, as a mental health professional, she works with at-risk youth to help them adapt or utilize their strengths at home and in school. She has over 10 years of experience working with children and their families with disabilities to help them achieve personal and career goals and to overcome adversity.

Jawana Kindred, MS, earned her master's in Counseling Psychology with a concentration in Rehabilitation Counseling from Alabama Agricultural and Mechanical University, Department of Education, Humanities and Behavioral Sciences Counseling Psychology Program. She received her undergraduate degree in Sociology from the University of North Alabama. She currently works at the Alabama Department of Rehabilitation Services as a Vocational Rehabilitation Counselor.

Denise Y. Lewis, PhD, LPC, NCC, is an Assistant Professor in the Department of Graduate Counseling at Grace College and Seminary. She is a Licensed Professional Counselor (LPC) and a nationally certified counselor. Her areas of specialization include counselor education, clinical counseling, multicultural and diversity issues in counseling, and spiritual and religious issues in counseling. Dr. Lewis's research interests focus on African American youth and families and involve evaluating and addressing systemic problems that impact their areas of wholistic functioning.

Phillip Derrell Lewis, PhD, CRC, LADC-C, serves as faculty at Langston University in the Department of Rehabilitation Counseling and Disability Studies. Dr. Lewis earned his doctorate in Rehabilitation Counseling Education and Law/Health Policy/Disability from The University of Iowa, his master's in Rehabilitation Counseling/Rehabilitation Administration from The University of Southern Illinois at Carbondale, and his Bachelor of Science in Social Work/Political Science from Rust College. He earned a BS degree in Social Work/Political Science from Rust College in Holly Springs, Mississippi. His research interests include, but are not limited to, rehabilitation services for persons with mental and physical disabilities, school-to-work transition for adolescents with disabilities, correctional rehabilitation counseling, suicide prevention, substance abuse counseling, bullying, triple negative breast cancer/cancer prevention, multicultural counseling, and agrability.

Ajasha Long, MS, is a fourth-year doctoral candidate in the Counseling Psychology program at Ball State University. She received her bachelor's degree in psychology in 2015 from Alcorn State University in Lorman, Mississippi. She obtained her master's degree in 2017 from Alabama A&M University in Huntsville, Alabama. She has a broad interest in health psychology, with a specific focus on chronic health conditions in the African American community. Ms. Long is an active member of the Indiana Association of Black Psychologists, where she serves as the Student Liaison for Ball State University. She also is a member of the American Psychological Association. In her spare time, she enjoys hiking, kayaking, reading, and listening to podcasts.

Danielle Dede Nimako, PhD, CRC, is an Assistant Professor in the Counselor Education Department at Emporia State University. She has clinical training in Autism Diagnostic Observation Schedule–2nd Edition (ADOS-II), Autism Diagnostic Interview–Revised (ADI-R), as well as a Transitioning Together Parent & Teen Group Facilitator and Trainer. Dr. Nimako has administrative, counseling, teaching, and research experience in a variety of settings, making her a well-rounded professional. Her research focuses on improving the quality of life for individuals with disabilities and their families in areas where access to resources is limited. She has a keen interest in training and educating rehabilitation practitioners, global disability issues, disability policies in developing countries, and multicultural issues in the field of rehabilitation counseling.

Chanda J. Pinkney, MA, is currently a doctoral student with the Department of Counseling and Higher Education at Ohio University, with her dissertation focusing on adult children of drug addiction. She earned her master's degree in Counseling from Pillar College and her bachelor's in Sociology from the University of Michigan. Ms. Pinkney has over 20 years of experience as a behavioral health professional and is an active member of the American Counseling Association and Chi Sigma Iota (Alpha Chapter). She is a proud native of Newark, New Jersey, and enjoys cozy murder mysteries and baking desserts from scratch in her spare time.

Malik Aqueel Raheem, EdD, is an Assistant Professor at Wilberforce University in the Clinical Rehabilitation Counseling program. Dr. Raheem earned his doctorate in counselor education and supervision from Northern Illinois University and his master's in Community Counseling from Chicago State University. He has made several national presentations on racial trauma and mental health issues with people of African descent.

Rebecca R. Sametz, PhD, CRC, LPC, ETS, CMCC, is an Assistant Professor and Director of the Masters of Science Clinical Rehabilitation Counseling program at Texas Tech University Health Sciences Center. Dr. Sametz is a Licensed Professional Counselor (LPC), Certified Rehabilitation Counselor (CRC), and certified Employment Training Specialist (ETS). She is currently the Director of Red Raider Pre-College Summer Academy, where she developed a weeklong program for youth with disabilities interested in attending postsecondary education. Previously, Dr. Sametz worked at a nonprofit as a Youth Career Development Specialist in which she partnered with local school districts in order to provide youth with disabilities community work experiences who were preparing for transition from school to work. Also, Dr. Sametz worked for the State of Michigan's agency for the Blind and Visually Impaired, providing career counseling and exploration services for adults and youth with disabilities, as well as serving as a job placement coordinator and job developer.

Jennifer Sánchez, PhD, CRC, LMHC, is an Associate Professor in the Department of Rehabilitation and Counselor Education at the University of Iowa. She received her PhD in Rehabilitation Psychology from the University of Wisconsin–Madison and her MEd in Rehabilitation and Mental Health Counseling from Florida Atlantic University. Dr. Sánchez possesses over 15 years of clinical, teaching, and research experience. She uses a biopsychosocial framework for diagnosis, conceptualization, and treatment of children, adolescents, and adults with neuropsychiatric disabilities, such as neurodevelopmental disorders (e.g., autism), mental illnesses (e.g., schizophrenia), substance use disorders (e.g., opioid use disorder [OUD]), and neurocognitive disorders (e.g., traumatic brain injury [TBI]), including co-occurring disabilities. Her varied forensic and civil work settings span inpatient psychiatric facilities, Veterans Administration (VA) facilities, state hospitals and agencies, K–12 schools and postsecondary education, community mental health centers, and homeless shelters and transitional housing. She has coedited 2 special issues, published over 30 peer-reviewed articles, and delivered more than 75 professional presentations. Committed to the field of rehabilitation, Dr. Sánchez is Chair of the NCRE Council on Psychiatric Rehabilitation, a national trainer for state–federal vocational rehabilitation (VR) agencies on using motivational interviewing to improve employment outcomes for VR consumers, and an Invited Member of the Iowa Healthcare Collaborative OUD Consortium. She serves on the editorial boards of the *Journal of Counseling & Development*, *Counselor Education and Supervision*, the *Journal of Rehabilitation Administration*, and the *Journal of Applied Rehabilitation Counseling*. Dr. Sánchez has received numerous awards for her professional accomplishments at institutional, regional, and national levels.

Perry Sanders, EdD, CRC, serves as Assistant Professor in the Department of Rehabilitation Counseling and Disability Studies at Langston University. He holds a Bachelor of Arts degree in Psychology from Southwestern Oklahoma State University, a Master of Science degree in Rehabilitation Counseling from Oklahoma State University, and a doctorate in Occupational and Adult Education from Oklahoma State University. He is a Certified Rehabilitation Counselor (CRC). Prior to coming to Langston University, he was employed for 23 years as Career Counselor under the Work Force Investment Act with the City of Tulsa. Prior to career counseling, he was a Rehabilitation Teacher of the Blind with the Division of Visual Services. He has served as a Governor's Appointee on the Oklahoma Rehabilitation Council and served on the Statewide Independent Living Council. He is a recipient of the Oklahoma Rehabilitation Council's Community Service Award.

Chrisann Schiro-Geist, PhD, CRC, D/ABVE, is a Professor at the University of Memphis Institute on Disability and has been a university educator for over 40 years. She has been on the faculty of the Illinois Institute of Technology and the University of Illinois at Champaign–Urbana. Dr. Schiro-Geist came to the University of Memphis as the Senior Vice Provost in 2004. She is currently in the department of Counseling, Educational Psychology and Research. Her research areas focus on a variety of social justice issues related to persons with disabilities and other underserved populations, especially as they pertain to issues of return to work.

Dr. Matthew Sprong, LCPC, CRC, is a Vocational Rehabilitation Counselor at the Department of Veteran Affairs and Assistant Professor of Clinical Mental Health Counseling at Lock Haven University.

Dr. Sprong's professional experiences involve counseling people with and without disabilities, drug and alcohol counseling, providing vocational rehabilitation to veterans, providing forensic testimony as a life care planner and vocational expert, serving as a Program Evaluator at a community-based rehabilitation program. He has over 35 peer-reviewed journal article publications in the area(s) of internet gaming disorder and video gaming behavioral functions, people with disabilities and coexisting substance related disorders, disability equity in postsecondary education, and service delivery issues for people with disabilities. He has published a coauthored textbook titled *The Substance Related Disorder Assessment: A Road Map to Effective Treatment Planning* and has given more than 60 professional presentations at international, national, state, and local conferences. Dr. Sprong is a Certified Rehabilitation Counselor, Licensed Clinical Professional Counselor, Certified Alcohol and Drug Counselor, and Certified Life Care Planner. Currently, Dr. Sprong serves as the Editor-in-Chief of the *Rehabilitation Professional* journal and serves on the editorial boards for the *Journal of Rehabilitation*, *Journal of Applied Rehabilitation Counseling*, *VEWAA*, and the *Journal of Addictive Behaviors, Therapy, and Rehabilitation.*

Robert (Rob) L. Stevens, PhD, CRC, LPC, is an Assistant Professor of Rehabilitation Science at Arkansas Tech University in Russellville, AR. Dr. Stevens received his doctoral degree in Counselor Education and Supervision from Ohio University. He is a Certified Rehabilitation Counselor and a Licensed Professional Counselor. His research areas are as follows: adjustment to life after an acquired chronic illness or disability and the intersectionality of disability and sexuality/gender identity. Dr. Stevens presents at state, regional, and national conferences to advocate for social justice and equality for all and is currently a board member of the National Association for Multicultural Rehabilitation Concerns.

John H. Tooson, PhD, CRC, earned his PhD and master's degree from the College of Education, Educational Services and Research with a major in Rehabilitation Counseling and Administration from The Ohio State University. In addition, he has earned a Master of Science in Health Care Administration and a Master of Science in Personnel Administration from Central Michigan University. His Bachelor of Science degree was earned at Central State University in Ohio. Dr. Tooson worked for the State of Ohio for 30 years in Rehabilitation and Workers' Compensation, providing rehabilitation services to industrially injured clients with disabilities. After retirement from the State of Ohio, he began working as a professor with the Graduate Rehabilitation Counseling program at Wilberforce University, where he is currently an Assistant Professor in the Clinical Rehabilitation Counseling Program and Acting Dean of the College of Graduate and Adult Continuing Education.

Thomas D. Upton, PhD, CRC, is a Professor in the Rehabilitation Counselor Training Program at the Rehabilitation Institute, Southern Illinois University Carbondale. He earned his PhD in Rehabilitation Counseling from the University of Iowa (2000). Additionally, Dr. Upton has varied rehabilitation experiences. These include work in two comprehensive rehabilitation centers, as a senior state/federal vocational rehabilitation (VR) counselor, a private consultant for a private VR firm, and a brain injury consultant. Dr. Upton serves as an editorial consultant for the *Journal of Applied Rehabilitation* and the *Journal of Rehabilitation.* His research interests include innovations in brain injury rehabilitation, rehabilitation counselor preparation, and disability attitudes.

Bilal Urkmez, PhD, CRC, is an Assistant Professor in counselor education in the Department of Counseling and Higher Education at Ohio University. Dr. Urkmez holds the PhD in Rehabilitation Counselor Education from Michigan State University at East Lansing. He also holds a MA in Rehabilitation Counseling from Wayne State University at Detroit. He has worked as a clinical rehabilitation counselor and school counselor. His research interests are promoting evidence-based practices and improving quality of life for people with disabilities. He is also interested in the effective vocational services and interventions among people with traumatic brain injuries. He is involved in a research team at Ohio University about parental involvement issue for parents who have children with disabilities and emotional regulation for college students with autism spectrum disorder.

CPSIA information can be obtained
at www.ICGtesting.com
Printed in the USA
LVHW021103170723
752531LV00007B/22